Centro de Estudios Puertorriqueños

CENTRO JOURNAL

VOLUME XXXIV • NUMBER I • SPRING 2022

The illustration is by cartoonist Clifford K. Berryman and appeared
in *The Washington Post* on March 9, 1900.

ISBN: 978-1-945662-56-0 (print); ISSN: 1538-6279 (print); 2163-2960 (electronic)
©2022 Centro de Estudios Puertorriqueños
Hunter College / City University of New York
695 Park Avenue, E-1429, New York, NY 10065
212.772.5690 • Fax 212.650.3673 • http://centropr.hunter.cuny.edu

CENTRO Journal is indexed or abstracted in: Academic Search Complete (EBSCO host); Alternative Press Index; America: History and Life; Cabell's Whitelist; Caribbean Abstracts; CONUCO-Consorcio Universitario de Indización; Gale; HAPI–Hispanic American Periodicals Index; Historical Abstracts; Left Index; MLA International Bibliography; OCLC PAIS; ProQuest; Scopus; Social Services Abstracts; Sociological Abstracts; Ulrich's Periodicals Directory; H.W. Wilson Humanities Abstracts; Worldwide Political Science Abstracts.

CENTRO JOURNAL
VOLUME XXXIV • NUMBER I • SPRING 2022

SPECIAL ISSUE: Back to the future: The Implications of *Balzac* One Hundred Years Later
GUEST EDITORS: Charles R. Venator-Santiago and José Javier Colón Morera

PAGE 5
INTRODUCTION
Back to the future: The Implications of *Balzac* One Hundred Years Later
Charles R. Venator-Santiago and José Javier Colón Morera

PAGE 21
The Sword of Libel: Jesús María Balsac and The Quest for Equality
Francisco Ortiz Santini

PAGE 37
The 'New' *Insular Cases* and the Territorial Clause:
From Temporary Incorporation to Permanent Un-incorporation
Jorge M. Farinacci Fernós

PAGE 53
Balzac v. People of Porto Rico and the Problem of the Liberal Narrative of
Citizenship, Why Puerto Ricans are Not Second-Class Citizens Today
Charles R. Venator-Santiago

PAGE 113
Balzac, US Citizenship and Territorial Incorporation in Puerto Rico
Edgardo Meléndez

PAGE 157
Balzac v. Porto Rico: Dead Letter after *Ramos v. Louisiana*?
Joel A. Cosme Morales

PAGE 189
The Undying Dead: Why a Century after *Balzac v. Porto Rico*
the *Insular Cases* Are as Important as Ever
Bartholomew Sparrow

PAGE 227

Puerto Rico without Puerto Ricans/"Puerto Ricans without Puerto Rico":
A Comment on *Balzac versus Porto Rico*, A Hundred Years Later
Madeline Román

BOOK REVIEWS

PAGE 255

Latino Orlando: Suburban Transformation and Racial Conflict,
by Simone Delerme
Reviewed by Alessandra Rosa

PAGE 259

"El feminismo no es nuevo": Las crónicas de Clotilde Betances Jaeger,
edited and with an introduction by María Teresa Vera-Rojas
Reviewed by Cristina Pérez Jiménez

PAGE 265

Poets, Philosophers, Lovers: On the Writings of Giannina Braschi,
edited by Frederick Luis Aldama and Tess O'Dwyer
Reviewed by Carmen Haydée Rivera

PAGE 269

*Revolution Around the Corner: Voices from the Puerto Rican Socialist Party in the
United States*, edited by José E. Velázquez, Carmen V. Rivera and Andrés Torres
Reviewed by Efraín Barradas

Introduction— Back to the future: The Implications of *Balzac* One Hundred Years Later

CHARLES R. VENATOR-SANTIAGO AND JOSÉ JAVIER COLÓN MORERA

ABSTRACT

The year 2022 marks the centennial of the Supreme Court's ruling in *Balzac v. People of Porto Rico* (*Balzac v. Porto Rico* 1922), perhaps the most consequential of the *Insular Cases*. *Balzac* affirmed the federal government's power to rule Puerto Rico and its residents separately and unequally within the US polity (Torruella 1988). All the efforts to get the United States Supreme Court to revoke this precedent explicitly have failed. In a way, it is "the elephant in the room" that the federal government is now trying to ignore—not very successfully—in the context of the apparent decay of the colonial system put in place through the Foraker Organic Act of 1900 (*Foraker Organic Act of 1900*).

Charles R. Venator-Santiago (charles.venator@uconn.edu) is an Associate Professor with a joint appointment in the Department of Political Science and El Instituto at the University of Connecticut. He coordinates various public archives including the Puerto Rico Citizenship Archives Project, the Puerto Rico Federal Status Archive Project, and the American Samoa Nationality and Citizenship Archives Project. He is the author of *Puerto Rico and the Origins of U.S. Global Empire: The Disembodied Shade* (Routledge, 2015).

José Javier Colón Morera (jose.colon9@upr.edu) is a Professor at the Political Science Department of the University of Puerto Rico, Río Piedras Campus. He has extensively researched human rights issues regarding Puerto Rico's territorial-colonial status. He has a Ph.D. in Political Science from Boston University and a J.D. from the University of Puerto Rico. Colón Morera is the co-author, with Ramón Bosque Pérez, of *Puerto Rico Under Colonial Rule* (SUNY Press, 2006), and various essays on the topic published in academic journals.

This special volume of the *CENTRO Journal* collects several articles about this monumentally important judicial precedent and its continuous presence in the most important and populated colony remaining in the world. The articles presented help us understand the enduring continuities and discontinuities of the application of the doctrine of territorial non-incorporation to Puerto Rico, a possession inhabited by US citizens.

The articles examine different dimensions of the legacy and continued impact of *Balzac*; it captures many of the complexities of this century of colonialism by judicial decree. Furthermore, they present us with information and analyses that expand our knowledge of the enduring impact of *Balzac*. We have organized the volume in three parts. The first section provides reflections that help contextualize or historicize *Balzac* and its continued relevance. The second cluster examines the relations between *Balzac* and the citizenship status of Puerto Ricans. Finally, the third examines various contemporary debates that arise from this case. These academic contributions shine a light on one of the most consequential Supreme Court rulings that shaped the status of Puerto Rico and Puerto Ricans within the US empire.

One of the challenges that scholars face when writing about *Balzac* is the dearth of historical materials and research on this ruling. Although various important articles and book chapters have addressed various dimensions of this case (Tauber 2006; Katz 1992; Kent 2018) (Aleinikoff 2002; Soltero 2006), we are only aware of one published book on the history of this ruling, namely Francisco Ortiz Santini's *Balsac vs el Pueblo de Puerto Rico: su historia; sus protagonistas* (2019). This volume opens with a special historical overview of *Balzac* and the historical context that shaped the case written by Ortiz Santini. Ortiz Santini's contribution provides one of the clearest and most concise explanations of the *Balzac* ruling, and both its historical relevance and enduring impact. Ortiz Santini's contribution invites the reader to wonder why more has not been written about this history and its relationship to important social and political movements in Puerto Rico.

As previously noted, *Balzac* applied the doctrine of territorial incorporation following the collective naturalization of the islands' residents under the terms of the *Jones Act of 1917*. This doctrine was invented between 1898 and 1901 to govern Puerto Rico and the other territories annexed in the aftermath of the Spanish-American War of 1898. Central to this constitutional interpretation was the invention of a distinction between incorporated territories, bound to become states of the Union, and unincorporated territories that could be held as mere possessions.

Also known as the Third View, the initial goal of this doctrine was to construct an alternative tradition of territorial expansionism to the prevailing anti-imperialist/colonialist and imperialist traditions (Lowell 1899). However, as the legal history of this doctrine or its constitutional interpretation demonstrates, the status ascribed to Puerto Rico and the other annexed territories was conceived as a temporary or transitional measure.

Jorge M. Farinacci Fernós's contribution explains how this constitutional doctrine became indefinite, and perhaps permanent. More than a century later, US federal government continues to rely on the doctrine of territorial incorporation to rule in a separate and unequal manner (Torruella 1988). A key question raised by this contribution is: Why are textualist and originalist judges continuing to reaffirm the distinction between an unincorporated and an incorporated territory, a distinction that has never existed in the constitutional text?

Two additional articles examine the relations between *Balzac* and the status of citizens residing in Puerto Rico within the US empire. Both articles examine historical debates about the ascription of an unequal citizenship status on the residents of Puerto Rico. However, each article is informed by different conceptual questions and visions of citizenship. Venator-Santiago's article takes two basic arguments laid out in *Balzac* as a starting point or premise for his argument. First, he notes that, according to *Balzac,* Puerto Rican-born citizens acquired the same citizenship status as mainland-born citizens. Second, and related to this claim, is a federalist interpretation that makes the application of the Constitution in Puerto Rico contingent on the status of the "locality" or, more specifically, on Puerto Rico's unincorporated territorial status. Thus, what explains whether a locally applicable constitutional provision is operative in Puerto Rico is not the citizenship status itself (or any citizen residing in the islands), but rather the constitutional status of the territory. It follows that because Puerto Rico is an unincorporated territory, the Court could arbitrarily declare that some constitutional provisions, like the Sixth Amendment's right to trial by jury, were not applicable in Puerto Rico.

Drawing on the legal histories of the citizenship legislation extended to Puerto Rico, Venator-Santiago makes two simple arguments. First, since the enactment of the *Nationality Act of 1940,* Venator-Santiago documents, birth in Puerto Rico is tantamount to birth in the United States and Puerto Rican–born citizens acquire the same citizenship as persons born in a state or incorporated territory. Second, he argues that ascriptive narratives of citizenship rely on a liberal narrative of membership that ignores how the status of Puerto Rico (a locality), not the status of its citizenship, mediates the relations between the citizen residing in Puerto Rico and the state. Venator-Santiago's argument is premised on a key question that has yet to be answered by the Supreme Court: Does Congress possess the power or authority to extend birthright or *jus soli* citizenship anchored on the Fourteenth Amendment to an unincorporated territory?

Edgardo Meléndez' contribution provides a careful and detailed analy-sis of the relations between *Balzac,* citizenship, and Puerto Rico's territorial status. Drawing on a detailed discussion of primary archival documents, Meléndez' article fills the gaps in *Balzac* with historical arguments by key policymakers and clarifies the ideological premises of Justice Taft's reason-ing in *Balzac.* Of specific interest is Meléndez' analysis of how Justice Taft decoupled the notion of territorial incorporation from the grant of citizen-ship. To be sure, in *Downes v. Bidwell* (1901), Justice White suggested that the doctrine of territorial incorporation enabled Congress to incorporate Puerto Rico either explicitly or implicitly. Congress could enact legisla-tion that explicitly incorporated or changed Puerto Rico's territorial status. Alternatively, Congress could implicitly incorporate Puerto Rico by enacting citizenship legislation for its residents, an act that could be interpreted as a gesture by Congress to "welcome" Puerto Ricans into the Anglo-American family. In *Balzac,* however, the Court modified this precedent by establish-ing that Congress could only incorporate Puerto Rico with legislation that explicitly incorporated Puerto Rico. Like other contributions in this volume, Meléndez' article raises the question of whether Congress' decision in 1906 to grant Puerto Ricans the ability to acquire a US citizenship via individual naturalization can help us rethink Justice Taft's arguments in *Balzac.*

For more than a century, Congress has affirmed the doctrine of territo-rial incorporation, a doctrine informed by racist rationales of the period in which it was decided. Congress has also refused to incorporate or change Puerto Rico's territorial status since then. In *Ramos v. Louisiana* (2020), Joel A. Cosme Morales argues, the Supreme Court essentially established a precedent that permits the Court to overturn past opinions informed by the racist ideologies of the period in which they were decided. Drawing on this precedent, Cosme Morales argues that the *Ramos* precedent effectively makes *Balzac* a dead letter case and that the Supreme Court should overturn the doctrine of territorial incorporation and the *Insular Cases* more generally. Cosme Morales' argument invites several interesting questions for consideration. First, why should the Court overturn the *Insular Cases*? After all, the *Insular Cases* were merely affirming federal legislation. Shouldn't this be a political decision? Or stated differently, why should political questions be resolved by the Courts? A second line of interesting questions revolved around the role that a century-old racist precedent continues to shape law and policy today. Why does the federal government continue to affirm the doctrine of separate and unequal today?

In recent years, both Congress and the Supreme Court rejected the idea that the Puerto Rican government exercise local autonomy over the islands' affairs. The enactment of PROMESA and the Court's ruling in *Puerto Rico v. Sanchez Valle* (2016) re-established that Puerto Rico was a creature of Congress, devoid of any significant level of substantive administrative sovereignty over its local affairs.

Bartholomew Sparrow's article contextualizes *Sanchez Valle* in the legacy of *Balzac*, affirming the federal government's powers to discriminate geographically against the residents of Puerto Rico. Sparrow notes that the Court has in large measure ceased citing the *Insular Cases* but continues to affirm the substance of its precedents. Sparrow's analysis raises the question, why does the Court continue to embrace an "invisible precedent," or, more precisely, the logic of precedents in part anchored on racist ideologies? Why is the Court today unable to overrule the precedents' established by the *Insular Cases*? What are the current geopolitical conditions that could support such conduct?

Drawing on interpretations from the field of sociology of law and second-generation systems theory, Madeline Román's contribution offers a conceptual reflection on the impact of *Balzac* today. This article provides an alternative way to make sense of the doctrine of territorial incorporation through various theoretical lenses. As an example of Román's description of a "higher level of analysis," one generating a conceptual reflection of historical debates over federalist and colonialist jurisprudence, it has considerable merit. Like other contributions of this volume, it raises important questions for future study. For example, Román invokes the narrative of the "state of exception" to explain the doctrine of territorial incorporation. Can a narrative of the state of exception raise new insights about the application of an anti-democratic constitution and its corresponding federal system in Puerto Rico? Can the comparison of Puerto Rico's territorial status within the US empire be compared to President Abraham Lincoln's suspension of the writ of habeas corpus, to indigenous reservations, or to Nazi concentration camps?

The Continuous Presence of *Balzac*

Let us focus on the *Balzac* ruling. A synopsis of this decision of the early 20th century by University of Puerto Rico's Professor Efrén Rivera Ramos, an expert on this matter, provides an excellent summary:

Jesús M. Balzac, a Puerto Rican journalist and labor leader from Arecibo, was convicted of two libel charges for publishing certain critical remarks against the American governor of Puerto Rico, Arthur Yager. Balzac alleged that his sentence was illegal because he had not been granted a trial by jury, as required by the Sixth Amendment of the US Constitution. *He further claimed that extending US citizenship to Puerto Ricans had the double effect of incorporating Puerto Rico to the United States, thus extending to its inhabitants all the rights bestowed in the federal Constitution.* In 1922, the Supreme Court presided by Judge William Howard Taft, who had been colonial Attorney General and Governor in the Philippines, Secretary of War and President of the United States, rejected the arguments presented by the Puerto Rican. He determined that concession of citizenship had not changed the condition of unincorporated territory of Puerto Rico, and that upon examination of the matter, the right to a trial by jury was not among the fundamental rights that should be granted to the residents of Puerto Rico as a matter of the federal Constitution. *The idea that citizenship would result in the dissolution of the colonial relationship was thus dispelled.* (Rivera Ramos 2019—author's translation and emphasis added)[1]

The importance of the doctrine of the *Insular Cases* with regard to Puerto Rico's historical development and the perpetuation of its colonial situation is crucial to understand *Balzac*. According to Efrén Rivera Ramos, the *Insular Cases* had several very relevant legal and political implications:

(a) they provided an explicit legal justification of the American colonial project in Puerto Rico.

(b) they played a central role in the constitution of a legal and political subject over which the American metropolitan state could exercise its power.

(c) they created a discursive universe within which all further discussion of the colonial problematic would have to be conducted, that is, they defined the "legitimate" discursive framework for subsequent political struggles in relation to the question of the political status of Puerto Rico and the legal and political entitlements of Puerto Ricans; and

(d) they constructed a context for action that facilitated the generation of practices which further reproduced both the conditions for the realization of the colonial project and the framework for its discursive validation. In these four significant respects—with their attendant consequences—the decisions and the doctrine they established became an important constituent element of the colonial project: a significant dimension of Puerto Rican reality as conditioned by the colonial experience. (Rivera Ramos 1996, 228)

Another relevant aspect of the Insular Cases is the fact that they give the US Congress what has been called the power to de-annex the territory—in other words, reverse the non-incorporated condition and to dispose of the territory.

The preeminence of the *Insular Cases* is acknowledged by those considered the major legal authorities on the subject. José Julián Álvarez González, for example, states that the *Balzac* ruling is most likely ineffectual regarding the right to a trial by jury in criminal cases in Puerto Rico.

He nevertheless is aware of its continuous bearing on the crucial subject of the effects of political incorporation as a previous step toward statehood (Álvarez González 2010). In other words, the part of the ruling that is still clearly relevant is mostly the one that has to do with Puerto Rico's political status, despite the efforts of Judge Gelpí—who openly opposes this doctrine of non-incorporation, as demonstrated in *Consejo de Playa de Ponce v. Rullán* (2008). Professor Álvarez González questions Judge Taft's interpretation in the *Balzac* ruling, asserting that concession of US citizenship will allow Puerto Ricans to enjoy full constitutional rights once they move to reside in the states (Álvarez González 2010). The migratory patterns, however, as unleashed by the *Balzac* interpretation, are enormous (Cohn et al. 2014). Another relevant aspect of the *Insular Cases* is the fact that they give the US Congress what has been called the power to de-annex the territory—in other words, reverse the non-incorporated condition and to dispose of the territory. This power was already exercised in the case of the Philippines (Brands 1992). Constitutionalist Christina Duffy Ponsa understands that is one of the main reasons behind and consequences of the *Insular Cases* doctrine (Duffy and Cepeda 2009).

In 1917, responding to multiple factors related to strengthening the hegemonic power of the US, and in a particular geopolitical context, Congress collectively naturalized the residents of Puerto Rico as citizens of the United States (Franqui-Rivera 2013). This came about after a previous legislation allowed the individual naturalization of a limited number of Puerto Ricans since 1906 (Venator-Santiago and Meléndez 2017). Much later, in 1940, Congress finally conceded that being born in Puerto Rico *is equivalent to being born in the United States,* as discussed by Venator-Santiago earlier (*Nationality Act of 1940*).

The *Balzac* precedent, a 1922 unanimous decision, had to resolve the controversy about the consequences of the collective naturalization of the residents in terms of their political status. The 1922 ruling clearly and unequivocally established that the incorporation of territories like Puerto Rico is an *explicit* prerogative of Congress. Such powers of administration of the territories is a political problem best attended to by the national legislative branch.

If the *Insular Cases* are so central to the administration of the territorial system, why is the Supreme Court reluctant to confront these cases? It would seem obvious that the racist connotations of the cases would lead the Federal Justice Department lawyers to keep a reasonable distance from precedents censured for their strong racist content. As a matter of fact, in the *Reid v. Covert* case, a number of Supreme Court judges clearly stated that it would not [further expand] the doctrine (*Reid v. Covert* 1957). They even warned against its dangers:

[I]t is our judgment that neither the [Insular] cases nor their reasoning should be given any further expansion. The concept that the Bill of Rights and other constitutional protections against arbitrary government are inoperative when they become inconvenient or when expediency dictates otherwise is a very dangerous doctrine and if allowed to flourish would destroy the benefit of a written Constitution and undermine the basis of our Government. (*Reid v. Covert* 1957, 14)

As this volume will demonstrate, *Balzac's* precedent is still used as a controlling principle, without explicitly recognizing its preeminence. The Federal government is embarrassed to cite cases in which the Court is closer, more than ever, to explicitly acknowledging that Puerto Rico constitutes a culturally separate entity (*Balzac v Porto Rico* 1922, 347). It is a subject that intertwines the racism of the beginning of the 20th century with an acknowledgment of the tremendous contemporary force of cultural nationalism.

Regarding the question presented in *Balzac* on whether collective naturalization of Puerto Ricans in 1917 had altered Puerto Rico's political status, the answer from the Supreme Court was unequivocal: "Had Congress intended to take the important step of changing the treaty status of Porto Rico by incorporating it into the Union, it is reasonable to suppose that it would have done so by the plain declaration, and would not have left it to mere inference" (*Balzac v. Porto Rico* 1922, 306).

The Court states in *Balzac*:

The Constitution, however, contains grants of power, and limitations which in the nature of things are not always and everywhere applicable and the real issue in the Insular Cases was not whether the Constitution extended to the Philippines or Porto Rico when we went there, but which ones of its provisions were applicable by way of limitation upon the exercise of executive and legislative power in dealing with new conditions and requirements. The guaranties of certain fundamental personal rights declared in the Constitution, as, for instance, that no person could be deprived of life, liberty, or property without due process of law, had from the beginning full application in the Philippines and Porto Rico, and, as this guaranty is one of the must fruitful in causing litigation in our own country, provision was naturally made for similar controversy in Porto Rico. Indeed, provision is made for the consideration of constitutional questions coming on appeal and writs of error from the Supreme Court of the Philippines, which are certainly not incorporated in the Union.

On the whole, therefore, we find no features in the Organic Act of Porto Rico of 1917 from which we can infer the purpose of Congress to incorporate Porto Rico into the United States with the consequences which would follow. (Balzac v. Porto Rico 1922, 312–3—emphasis added)

The *Insular Cases* were also not cited in the *Sánchez Valle* ruling, which states that the ultimate source of sovereignty in the Commonwealth of Puerto Rico's territorial treaty is Congress, for purposes of the double jeopardy federal doctrine (*Puerto Rico v. Sánchez Valle* 2016). They also were not cited in the *Aurelius* case, which validated the process by which the members of the Financial Oversight and Management Board [of Puerto Rico] would be chosen (*Financial Oversight v. Aurelius* 2020).

The reverberating effects of the judicial norm set in *Balzac v. Porto Rico* are still forcefully felt. Its presence reaffirmed in 1922, by a unanimous court decision, the non-incorporated nature of Puerto Rico as a territory composed of US citizens, a territory that belongs to the United States. The decision has been at hand in recent crucial human rights litigation.

The Federal Government's discriminatory policy toward Puerto Rican residents in the foreign-domestic locality is constantly referred to as a problem for those struggling for more equitable remedies to generalized poverty in the territories. For example, *many friends of the court* involved in the *Vaello Madero* litigation, which asked for parity in federal funds in the SSI program for Puerto Rican residents, have requested the explicit reversal of *Balzac* (Puerto Rico Governor 2021; Latino Justice 2021). Many recognize this legal precedent as the primary justification for racist colonial forms of differentiation.

The facts of the *Vaello* case illustrate the centrality of locality in the administration of Puerto Rico as a "foreign in a domestic sense location." Vaello Madero, a Puerto Rican, lived in New York from 1985 to 2013 and had qualified to receive Supplemental Security Income (SSI) benefits (*United States v. Vaello Madero* 2020). However, he moved to Puerto Rico in July 2013, and in June 2016, the Social Security Administration (SSA) stopped sending his SSI payments. In defense of a disparate treatment to Puerto Ricans residing in Puerto Rico, the Federal Government has used, in both a discreet and forceful manner, the "insular cases" doctrine extensively. In the *Vaello Madero* case, the last of a number of recent legal disputes about Puerto Rico in the US Supreme Court, the US Department of Justice has used the non-incorporated logic extensively. This assertion by the Justice Department, under President Trump's tenure, is very explicit:

Indeed, the Constitution itself distinguishes between States and Territories for a variety of purposes, including representation in Congress; participation in presidential elections; congressional power; delegation of legislative power; appointments of officers; judicial tenure; and double jeopardy. Congress, too, has enacted a variety of laws that distinguish Territories from States—including tax laws; bankruptcy laws; civil-rights laws; and healthcare laws. Put simply, a Territory differs from a State, and the Constitution allows Congress to recognize that difference. (Petition Writ of Certiorari 2020, 11)

The Trump administration's reliance on the Insular cases in the course of the *Vaello* case was very strong:

Congress has a legitimate interest in avoiding a one-sided fiscal relationship under which *Puerto Rico shares the financial benefits but not the financial burdens of statehood,* and declining to include Puerto Rico in the SSI program is a rational means of furthering that interest. (Petition Writ of Certiorari 2020, 12—emphasis added)

President Biden's position is similarly strong in the assertions of broad authority over a non-incorporated territory and its centrality to the process leading to decisions about the political future of territories. For example, in the same Vaello dispute, the Federal government argues for a separate territorial policy. The Biden administration also uses the political status controversy to ask the Federal courts to stay away from claims of parity on federal funds for Puerto Rico:

The Admission Clause commits to Congress the responsibility to decide when to admit a Territory into the Union and thereby provide it with the benefits associated with statehood. Interpreting the equal-protection guarantee to require Congress to accord Territories the same treatment as States would upset that textual allocation of responsibility. (Brief for the United States 2021)

The *Vaello Madero* case refers to the living conditions of a poor and vulnerable Puerto Rican population of several US territories, with already dire poverty and inequality indicators (Vázquez-Colón 2020). The normative implications of the support of non-incorporation by the Federal Government are substantial. The positions assumed by the US executive branch, regardless of the partisan powers in charge, are still based on the normative and political logic of *Balzac* (Brief for the United States 2021). The *Balzac* ruling of 1922, in this context, is having an important role as an "invisible precedent." Before the US Supreme Court, the Executive Branch of the Federal government would defend its constitutional prerogatives to determine the level of public costs of Federal funds expenditure in this Caribbean territory, as well as its tax policies. On the other hand, progressive sectors refuse to uphold some of the implicit doctrines of the *Insular Cases* (Equally American 2021).

Its doctrine is central in the decision of the US Congress to evade an issue for which it does not have the political will to advance: an explicit decolonial agenda.

All these recent political and judicial events force us in academia to confront the continuing colonial legacy that *Porto Rico v Balzac* represents.

Its doctrine is central in the decision of the US Congress to evade an issue for which it does not have the political will to advance: an explicit decolonial agenda. It is our duty to keep insisting on the damaging effects of this onerous presence of the past, and to create conditions providing a new normative understanding for Puerto Rico.

NOTES

[1] Jesús M. Balzac, un periodista y líder obrero puertorriqueño de Arecibo, fue encontrado culpable de dos delitos de libelo por publicar ciertas expresiones críticas del gobernador estadounidense de Puerto Rico, Arthur Yager. Balzac reclamó que su condena había sido ilegal, pues no se le había celebrado un juicio por jurado, como requiere la Enmienda Sexta de la Constitución de los Estados Unidos. Alegó que la extensión de la ciudadanía estadounidense a los puertorriqueños había tenido el doble efecto de incorporar a Puerto Rico a los Estados Unidos y hacer extensivos a sus habitantes todos los derechos consignados en la Constitución federal. En 1922, el Tribunal Supremo, presidido por el Juez William Howard Taft, quien había sido Procurador General, Gobernador colonial de Filipinas, Secretario de Guerra y Presidente de los Estados Unidos, rechazó el argumento del puertorriqueño. Determinó que la concesión de la ciudadanía no había tenido el efecto de terminar con la condición de territorio no incorporado de Puerto Rico y que, examinada la cuestión, el derecho a juicio por jurado no constituía uno de esos derechos fundamentales que debían reconocérseles a los residentes de Puerto Rico como cuestión constitucional federal. Se disipaba así la idea de que la ciudadanía tendría como consecuencia la disolución de la relación colonial (**Rivera Ramos 2019**).

REFERENCES

Aleinikoff, T. Alexander. 2002. *Semblances of Sovereignty: The Constitution, the State, and American Citizenship.* Cambridge, MA: Harvard University Press.

Álvarez González, José Julián. 2010. Derecho constitucional de Puerto Rico y relaciones constitucionales con los Estados. Bogotá: Temis.

Balzac v. Porto Rico. 1922. 258 U.S. 298.

Brands, H. W. 1992. *Bound to Empire: the United States and the Philippines.* New York: Oxford University Press.

Brief for the United States. 2020. No. 20-303, 29, June.

Cohn, D'Vera, Eileen Patten, Eileen and Mark Hugo Lopez. 2014. Puerto Rican Population Declines on Island, Grows on U.S. Mainland. Pew Research Center. <https://www.pewresearch.org/hispanic/2014/08/11/puerto-

rican-population-declines-on-island-grows-on-u-s-mainland/>.

Consejo de Playa de Ponce v. Rullán. 2008. 586 F. Supp. 2d 22.

Downes v. Bidwell. 1901. 182 U.S. 244.

Duffy Ponsa, Christina and Adriel I. Cepeda Derieux. 2009. Los Casos Insulares: doctrina desanexionista. *Revista Jurídica de la Universidad de Puerto Rico* 78(3), 661–99.

Equally American. 2021. Members of Congress Press Biden-Harris DOJ To Reject Insular Cases, <https://www.equalrightsnow.org/members_of_congress_press_biden_harris_doj_to_reject_insular_cases>.

Franqui-Rivera, Harry. 2013. Mitología nacional: ciudadanía norteamericana para la gente de Puerto Rico y servicio militar. *MEMORIAS, Revista digital de Historia y Arqueología desde el Caribe colombiano* 10(2), 5–21.

Financial Oversight and Management Board for Puerto Rico v. Aurelius Investment, LLC. 2020. 140 S.Ct. 1649.

Jones Act of 1917. 1917. Pub. L. No. 64-368, 39 Stat. 951.

Katz, Robert A. 1992. The Jurisprudence of Legitimacy: Applying the Constitution to U.S. Territories. *University of Chicago Law Review* 59(2), 779–806.

Kent, Andrew. 2018. The Jury and Empire: The Insular Cases and the Anti-Jury Movement in the Gilded Age and Progressive Era. *Southern California Law Review* 91, 375–465.

Latino Justice PRLDEF Amicus Brief. 2021. 7 September.

Lowell, Abbott Lawrence. 1899. The Status of Our New Possessions—A Third View. *Harvard Law Review* 13(3), 155–76.

Nationality Act of 1940. 1940. Pub. L. No. 76-853, 54 Stat. 1137.

Ortiz Santini, Francisco. 2019. *Balsac vs el Pueblo de Puerto Rico: su historia; sus protagonistas.* N.p.: Editorial My Book Creations.

Petition for a Writ of Certiorari. 2020. *United States of America v. Vaello Madero,* September.

Puerto Rico v. Sanchez Valle. 2016. 579 U.S. 59, 136 S. CT. 1863.

Puerto Rico Governor Pedro Pierluisi and the New Progressive Party Amicus Brief in support of Respondent. 2021. 7 September.

Ramos v. Louisiana. 2020. 140 S. Ct. 1390.

Reid v. Covert. 1957. 354 U.S. 1.

Rivera Ramos, Efrén. 1996. The Legal Construction of American Colonialism: the Insular Cases *Revevista Jurídica de la Universidad de Puerto Rico* 65, 225–303.

_____. 2001. *The Legal Construction of Identity: The Judicial and Social Legacy of American Colonialism in Puerto Rico*. Washington, DC: American Psychological Association.

_____. 2019. El discurso de la ciudadanía: mitos y realidades. *80grados* 26 April. <https://www.80grados.net/el-discurso-de-la-ciudadania-mitos-y-realidades/>.

Soltero, Carlos R. 2006. *Latinos and American Law: Landmark Supreme Court Cases*. Austin: University of Texas Press.

Tauber, Alan. 2006. The Empire Forgotten: The Application of the Bill of Rights to U.S. Territories. *Case Western Reserve Law Review* 57(1), 147–78.

Torruella, Juan R. 1988. *The Supreme Court and Puerto Rico: The Doctrine of Separate and Unequal*. Río Piedras: Editorial de la Universidad de Puerto Rico.

Vázquez-Colón, Brenda A. 2020. Expuesto nuevamente el rostro de la desigualdad, Se trata de un desafío real para la Isla poder mejorar su entorno social y económico. *El Vocero* 23 October. <https://www.elvocero.com/economia/expuesto-nuevamente-el-rostro-de-la-desigualdad/article_04958130-14cc-11eb-ab90-b3b3be644064.htm>.

Venator-Santiago, Charles R and Edgardo Meléndez. 2017. U.S. Citizenship in Puerto Rico: One Hundred Years After the Jones Act. *CENTRO: Journal of the Center for Puerto Rican Studies* 29(1), 14–37.

United States v. Vaello-Madero. 2020. 956 F.3d 12, 15 (1st Cir.).

The Sword of Libel: Jesús María Balsac and The Quest for Equality

FRANCISCO ORTIZ SANTINI

ABSTRACT

When Jesús María Balsac marched to Washington by means of his appeal, Puerto Rico was enduring one of the most convulsive periods in its history. The colonial government employed brute force to repress the outgrowing pro-workers and pro-statehood movement headed by leaders such as Santiago Iglesias Pantín, Esteban Padilla and Balsac himself. But brute force was not the only means utilized to subjugate the defiant *socialistas*. Freedom of speech was also impaired and even used as a means for retaliation. As anticipated by Padilla, the colonial administration of Governor Arthur Yager targeted the Partido Socialista's leadership in the city of Arecibo with criminal libel. And then, the *Balzac* legal affair got started. This paper is a reflection upon these events, how they still influence our lives, and why I chose to write about it. [Keywords: Balzac, freedom of speech, Insular Cases, Colonial Rule, Puerto Rico, US Supreme Court]

Francisco Ortiz Santini (Francisco.ortiz8@upr.edu), a lawyer in private practice and part-time professor at the School of Communication and Information of the University of Puerto Rico, Río Piedras campus, is originally from Aibonito, Puerto Rico. He has a doctorate in Philosophy and Letters with a concentration in History, obtained at the Center for Advanced Studies of Puerto Rico and the Caribbean. He is fond of genealogy and the use of open-source applications for computers.

"This will give you an idea of the amount of scum falling upon us,
and all we are ready to carry through this time if they seize our rights."
(Esteban Padilla to Santiago Iglesias Pantín, May 1918)

A Brief Introduction

El profesor Juan Manuel García-Passalacqua was obsessed with *Balzac* the case, and also with *Balsac* the man, who stood trial for it. At the beginning, I was not. I did not want to anchor my Ph.D. thesis on a legal case; not even if it was *that* case. Why? Because I was already an attorney at the time, and just felt it would be more challenging to engage in some subject beyond law, in order to prove—at least to myself—I was "worthy" of my doctoral degree. But as anyone who knew him well enough, *Juanma* was nothing if not persistent. He was so utterly convinced about the worthiness of the *Balzac* quest that I ended conceding and gave it a shot. Due to a monograph previously submitted by another student, we already knew our subject was some sort of labor "crusader" who enabled *escuelitas* (small classrooms) to indoctrinate cane workers in the virtues of syndicalism and socialism. Getting hold of ancient Puerto Rican court records was not difficult to achieve so, why not?

And then, I was in shock. Things started to unravel the moment I noticed Santiago Iglesias Pantín paid a small fortune—in those long-gone days' money—for a bond on behalf of Jesús María Balsac's gambit to the United States Supreme Court. For starters, I just learned Puerto Rico's paramount labor leader was behind the case, and Balsac's last name was misspelled by both our court system as well as the US.[1] So, there was a story to be uncovered and told not just behind the case, but also the man as well after all. From then on, I was hooked and pursued the story.

Anatomy of a case: dramatis personae

As often happens, further research showed this legal saga was not limited to Iglesias Pantín and Balsac himself. There was their fellow partner Esteban Padilla. Also, the labor leader Samuel Gompers, a key player in all concerted efforts to bring the Puerto Rican question before the United States Supreme Court *and* Congress. There was also Jackson H. Ralston, an attorney well-versed in labor, constitutional and territorial affairs, but one who ultimately knew deep down Balsac's quest to be a lost cause. And, of course, this is a story about a supreme colonialist, William H. Taft. Let us take a brief look at the later.

Far from a natural-born leader, the future US President and Chief Justice was a man of limited intellectual resources or initiative. Taft chose to study law in his native Cincinnati, having much more prestigious universities at hand. He was not interested in a private practice of the law nor in bringing on litigation. He preferred for the controversies to come to him and, as such, only work posts in the executive and judiciary branches of the federal government would fit the bill. He "always had [his] plate the right side up when offices were falling" (Pringle 1939, 57). As pointed out by another of his biographers, "Taft's appointment as Solicitor General rested largely on political grounds, and not because of his mastery of constitutional law" (Burton 1998, 44). Due to his family and political connections,

[t]he fates were, as always, pushing Taft higher and higher. Perhaps he was the only man in American political history who can, with complete accuracy, be described as a creature of destiny. (Pringle 1939, 107)

But not even being a judge could spark a lightning of creativity in Taft, who was perfectly at home with literal interpretations of written law. And he was a conservative man; very much so. Among Taft's enemies, organized syndicalism would be seen as preponderant. He would promptly be dubbed "the injunction judge." He would not hesitate in wishing death or harm to labor activists, but inflicted by hands other than his own (Pringle 1939).

Initially, Taft opposed his country's imperialist ventures. But once Spain was defeated, he had minimal objections to relocate a half globe away with the Second Philippines Commission, and later becoming the first colonial Governor of the archipelago. All his objections were dissipated once he secured the right not only to—along with Secretary of State Elihu Root—draft the rules for the Commission, but to preside it (Pringle 1939; Burton 1998). Taft was not made to achieve leadership by his own means or initiatives. It had to be handed to him, on a silver plate nonetheless.

Meanwhile, by the turn of the 20th century Santiago Iglesias Pantín and Samuel Gompers were becoming acquainted. The syndicalist and former

Spanish anarchist made a pact to, in order to receive the American Federation of Labor's blessing as its representative in Puerto Rico, transform himself into a "moderate" labor leader (Mandel 1963; García and Quintero Rivera 1997). On his part, Gompers shared with William H. Taft a "natural" antipathy for the people of some of the territories acquired after 1898 (Bedford 1995). Fortunately—I suppose—Puerto Ricans were not among those. He was terrified when—taken by the hand by Iglesias Pantín—he visited the island for the first time in 1904 and saw the terrible conditions most of its inhabitants were enduring, notwithstanding General Nelson Miles' promises to the contrary. For Iglesias Pantín, that first Gompers visit galvanized the alliance between the insular and continental syndicalist movements.

The pretentious "Attorney for Porto Rico" sued Zeno Gandía for libel, in much the same way as Balsac would be hit six years later by colonial Governor Arthur Yager.

Gompers and Iglesias Pantín were already seasoned warriors in the political arena. Both risked jail on several occasions or were actually put behind bars for a while. Gompers, however, could count on Jackson H. Ralston, attorney at law, to steer away the willing jailers. A fascinating character by himself and a successful trial lawyer, Ralston ably represented interests as diverse as the then Oregon territory or the Philippines government (Dennis 1946). After successfully representing territorial and labor interests, it was small wonder he chose to stand for Jesús María Balsac before the US Supreme Court.

But before Balsac, there was doctor Manuel Zeno Gandía. One of the greatest Puerto Rican novelists and journalists, Zeno Gandía was indignant with one particular guy from the North, who as an attorney was taking advantage by suing the island's government while retaining a public post financed with insular money. Not that different from what is happening with our current—and equally imposed—Financial Oversight and Management Board, I would guess. In the little known 1912 case of *Gandía v. Pettinghill*, Zeno Gandía was sued for criticizing a person only known as NBK Pettinghill. According to the courts' findings, Zeno Gandía charged

Pettinghill of, at least, immoral behavior, because "while United States Attorney for Porto Rico, carried on a private practice also, and even acted as a lawyer on behalf of persons bringing suit against the government of Porto Rico" (*Gandía v. Pettinghill* 1912, 457). The pretentious "Attorney for Porto Rico" sued Zeno Gandía for libel, in much the same way as Balsac would be hit six years later by colonial Governor Arthur Yager. In those days, and as recently as in the 1990s, libel was a double-edged sword in Puerto Rico, with both civil and criminal ramifications.

The *Gandía* case would be ultimately decided by the US Supreme Court in favor of Dr. Zeno Gandía. It was a unanimous judgment, penned by renowned jurist Oliver Wendell Holmes. But while deciding in favor of the defendant, Justice Holmes could not help but insert racist overtones in his prose. He stressed that finding in the defendant's favor still required "making reasonable allowance for the somewhat more exuberant expressions of meridional speech" (1912, 458). This cursed phrase would resurface as a mark for libel prosecution in the colonies, as the supreme courts of both the US and the Philippines (by then well under US rule) so stated in the *Balzac* decision itself, and in another one issued by the later court just months after the former's (*The People of the Philippine Islands vs. Isaac Pérez* 1923).

But Holmes was something else beyond a racist. He authored the infamous 1927 *Buck v. Bell* decision, allowing the use of forced sterilization on one Mrs. Carrie Buck, "a feeble-minded white woman..., the daughter of a feeble-minded mother..., and the mother of an illegitimate feeble-minded child" (274 US 200, 205). For the so-called great jurist, "[t]hree generations of imbeciles [were] enough" (274 US 200, 207). In *Balzac*, he concurred in the judgment of an otherwise unanimous decision.

One could not help but wonder how people like Zeno Gandía and Balsac were able to cope with a colonial regime that kept remembering them—albeit in an elegant style—their racial distinctiveness, not to mention inferiority. Racism permeated the relations between colonial administrators and their Puerto Rican subjects, every step of the way (Erman 2018). Such was the case, for example, with then President Thomas Woodrow Wilson. Having received the assistance of labor for the 1912 presidential election, Wilson could not afford to alienate leaders such as Gompers. At the same time, he could not care less about the welfare of Puerto Rican workers. It was Wilson who named his old friend Arthur Yager as colonial Governor. When workers started clashing with their employers, Wilson's delayed maneuvering in support of his friend was crucial in dissipating Gompers' mounting demands for the Governor's removal. And so, it was Governor Yager's increasing struggle with insular labor what set the stage for the Balsac prosecution.

Jesús María Balsac was not merely a rank-and-file member of the Federación Libre de Trabajadores (FLT). He was well educated and knew how to print—a singular asset in those years with no internet nor television. Newspapers and the telegraph ruled the day. Balsac was author or collaborator in no less than four books in which he wrote about politics, justice and, of course, workers' rights. He regarded Esteban Padilla—perhaps, along with Luisa Capetillo, the most militant and active labor leader in Puerto Rican history—as his brother-in-arms. But Iglesias Pantín had a special place in his heart, calling him *mi maestro* ("my mentor"). Padilla and Balsac were also deeply involved in political struggles, especially in the coastal city of Arecibo. There, they assisted in the foundation of the local Partido Obrero Insular, a direct precursor to the powerful Partido Socialista that would dominate Puerto Rican politics in the coming decades. But aside from political conflicts, there was violence. A lot, actually.

Years before Pedro Albizu-Campos signaled armed resistance from the Partido Nacionalista, labor set a precedent. Telegraph communications among labor activists depicted daily incidents of physical violence between workers on strike and the police. Intimidation and repression by the colonial authorities and plantation owners against labor members were continual. For instance, Jorge Bird, general manager of the Fajardo Sugar Company, sent a message to Santiago Iglesias Pantín stating that he would be shot dead if something happened to the former or his family. Communications were curtailed, because the Bureau of Insular Telegraph applied a prior restraint to labor messages due to its contents. Tellingly, in a note published in April 1918, labor declared that "[i]f the government allowing these abuses is a democratic government, damned be the democracy!!"

The first movement seriously aimed at destabilization of the colonial regime was a mix of socialist and annexation ideals (García-Passalacqua 1993; Silén 1980). In order to avoid facing an "elephant in the room" contradiction of fighting a colonial government while at the same time aspiring to statehood, labor leadership brushed aside or openly ignored the systemic racism coming from the North. It postured instead that all blame for the current toxic atmosphere rested on the shoulders and personal failings of colonial administrators who opposed equal treatment for all Puerto Ricans. At the same time, it built alliances with sectors sympathizing with their cause such as, precisely, the American Federation of Labor (AFL) (Silén 1995).

With the AFL's assistance and support, including a salary for Iglesias Pantín, the Federación Libre de Trabajadores morphed into the locally based Partido Obrero Insular, in order to compete for control of the Arecibo municipality. With Esteban Padilla and Jesús María Balsac as heads of the monumental effort, Arecibo's fields formed the center of a perfect storm engulfing the whole island. Labor reports of systematic violence and suppression of expression, by both private individuals and the colonial regime, continued. It was then when Padilla warned Iglesias Pantín about "the amount of scum falling upon us" in May 1918. "Capitalist" newspapers were reporting at the time that Balsac was a target of a criminal ongoing prosecution, as a result of two opinion columns he penned in his own newspaper, *El Baluarte* ("The Fortress").

The articles in question, drafted in well-worded, cultured and even poetic language, were nonetheless merciless and highly condemning of Governor Yager. Even fellow labor journalists conceded the wording as "rude." And so the article got the Governor's attention. Rumors started spreading about an ongoing criminal investigation against Balsac. Even from such an early phase, labor was quite sure about what it intended to pursue, beyond Balsac's freedom of course. A well-known Partido Unión de Puerto Rico attorney and also related to labor—one named José de Jesús Tizol—was retained as counsel. On May 9, 1918, two members of the Junta de Defensa Pro-Balsac, Esteban Padilla and J. Santos Rodríguez, published in labor's newspaper *Unión Obrera* a joint article informing about Balsac's cases and stating, in unequivocal terms, the goals pursued:

Mr. Tizol and us believe this matter must be brought on appeal to the Mainland if needed (and it is almost for sure it will be) and make of it an exemplary case defining once and for all the condition of the Puerto Rican producer regarding the public rights and citizenship supposedly guaranteed by both the Ameri-

**can Constitution and Flag, guarantees denied these days in Puerto Rico by
the unfair and biased actions of the local government. For that, considerable
resources are required, several hundreds of dollars and diligent and enthusiastic action, for it would not be a surprise for those hearings to take place on or
before May 20, which is why we appeal to all our conscious workers' solidarity,
those who aspire to more wealth, social and public liberties.**

On May 31, 1918—at the same time Governor Yager was striping the
Partido Obrero Insular of a well-earned electoral victory in Arecibo—the
District Attorney filed two indictments for violation of Penal Code's Articles
243 and 244, criminal libel, against Balsac.

As can be expected, labor media paid particular attention to the proceedings. Balsac was informed of the charges pressed against him, and a trial
was scheduled. However, attorney de Jesús Tizol forced constant delays by
asking for several continuances due to schedule conflicts. It was clear, at
least from my standpoint, that he was dragging his feet, trying to fatigue the
District Attorney. But the tactic only worked so far and the trial court forced
the defense to stand trial on a mutually agreed date that, nonetheless, de
Jesús Tizol tried once again to thwart. Among the final arguments brought
by the defense and almost as an afterthought, a trial by jury was requested. It
was the very first time such a particular request was made, and was as such
denied by presiding judge Enrique Lloreda Casabo.

The trial took place in one single day, July 29, 1918. The District
Attorney's witnesses' roster showed he had the government's full support.
It included such people as Ramón Alfonso Rivera (Arecibo's Postmaster),
all the way to José Coll Vidal (journalist and director of *La Democracia*
newspaper). Several fellow labor members testified on Balsac's behalf, but
it was clear he was the author and publisher of the articles. He did not testify. And he was found guilty. A request for Balsac to remain free pending
appeal was granted. Prison was avoided—at least for the time being—and an
unexpected, federal-related request for a trial by jury was brought up and
preserved, for future use.

The next step would be the Puerto Rico Supreme Court. But a couple of
hurdles—one almost fatal and the other most certainly—were present. The
first involved nearly losing the appeal on procedural grounds, due to the

lack of counsel. For reasons as yet unknown, attorney de Jesús Tizol became unavailable, forcing Balsac to file a sworn statement detailing his efforts to contact the former. In the last minute, labor came to the rescue in the form of two lawyers intimately related to the movement: Abraham Peña Romero and José Soto Rivera.

With the Puerto Rico Supreme Court now duly "primed," it should have come as no surprise Balsac had not a chance.

The second obstacle to Balsac's and the Federación Libre de Trabajadores' quest came from the United States Supreme Court, by means of a couple of decisions handed down in January, 1918. They involved two 1917 criminal cases: *People of Porto Rico v. Tapia*[2] and *People of Porto Rico v. Muratti*. A brief explanation is required. As soon as the American citizenship was "given" to all Puerto Ricans in March 1917, both the US Federal District Court and the Puerto Rico Supreme Court took for granted it meant incorporation into the Union. So much so, that it required reversing otherwise legitimate murder convictions.

And so, in delivering the opinion in *Muratti* (1917), American Associate Justice Adolf Grant Wolf—sitting as such in the Supreme Court of Puerto Rico—found the matter at hand to be as clear as a simple equation: "a + b + c = a + c + b."[3] By quoting US Supreme Court decisions such as 1901 *Downes v. Bidwell* and *Rasmussen v. United States*, Justice Wolf sustained that

the irreversible tendency and force of these decisions are necessarily in favor of having Puerto Rico as an integral part of the United States, just as Louisiana, Florida and other territories before admission as states, such as Hawaii, the District of Columbia and Alaska nowadays. (25 DPR 568, 572)

On appeal in both cases, the US Supreme Court took little time in making clear to the lower courts they simply "did not get the memo" in what regarded Puerto Rico. Citing a plethora of *Insular Cases*, the Court summarily reversed the US District Court in *Tapia*. Then, and quoting *Tapia* as sole authority, *Muratti* met the same fate by means of another summary reversal. With the Puerto Rico Supreme Court now duly "primed," it should have come as no surprise Balsac had not a chance. And none he got. The trial court's judgment was unanimously affirmed, including the dismissal of the trial-by-jury claim, upon the authority set forth in *Tapia* and *Muratti*.

Against this backdrop of legal drama taking place in Puerto Rico, new Supreme Court Chief Justice William Howard Taft was getting comfortable or, at least, trying to. But since he was not a natural-born leader, he found it difficult to get along with fellow justices, let alone forging consensus. The Taft court was delivering fractured 5-to-4 decisions aplenty, including cases involving labor matters (Pringle 1939; Burton 1998). That, alone, did not bode well for a *Balzac* appeal fueled by labor's ideology and money.

But labor would have none of it, since the *Balzac* proceedings were heralded as the "exemplary case defining once and for all the condition of the Puerto Rican producer regarding the public rights and citizenship supposedly guaranteed by both the American Constitution and flag," as stated in *Unión Obrera*. But the need for money—a lot of it—was of great concern. Manuel Alonso, General Secretary of the FLT announced a "pro-prosecuted" collect, with special emphasis on the *Balzac* appeal. Meanwhile, the AFL retained Jackson Ralston as main counsel for Balsac, to be compensated by the FLT. With the appeal in place, the AFL engaged in its own quest for Puerto Rican incorporation into the Union by means of a congressional law project known as the Nolan Bill.

The Nolan Bill (law project 9934) was one of several bills aimed at modifying the current status of Puerto Rico (Trías Monge 1997). Its main sponsor, Republican Congressman from California John I. Nolan, was a labor activist who came to Washington with the helping hand of Gompers and the AFL. His ascension to Congress also shows the political clout held by Gompers over both main US political parties. Of all the law projects then jockeying for support, the Nolan Bill was the only one explicitly proposing to hold Puerto Rico as an incorporated territory. It received the unconditional endorsement from the FLT, which stated that "[e]xcept for the bill making Puerto Rico an incorporated territory of the United States and thus placing the Island on the path to statehood, none of the other projects will solve Puerto Rico's political and economical situation in the right way and according to the free institutions of the American government" (Los puertorriqueños quieren hacer de la Isla un Estado 1922—author's translation).

In effect, labor was pulling its considerable muscles on behalf of the Puerto Rican cause in not one, but in two of the three branches of the Federal government, at once. In the judiciary, FLT's money and AFL's contacts enabled the *Balzac* appeal to be well-represented before the US Supreme Court by such a renowned attorney as Ralston. On the other hand, a concurring, equally aimed offensive was taking place in Congress, pushed forward by Samuel Gompers' AFL in the form of the Nolan Bill. Territorial incorporation was their lone target.

The Nolan Bill would die in Congress with little fuss (Trías Monge 1997). In the Supreme Court, a similar fate was awaiting the *Balzac* appeal. In an unusual finding of consensus, a unanimous court found against the appellant. It did not matter labor was bringing up the case. Neither did that Chief Justice Taft was authoring the opinion and judgment. There was no dissent to be found; not a single voice supporting implied incorporation as postured by Ralston, even though it has been previously found so in a case concerning the Alaskan territory (*Rassmussen v. United States* 1905).[4] Not even a solitary and sympathetic voice for labor was heard. In the clearest of terms, Chief Justice Taft ruled that

Congress has thought that a people like the Filipinos or the Porto Ricans, trained to a complete judicial system which knows no juries, living in compact and ancient communities, with definitely formed customs and political conceptions, should be permitted themselves to determine how far they wish to adopt this institution of Anglo-Saxon origin, and when. (*Balzac v. People of Porto Rico* 1922, 310)

In his opinion for the court, the Chief Justice even found the juncture to send a message to the Puerto Ricans. When remembered of the *Tapia* and *Muratti* cases, Taft stated that "[c]ounsel have urged us in the cases at the bar to deal with the questions raised more at length in exposition of the effect of the Organic Act of 1917 upon the issue, and we have done so" (*Balzac v. People of Porto Rico* 1922, 313–4). In a brief letter, dated April 18, 1922, to Santiago Iglesias Pantín about the result, Jackson Ralston stated:

I am enclosing herewith opinion in the case of Balzac vs. People of Porto Rico with regard to the nature of which you have undoubtedly been fully informed by telegraph.

I regret the outcome. But under the circumstances any other result was impossible.

A few more words

Taken alongside the Nolan Bill effort, the *Balzac* case constitutes the closest Puerto Rico has been to achieving Statehood—or at least an incorporated territorial status—with assistance from a sympathetic and powerful movement from within the United States. It combined the will and resources of two of the most influential and muscular organizations in both the United States and Puerto Rico, as both the American Federation of Labor and the Federación Libre de Trabajadores certainly were. The former had access and influence in both the Executive and Legislative branches of power in the federal government, as well as in both political main parties. President Woodrow Wilson may have tried to diverge from AFL's Samuel Gompers demands, but could not ignore him. Colonial Governor Arthur Yager may have tried to ignore Federación Libre de Trabajadores' Santiago Iglesias Pantín, but could not avoid dealing with him.

After the 1917 *Tapia* and *Muratti* cases, there should have remained very little incentive to push the incorporation issue again before the US Supreme Court. The Puerto Rico Supreme Court certainly learned its lesson, when confirming the judgments against Balsac. The local courts' judgments finding incorporation in both *Tapia* and *Muratti* forced the US Supreme Court's hand to intervene and set the record straight. There were no such qualms in *Balzac*. The Puerto Rico Supreme Court acknowledged it could not risk another summary, humiliating reversal on behalf of incorporation. So, brief, terse judgments were delivered against Balsac in the insular realm. That should have been it. But it was not. At least, not for labor, both insular *and* continental.

On the contrary, labor seemed to be following a well-choreographed strategy, knowing perfectly well *Balzac* would end up in Washington. It stated so as early as May 1918, even before criminal charges against Balsac were announced. They were expecting the "scum falling upon" them, as Esteban Padilla foretold Santiago Iglesias Pantín, and were ready to act upon it, as if a door was suddenly open. Taking into account poverty at the time, lots of money was collected on Balsac's behalf. Or perhaps I should better say on *Balzac*'s behalf. Iglesias Pantín even put his own money on the table in order to make the appeal to Washington a reality.

Meanwhile, continental labor put in play no other than Jackson H. Ralston to take care of *Balzac*. At the same time, Congressman Nolan and continental labor were acting upon incorporation in Congress. To the best of my knowledge, this dual offensive on behalf of incorporation for Puerto Rico was unprecedented, nor has happened again ever since. The only other event involving both Congress and the Supreme Court acting at once regarding the Puerto Rican status took place in 2016 and was not aimed at incorporation, but on the contrary to reaffirm territorial status: the one-two punch of *Puerto Rico v. Sánchez-Valle* (2016) and PROMESA (2015-2016).

Hence, the *Balzac* case is not merely a historic event, but an inflection point. It was part of a larger project, concocted by powerful syndical movements from both the metropolis and the colony: the most ambitious and well-funded in favor of incorporation. And it failed. It also shows how difficult it was—and remains—to defeat colonialism.

NOTES

[1] No explanation so far for the misspelling, besides the obvious possibility that *Balzac* with z was much more commonly known—then as well as nowadays—than *Balsac* with an "s."

[2] In *Tapia*, the federal District Court of the United States for the District of Puerto Rico dismissed a criminal complaint against defendant.

[3] "To sustain that incorporation has not yet arrived here is like saying the acquisition of a Territory, plus an organized government, plus citizenship in the case of Porto Rico does not equal the acquisition of a Territory plus citizenship, plus the organized government, the Alaska case, or what is the same, to deny the algebraic truth that a + b + c = a + c + b." (*People of Porto Rico v. Muratti* 1917, 577)

[4] In rejecting the *Rassmussen* decision as binding precedent, the Chief Justice stated that Alaska was a very different case from that of Porto Rico. It was an enormous territory, very sparsely settled and offering opportunity for immigration and settlement by American citizens. It was on the American Continent and within easy reach of the then United States. It involved none of the difficulties which incorporation of the Philippines and Porto Rico presents[.] (*Rassmussen v. United States* (1905, 632–3)

REFERENCES

Balzac v. People of Porto Rico. 1922. 258 US 298.

Buck v. Bell. (1927) 274 US 200.

Burton, David H. 1998. *Taft, Holmes, and the 1920s Court: An Appraisal*. Madison, NJ: Fairleigh Dickinson University Press.

Downes v. Bidwell. 1901. 182 US 244.

Duffy, Herbert S. 1930. *William Howard Taft*. New York: Minton, Balch.

Erman, Sam. 2018. *Almost Citizens: Puerto Rico, the US Constitution and Empire*. New York: Cambridge University Press.

Gandía v. Pettinghill. 1912. 222 US 452.

García Passalacqua, Juan Manuel. 1993. *Dignidad y jaibería: temer y ser puertorriqueño*. San Juan: Editorial Cultural.

Los puertorriqueños quieren hacer de la Isla un Estado. 1922. *Justicia* 6 February.

Padilla, Esteban and J. Santos-Rodríguez. 1918. Pro J. M. Balsac. *Unión Obrera* 9 May.

People of Porto Rico v. Muratti. 1917. 25 DPR 568.

People of Porto Rico v. Tapia. 1917. DCUS of PR.

Puerto Rico v. Sánchez-Valle. 2016. 579 US.

Pringle, Henry F. 1939. *The Life and Times of William Howard Taft: A Biography*. Vols. 1 & 2. New York: Farrar & Rinehart.

PROMESA—Puerto Rico Oversight, Management, and Economic Stability Act. 2015-2016. Last accessed 25 April 2021. <https://www.congress.gov/bill/114th-congress/house-bill/5278/text/>.

Rassmussen v. United States. 1905. 197 US 516.

Silén, Juan Ángel. 1980. *Historia de la nación puertorriqueña*. San Juan: Editorial Edil.

_____. 1995. *Apuntes para la historia del movimiento obrero puertorriqueño*. San Juan: Librería Norberto González.

The People of the Philippine Islands vs. Isaac Pérez. 1923. Last access 2 August 2021. <http://www.lawphil.net/judjuris/juri1923/dec1923/gr_l-21049_1923.html/>.

Trías Monge, José. 1997. *Puerto Rico: The Trials of the Oldest Colony in the World*. New Haven, CT: Yale University Press.

The "New" *Insular Cases* and the Territorial Clause: From Temporary Incorporation to Permanent Un-incorporation

JORGE M. FARINACCI FERNÓS

ABSTRACT

The *Insular Cases* split the Territorial Clause atom by formally distinguishing, for the first time, between so-called incorporated and un-incorporated territories. The former was the "classical" definition of the Clause; the latter constituted a doctrinal innovation that did not imply the start of the annexation process. *Balzac v. Porto Rico* reinforced the distinction and made clear that un-incorporation could be a permanent condition. Recently, the Supreme Court announced a series of decisions regarding the territories, particularly Puerto Rico, that do not mention the incorporated/un-incorporated distinction—refering to "territories" in general, without any additional characterization. This paper analyzes the journey of the Territorial Clause from its singular, classic, incorporated version, through its split into two distinct categories (classic and new) in the *Insular Cases* and *Balzac*, to its present form as a singular, un-incorporated version that appears to silently replace the classic version. The possibility of a populated territory remaining in permanent limbo signals that current U.S. law views colonialism as constitutionally valid. [Keywords: territories, constitution, colonialism, courts, incorporation, subordination]

Jorge M. Farinacci Fernós (jofarin@hotmail.com) is Associate Professor at the Interamerican University of Puerto Rico School of Law. He has published several law review articles and books, mostly regarding constitutional theory and history, including *La constitución obrera de Puerto Rico* (Huracán, 2015), *Hermenéutica puertorriqueña: cánones de interpretación jurídica* (InterJuris, 2019), and *La carta de derechos* (Editorial de la Universidad Interamericana, 2021). He is a member of the Editorial Board of *AMICUS: Revista de Política Pública y Legislación* and is the former Alternate Electoral Commissioner for the Citizen's Victory Movement.

Introduction

Until recently, the story of the Territorial Clause of the U.S. Constitution consisted of two great chapters, divided by the fault line established in the *Insular Cases* more than a century ago. Before these cases were decided by the Supreme Court of the United States, the Territorial Clause constituted a single normative unit: acquired territories were expected to continue their journey into eventual admission as states of the Union. In that sense, the general rule was that newly acquired lands were treated as incorporated territories, itself a temporary and transitional condition before statehood could be achieved, provided some preliminary requirements were met.

After the *Insular Cases*, the territorial atom was split in two: (1) incorporated territories, which tracked the previous historical practice under the Clause, and (2) unincorporated territories, which had not, and need not ever, start the admission process as states of the Union, and thus could remain in that situation indefinitely. This second chapter of the Territorial Clause story has dominated for decades.

This article argues that a third chapter is currently being written: the incorporated/unincorporated dichotomy has been mostly abandoned, in favor of a new singular doctrine within a reunified Territorial Clause. However, this has not had the effect of reestablishing the pre-*Insular Cases* legal order of incorporation as the general rule.

Quite the opposite: the newly reunified Territorial Clause has been wholly taken over by the unincorporated variant that was created in the second chapter. In other words, the Territorial Clause has now come full circle: while the first chapter only included the incorporated version of the Clause and the second chapter split the Clause in two–incorporated/unincorporated, the third chapter returns the Clause to a singular approach, but one where the unincorporated variant has completely displaced the original tenant of incorporation. The doctrinal two-step is now being completed.

As currently used by the Supreme Court of the United States, it seems there are no longer incorporated or unincorporated territories; there are just territories, and the unincorporated version now appears to wholly supply its normative definition. The equivalency, even if only partial after the *Insular Cases*, between territorial status and incorporation has been wholly abandoned. Colonialism has now become an accepted feature of U.S. constitutional law and, according to the Supreme Court, seems to be here to stay.

This essay addresses the previously outlined three chapters of the Territorial Clause's story. In particular, it focuses on how the more recent chapter constitutes a wholesale departure from the original; a sort of slow-moving doctrinal coup that started in 1901 and accelerated a hundred years ago with the *Balzac* decision. Part I narrates the pre-*Insular Cases* world, when the Territorial Clause only, or at the very least mostly, meant incorporation and eventual statehood. Part II tackles the widely studied nuclear fusion carried out by the *Insular Cases,* which split the Clause into two separate versions of the territorial status, and how the dichotomy that emerged survived for more than a century. Part III addresses what can be described as the *"New" Insular Cases*; a series of decisions handed down by the U.S. Supreme Court from 2016 to 2020 in the context of Puerto Rico's ongoing territorial/colonial condition, which seem to completely ignore the incorporated/unincorporated dichotomy and reunite the Territorial Clause under the unincorporated flag. The legal coup is now complete and victorious. Incorporation has been discarded and un-incorporation now reigns supreme.

Chapter One of the Territorial Clause Story:
Territorial Status as Incorporation

In the beginning, there was the Territorial Clause, found in Section 3, Article IV, of the U.S. Constitution. Tellingly, Article IV refers to the "States," while Section 3 specifically focuses on "New States." In other words, the clause dealing with *territories* is found under the same constitutional provision that deals with the admission of *new states* into the Union. Section 3 reads:

New States may be admitted by the Congress into this Union; but no new States shall be formed or erected within the Jurisdiction of any other State; nor any State be formed by the Junction of two or more States, or parts of States, without the Consent of the Legislatures of the States concerned as well as of the Congress.

The Congress shall have Power to dispose of and make all needful Rules and Regulations respecting the Territory or other Property belonging to the United

States; and nothing in this Constitution shall be so construed as to Prejudice any Claims of the United States, or of any particular State. (U.S. Const. art. VI, § 3—the highlighted portion refers to the Territorial Clause.)

As can be appreciated, the structure of Section 3 links the admission of new states with the administration of those territories currently owned by the United States. It would seem, therefore, that the territorial condition was somehow related to the admission of new states.[1] In other words, that territoriality and admission were conceptually linked within the constitutional structure.

History confirms this structural and conceptual connection. Prior to the Spanish-American War in 1898, the common wisdom was that territories "would, in the long run, form part of the United States" (Serrano Geyls 2005, 16). As Professor Serrano Geyls explains, "From the moment of acquisition the new territories were destined to become states of the Union and every step related to their government, taken by Congress and the executive, was with this aim in mind" (Serrano Geyls 2005, 16).

The first historical example of this phenomenon was the Ordinance for the Northwest Territories of 1787, adopted at the time of the founding. According to Román and Simmons, "The genesis of the Territorial Clause took place at the Constitutional Convention in 1787 when the founding fathers briefly contemplated the future acquisition of new lands by the United States" (2002, 449). For his part, Santana states that "[t]he ordinance itself influenced the drafting of the Territorial Clause of the Constitution during the Philadelphia Convention" (Santana 2014, 436). Likewise, these territories "were intended to eventually be admitted as states with equality of privileges" (Román and Simmons 2002, 450). Specifically, "the Northwest Ordinance contained a three-stage governmental structure, ending in full statehood" (Duffey 1995, 939; Santana 2014, 437).

As a result of the experience of the Northwest Ordinance of 1787—which Duffey describes as the "first authoritative national document in the long history of American expansion" (1995, 953)—it was understood that the territorial condition was thus *temporary and transitional*, part of an ongoing and uninterrupted process that would culminate in admission as a state of the Union: "Although the Constitution granted power to the federal government to admit new states and to govern over the territories, it did not expressly guarantee that these territories would become states. However, the territorial condition was considered transitory and temporary" (Román and Simmons 2002, 450).

The experience of the Northwest Ordinance of 1787 started a historical practice that was repeated during different periods of American expansion prior to 1898: "[W]ith few exceptions each subsequent territory followed the same process to transition to statehood after the formation of the Union" (Santana 2014, 436–7). In other words, "the Northwest Ordinance of 1787 encompassed the underlying theme and tradition of the United States territorial expansion: eventual statehood and full incorporation of their inhabitants as citizens...It eventually became the archetype for development of all territorial acquisitions" (Román and Simmons 2002, 450).

Colonialism was not intended to be an acceptable constitutional condition.

Duffey explains that "[t]he central difference between the imperialism of the Ordinance and that of Britain was that the Ordinance promised the communities it regulated full statehood once they became sufficiently populous, while contemporary British conceptions of colonial rule contained no viable alternative to subordinating the colonies" (1995, 955). As such, "the Northwest Ordinance of 1787 set forth the Founding Father's image that territorial acquisition would eventually lead to statehood" (Duncan 2016, 525).

The transitional and temporary nature of the territorial condition was born of the "fear of perpetual ownership of these territories by the Confederacy" (Santana 2014, 446–7). In other words, the United States was not supposed to permanently possess and rule over substantially populated territories. Colonialism was not intended to be an acceptable constitutional condition. Territoriality was treated as an interim status as part of a wider process of admission. Incorporation was the key normative component that described the constitutional status of territories.

Once a territory had achieved sufficient population levels and had acquired adequate forms of political self-organization, then the process towards statehood would reach its final phase. The granting of U.S. citizenship was also considered a requirement for statehood, since "citizenship was linked with incorporation, and that incorporation was linked with eventual statehood for the territory" (Torruella 2007, 326). As Román and Simmons explain, "It was understood that the territories would eventually become states as soon as Congress deemed the people of the territories prepared" (2002, 450). In other words, it was more a matter of *when*, not *if*. This view was expressly adopted by the Supreme Court of the United States in *Shively v. Bowlby* in 1894:

And the territories acquired by [C]ongress, whether by deed of cession from the original states, or by treaty with a foreign country, are held with the object, as soon as their population and condition justify it, of being admitted into the Union as states, upon an equal footing with the original states in all respects... (*Shilvey v. Bowbly* 1894, 49)

In order to complete the full picture of the Territorial Clause's first chapter, two additional points must be made. First, that, almost by definition, in order for the Territorial Clause to be applicable, the United States would have had to acquire some territory in the first place. Although the Territorial Clause does not explicitly empower Congress to acquire territory, "[t]he power of the United States to acquire and govern territory is no longer an open question" (Serrano Geyls 2005, 14). Specifically, the United States was able to acquire new territories by conquest or treaty, as an inherent power of sovereignty (Serrano Geyls 2005, 14). As such, "[i]n spite of the fact that the Constitution is silent on territorial acquisition, the Constitution does provide for the incorporation of states into the Union" (Duncan 2016, 525). And second, that, from the Northwest Ordinance of 1787 on, the United States continued on a constant expansionist march (Torruella 2007, 287). For the most part, that expansion was mostly within contiguous lands, what today constitutes the "continental" United States. The latter part of the 19th century saw the acquisition of noncontiguous lands that were not primarily populated by U.S. citizens (Torruella 2007, 288; Serrano Geyls 2005, 16).

Such was the doctrinal state of things before the *Insular Cases*: "The national policy up to the year 1898 had been that of considering territories as future states of the Union" (Serrano Geyls 2005, 17). Then came the

Spanish-American War of 1898, and thus began the second chapter in the history of the Territorial Clause.

Chapter Two of the Territorial Clause Story:
Splitting the Territorial Clause Atom, the Insular Cases, and the Birth of the Unincorporated Territory Doctrine

American territorial expansionism reached its imperialistic zenith at the end of the 19th century. The outbreak of the Spanish-American War in 1898 allowed the United States to come into possession of new lands that differed from those it had previously acquired. First, they were not contiguous with the rest of the country. Second, they were substantially populated, mostly by non-Anglo peoples of different cultures. Maybe more important, American intentions and designs had drastically changed: "It was thought by the political departments of the government that these new territories...were not fit to become States of the Union and would perhaps always remain as mere possessions of the United States or would eventually obtain their independence" (Serrano Geyls 2005, 17). Expansion had shifted from enlarging the country proper to amassing new possessions for economic and military exploitation and advantage (Torruella 2007, 289–90).

Since the U.S. Constitution only recognizes states and territories as forms of political organization within the United States, the new American expansionist project required a doctrinal shift with regard to the Territorial Clause, so as to prevent the new territories from beginning their journey toward statehood. The only available avenue for that shift was to split the territorial atom in two, creating a new constitutional condition that would not embark on the road to statehood.

The distinction between incorporated and un-incorporated territories was the result of this doctrinal fission. Note that the *original* content of the Territorial Clause was retained through the *incorporated territory* doctrine. The innovation was the addition of the *unincorporated territory* doctrine as part of the legal content of the Territorial Clause. This doctrine originated with Justice White's concurrence in *Downs v. Bidwell* (1901).[2]

With regard to *incorporated territories*, these have begun their march toward statehood. This means that the U.S. Constitution becomes fully applicable and that the territorial condition will eventually end. This merely reflects the classic normative content of the Territorial Clause prior to 1901.

As to *unincorporated territories*, these belong to, but are not a part of, the United States. As a result, the inhabitants of these territories only enjoy those federal constitutional rights that are deemed to be fundamental—a very scarce list when the *Insular Cases* were handed down in 1901—and are subject to Congress's plenary powers, which acts as the general legislature of the territory, unconstrained by the limitations of Article I of the U.S. Constitution.

Unlike their incorporated brethren, unincorporated territories have not begun, and need not ever begin at all, the march toward becoming a state of the Union. In other words, it can be a permanent condition of indefinite duration. Only when an unincorporated territory becomes an incorporated one, then the said march would have begun. But there would be no guarantee that such a transformation from unincorporated to incorporated would ever occur. Until that day came, if it did, the unincorporated territory could remain as such indefinitely. The other available avenue would be the independence of the territory.

This clause splitting was done through a series of cases that became known as the *Insular Cases*. Their reasoning was flawed, and their racist intent was plainly transparent. In short, the Court needed to create a new constitutional entity that would be subject to the plenary powers of Congress, but on a permanent, instead of temporary, basis. Furthermore, these territories need not ever start their journey toward statehood, denying them the transitional nature of the incorporated territory.

Yet the atom splitting allowed the United States to benefit from its ownership and direct control over these territories, without committing itself to integrate them into the federation as equal members. This was done through Congress' ability to wield plenary powers over the territories, without being bound by Article I of the Constitution. When it came to unincorporated territories, Congress gaveth and Congress taketh away.

The dual content of the Territorial Clause, which now encompassed both the incorporated and incorporated versions of territories, became the new established doctrine. In *Porto Rico v. Balzac* (1922), the U.S. Supreme Court went even further and cemented the bright-line difference between the two manifestations of the Territorial Clause. Unless Congress clearly and expressly determined to incorporate a territory, thus starting the clock for statehood, a territory could remain unincorporated permanently, subject to Congress' plenary powers and with only limited protections from the federal Constitution.

Curiously enough, as previewed, this situation created a different alternative path for unincorporated territories: independence and separation from the United States. In other words, while incorporated territories would have started their journey toward seemingly irreversible annexation, unincorporated territories seemed more likely to achieve independence than becoming a state of the Union. Such was the experience with the Philippines, which, after becoming a territory of the United States, was finally granted its independence through an Act of Congress in 1934.

In the end, "[a] new political division had thus been added to the American system. Prior to [the *Insular Cases*], the Union was to be considered composed only of States and Territories. Now it was formed by States, Incorporated Territories and Unincorporated Territories" (Serrano Geyls 2005, 23). But, as we are about to see, it looks like the Supreme Court has reverted to its previous dichotomy: states and territories. Yet the definition of territory now used is not its pre-*Insular Cases* articulation.

One of the rationalizations given for this atom splitting was the treaty-oriented notion that previous territories were eventually incorporated as States because of particular treaty agreements (Duncan 2016, 524). For example, "In its agreement with France, the United States agreed that the territory it would acquire would be incorporated into the rest of the United States and admitted to the Union as soon as possible" (Duncan 2016, 524).

But these rationalizations seem quite thin. More than a measured legal analysis, the atom splitting done in the *Insular Cases* and fortified in *Balzac* was the result of geopolitics and legalized imperialism. Yet, for a time, the dichotomy seemed to, at least, be settled. Thus, unincorporated territories had to either (1) accept their condition, or (2) engage in political action to either persuade Congress to incorporate them—thus initiating the journey toward statehood—or to recognize their independence.

The story of the latter half of the 20th century was one of the *unincorporated territory*. After the admission of Alaska and Hawaii as states of the Union, no further admissions were made. Moreover, no further *incorpo-*

rations were made either. In that sense, incorporated territories became theoretical creatures. This allowed the unincorporated variant to fill first the physical world and then the legal space of the Territorial Clause. Then came the *New Insular Cases*.

Chapter Three of the Territorial Clause Story?
How Un-Incorporation Reunified the Territorial Clause

The U.S. Supreme Court repeated the incorporated/unincorporated binary formulation for several decades after *Balzac*. But the seeds for a third chapter were brewing early on.

For example, in *Granville-Smith v. Granville-Smith*, the Court stated that "[b]eginning with the Treaty of Paris, the United States acquired by conquest, treaty or purchase outlying territories for which statehood was not contemplated" (1955, 4–5). The Court then cited as legal and historical authority the *Insular Cases*: "The position of these territories in our national scheme gave rise to a lively political controversy. Answers to some of the constitutional issues that arose were unfolded in a series of decisions best formulated, perhaps, in opinions by Mr. Chief Justice White and Mr. Chief Justice Taft" (1955, 5). In particular, the Opinion stated that "[a] vital distinction was made between 'incorporated' and 'unincorporated' territories" (1955, 5). According to the Court, the "first category had the potentialities of statehood like unto continental territories," while the "second category described possessions of the United States not thought of as future States" (1955, 5).

Other direct references to the dichotomy can be found in later Opinions issued by the Supreme Court, although they seemed to weaken as time went by in favor of an unincorporated takeover.[3] After two cases in 1990 referenced the distinction, the Supreme Court went silent on the issue until a brief, indirect mention in 2003 (*Nguyen v. U.S.*, 2003, 71).[4] The last reference to the dichotomy before 2016 was *Boumediene v. Bush* in 2008, and then only in the Court's unofficial syllabus.[5]

For decades, lower federal courts have also constantly referenced the incorporated/unincorporated territory dichotomy. Even after the Supreme Court ceased mentioning the dichotomy starting in 2015, lower federal courts continued using it. As of 2021, it is still clearly present in their decisions.[6]

But now it seems that the Supreme Court has shifted toward a complete two-step changeup of the Territorial Clause story. First, it has recently ceased referencing both versions of the Clause. It now speaks of territories without suffixes. In other words, it has reunified the territorial atom. And second, the actual substantive content of the newly reunified Territorial Clause has been totally taken over by the un-incorporation doctrine. Now, there are just territories; and the new default position seems to be un-incorporation, which can still be permanent and indefinite.

Puerto Rico seems to be ground zero for this doctrinal coup. After years of silence, since 2016 the U.S. Supreme Court has shown a substantial interest in Puerto Rico. Three cases have been decided on the merits since then (*Puerto Rico v. Sanchez Valle* 2016; *Puerto Rico v. Franklin California Tax-Free Trust* 2016; *FOMB v. Aurelius Investment* 2020), with a fourth on its way (*United States v. Vaello-Madero*). All three decisions were penned by different Justices. In none of them does the Court refer to the incorporated/unincorporated dichotomy.

No further elaboration was offered, but the result was striking: Congress can directly govern Puerto Rico as it sees fit, as if it were its general legislature.

In *Puerto Rico v. Sanchez Valle*, the Supreme Court stated that Puerto Rico "became a territory of the United States in 1898, as a result of the Spanish-American War" (2016, 2). A similar characterization was made of the Philippines prior to their independence, identified as "[t]hen a U.S. territory" (*Puerto Rico v. Sanchez Valle* 2016, 10). All in all, the Court referred to "U.S. territories" in general, without differentiating between incorporated and unincorporated ones. But the Court did signal that the unincorporated variant has become doctrinally dominant: "Congress has broad latitude to develop innovative approaches to territorial governance" (*Puerto Rico v. Sanchez Valle* 2016, 16). Yet *Sanchez Valle* was just the beginning.[7]

Puerto Rico v. Franklin California Tax-Free Trust (2016) was handed down the same term as *Sanchez Valle*. This second case cemented the new view that there are only territories—as a singular concept—and that Congress can wield a free hand indefinitely. Echoing *Sanchez Valle*, the Court drives through familiar ground, stating that Puerto Rico "became a Territory of the United States in 1898" (*Puerto Rico v. Franklin California Tax-Free Trust* 2016, 7). No further elaboration was offered, but the result was striking: Congress can directly govern Puerto Rico as it sees fit, as if it were its general legislature.

But the *coup de grace* was the U.S. Supreme Court's decision in *FOMB v. Aurelius*, handed down in 2020. There the Court had to decide whether the Fiscal Oversight Board created by Congress pursuant to the PROMESA statute—which established a special bankruptcy process for Puerto Rico after the Court had previously held in *Puerto Rico v. Franklin California Tax-Free Trust* that Puerto Rico could neither adopt its own bankruptcy statute nor avail itself of the protections of the federal Bankruptcy Code—was subject to the Appointments Clause of the U.S. Constitution.

If the Board members were characterized as federal officers, then they would be subject to the Clause and the Act's appointment structure would be unconstitutional since most members were not appointed by the President and confirmed by the Senate. On the other hand, if they were identified as territorial officers, then the Clause would be inapplicable and Congress's appointment mechanism would be a valid exercise of its plenary powers under the Territorial Clause, part of its "broad latitude to develop innovative approaches to territorial governance" (*Puerto Rico v. Sanchez Valle* 2016, 16).

After 1952, all Puerto Rican offices were created either by its Constitution or the statutes adopted by its elected Legislative Assembly. Evidently, the Fiscal Oversight Board is nowhere mentioned in the 1952 Puerto Rico Constitution nor in any of the statutes enacted under its authority. On the contrary, it was entirely the product of Congress' designs. How then could they be territorial officers? According to the Court, because Congress said so in its PROMESA statute. In other words, Congress has the power under the Territorial Clause to design a territory's internal governmental structure. While Congress had delegated some of that power to Puerto Ricans by authorizing the calling of a constitutional convention and then approving its 1952 Constitution, it had not relinquished its power. The PROMESA statute, which included a *de facto* amendment to the Puerto Rican territorial government structure, was held to be an instance in which Congress took some of that power back and exercised it directly and properly under the U.S. Constitution.

As to the territorial condition, the Supreme Court again only made reference to a singular doctrinal unit, eschewing the incorporated/unincorporated dichotomy. The Court explained that "for certain localities, there will be no state government capable of exercising local power" (*FOMB v. Aurelius Investment* 2020, 9). Accordingly, the Territorial Clause of the U.S. Constitution gives Congress the power to *govern* the territories, exercising the normal powers of a general legislature.

That power to govern applies to "entities that fall within the scope of Article IV" (*FOMB v. Aurelius Investment* 2020, 13). Note the use of the word "entities" as a catch-all description for non-states or territories. As to these, "Congress may structure local governments under Article IV and Article I in ways that do not precisely mirror the constitutional blueprint of the National Government" (*FOMB v. Aurelius Investment* 2020, 13).

This new formalistic—and seemingly simplistic—approach to Puerto Rico and the other (unincorporated) territories could also be the result of judicial indifference: the Court simply wants to avoid any language or statement that could be interpreted as "judicializing" a political matter that is entirely up to Congress and the Executive Branch. But even if this were so, the Court is nonetheless giving legal blessing to the current colonial reality, which could even embolden Congress to further entrench it. One could speculate that cases like *Sanchez Valle* and *Franklin California* actually signaled to Congress that it need not worry about dichotomies, incorporation or colonialism, paving the way for PROMESA.

One final note: some of the parties in *FOMB v. Aurelius Investment* specifically asked the Court to address and overrule the original *Insular Cases*. The Court explicitly rejected that invitation: "[W]e need not consider the request by some of the parties that we overrule the much-criticized *Insular Cases* and their progeny" (*FOMB v. Aurelius Investment* 2020, 21).

This statement implies that the *Insular Cases* are still good law; otherwise, there would be a need to overrule them. But what exactly are they still good law about? In five years and three Opinions, the Supreme Court has consistently omitted *any* reference to the incorporated/unincorporated distinction. In fact, it appears to have settled on a very formalistic approach to the constitutional structure pertaining to entities within the United States that are not the federal government or some other particular sphere that has special constitutional status. According to the modern Court, there are either states or territories: no more, no less. If any, the continued relevance of the old *Insular Cases* would be to give continued normative life to the unincorporated variant that has entirely taken over the Territorial Clause.

Final Thoughts

The U.S. Supreme Court may yet still keep the original *Insular Cases* alive and maybe even continue to nominally reference the unincorporated/incorporated territory binary. But a doctrinal shift is already under way. First, through an insistence on a more formalistic dichotomy: states and territories, period. In other words, to weaken the importance of suffixes as doctrinal accessories. As much as possible, a general reference to "territories" will suffice. Second, that the unincorporated version first articulated in the old *Insular Cases* has become the general norm for territories: instead of being an anomaly, it has become the dominant strain. From now on, the default rule for territories seems to be permanent and indefinite un-incorporation. Before the "new" *Insular Cases*, colonialism was ever present in the legal formulation of Puerto Rico's relationship with the United States. But colonialism managed to at least hide behind legal niceties. No more. It now seems that colonialism is front and center when it comes to that relationship, and, according to the Supreme Court, it is constitutionally valid. Let us hope that this is not the last chapter in the Puerto Rican story.

NOTES

[1] It also suggests that, in the constitutional context, there are only two possible alternatives: being admitted as a state or becoming a territory of the United States.

[2] See Rivera Ramos (1996). Professor Rivera Ramos explains how White's concurrence, which articulated the unincorporated territory proposition, eventually became the dominant position (1996, 247).

[3] See *Reed v. Covert*, 354 U.S. 1, 13-14 (1957) and 53 (Frankfurter, concurring); *Glidden v. Zdanok*, 370 U.S. 530, 547 (1962); *Examining Bd. of Engineers v. Flores de Otero*, 426 U.S. 572, fn. 30 (1976) ("The former category encompassed those Territories destined for statehood from the time of acquisition...The latter category included those Territories not possessing the anticipation of statehood"); *Torres v. Com. of Puerto Rico*, 442 U.S. 465 (1979) (several references to the dichotomy); *U.S. v. Verdugo-Urquidez*, 494 U.S. 259, 268 (1990) (stating that an unincorporated territory as "one not clearly destined for statehood"); *Ngiraingas v. Sanchez*, 495 U.S. 182, 186 (1990).

[4] "[U]ntil Congress established Guam as an unincorporated Territory with the passage of the Organic Act of Guam in 1950."

[5] Stating that one of the *Insular Cases* "resulted in the doctrine of territorial incorporation, under which the Constitution applies in full in incorporated Territories surely destined for statehood but only in part in unincorporated Territories.".

[6] See, for example, *Eche v. Holder*, 694 F.3d 1026, 1030-1031 (9th Cir. 2012) ("The Court reached this *sensible result* because unincorporated territories are not on a path to statehood"—emphasis added); *Hernandez v. U.S.*, 757 F.3d 249, 260 (9th Cir. 2014); *Thomas v. Lynch*, 796 F. 3d 535, 539-540 (5th Cir. 2015); *Tuaua v. U.S.*, 788 F.3d 300 (D.C. Cir. 2015); *Davis v. Commonwealth Election Commission*, 844 F. 3d 1087, 1095 (9th Cir. 2016) (describing the Northern Marianas as "an unincorporated territory"); *U.S. v. Obak*, 884 F. 3d 934, 938 and fn. 3 (9th Cir. 2018) (describing Guam as an unincorporated territory); *Vooys v. Bentley*, 901 F. 3d 172, fn. 10 (3rd Cir. 2018); *Davis v. Guam*, 932 F. 3d 822, 825 (9th Cir. 2019); *Government of Guam v. United States*, 950 F. 3d 104, 108 (D.C. Cir. 2020) ("Guam remained, as it had been since the Treaty of Paris in 1898, an 'unincorporated territory of the United States.'"); *U.S. v. Baxter*, 951 F. 3d 128, fn. 11 (3rd Cir. 2020) ("That is, the [Virgin Islands] has not been 'incorporated' into the United States on a path to statehood."); *U.S. v. Cotto-Flores*, 970 F.3d 17, 50 (1st Cir. 2020, Torruella, concurring).

[7] Even Justice Breyer in dissent seemed to accept that the unincorporated territory

had become the new dominant strain of the Clause: "In the usual course, a U.S. Territory becomes a State within our Union *at the invitation of Congress*" (*Puerto Rico v. Sanchez Valle* 2016, 3; Breyer, J., dissenting—emphasis added).

REFERENCES

Balzac v. Porto Rico. 1922. 258 U.S. 298.

Boumediene v. Bush. 2008. 553 U.S. 723.

Downs v. Bidwell. 1901. 182 U.S. 221.

Duncan, John. 2016. Uti Possidetis: Is Possession Really Nine-Tenths of the Law–
The Acquisition of Territory by the United States: Why, How, and Should
We. *McGeorge Law Review* 38(2), 513–44.

Duffey, Denis P. 1995. The Northwest Ordinance as a Constitutional Document.
Columbia Law Review 95, 929–68.

FOMB v. Aurelius Investment. 2020. 590 U.S.

Granville-Smith v. Granville-Smith. 1955. 349 U.S. 1.

Nguyen v. U.S. 2003. 539 U.S. 69.

Puerto Rico v. Franklin California Tax-Free Trust. 2016. 579 U.S. __, 136 S.Ct. 1938.

Puerto Rico v. Sanchez Valle. 2016. 579 U.S. __, 136 S.Ct. 1863.

Rivera Ramos, Efrén. 1996. The Legal Construction of American Colonialism: The
Insular Cases (1901-1922). *Revista Jurídica de la Universidad de Puerto
Rico* 65, 225–328.

Román, Ediberto and Theron Simmons. 2002. Membership Denied: Subordination
and Subjugation under United States Expansionism. *San Diego Law
Review* 39, 437–524.

Santana, Willie. 2014. Incorporating the Lonely Star: How Puerto Rico Became
Incorporated and Earned a Place in the Sisterhood of States. *Tennessee
Journal of Law & Policy* 9(3), 433–74.

Serrano Geyls, Raúl. 2005. The Territorial Status of Puerto Rico and its Effect on
the Political Future. *Revista Jurídica de la Universidad Interamericana de
Puerto Rico* 39, 13–66.

Shively v. Bowlby. 1894. 152 U.S. 1.

Torruella, Juan R. 2007. The Insular Cases: The Establishment of a Regime of
Political Apartheid. *University of Pennsylvania Journal of International
Law* 29, 283–347.

Balzac v. People of Porto Rico and the Problem of the Liberal Narrative of Citizenship, Why Puerto Ricans are Not Second-Class Citizens Today

CHARLES R. VENATOR-SANTIAGO

ABSTRACT

Describing Puerto Ricans as second-class citizens affirms an ahistorical liberal narrative of citizenship. Drawing on the legislative histories of the citizenship laws for Puerto Rico, this article argues that in 1940 Congress began to enact *jus soli* or birthright citizenship for Puerto Rico, anchored in the Citizenship Clause of the Fourteenth Amendment. In *Balzac v. People of Porto Rico* (1922), the Supreme Court affirmed the principle that locality, not citizenship, determined the application of the Constitution in Puerto Rico. This article demonstrates the representation of Puerto Ricans as second-class citizens is not only historically inaccurate, but also obscures some of the fundamental dimensions of power established by the doctrine of separate and unequal. [Keywords: Puerto Rico, Balzac, citizenship, empire, unincorporated territory]

Charles R. Venator-Santiago (charles.venator@uconn.edu) is an Associate Professor with a joint appointment in the Department of Political Science and El Instituto at the University of Connecticut. He coordinates various public archives including the Puerto Rico Citizenship Archives Project, the Puerto Rico Federal Status Archive Project, and the American Samoa Nationality and Citizenship Archives Project. He is the author of *Puerto Rico and the Origins of U.S. Global Empire: The Disembodied Shade* (Routledge, 2015).

We cannot find any intention to depart from this policy in making Porto Ricans American citizens, explained as this is by the desire to put them as individuals *on an exact equality with citizens from the American homeland,* to secure them more certain protection against the world, and to give them an opportunity, should they desire, to move into the United States proper and there without naturalization to enjoy all political and other rights.
(*Balzac v. People of Porto Rico* 1922, 311—emphasis added)

Five years after Congress gave Puerto Rican citizens a choice to either retain their status or acquire a United States citizenship under the terms of the collective naturalization provision of the *Jones Act of 1917,* a unanimous Supreme Court ruled in *Balzac v. People of Porto Rico* that island-born citizens acquired a citizenship "equal" to those born in the "homeland." Writing for the Court, Justice William H. Taft further established that Puerto Rican-born citizens who migrated to the "United States proper" would enjoy the same political and civil rights available to other citizens. This interpretation affirmed a principle of United States federalism that recognized a constitutional difference between states and territories or, as Justice Taft further argued, it was the status of the locality, not the citizenship, which determined the application of the Constitution. *Balzac,* perhaps the most consequential of the so-called *Insular Cases* (Rivera Ramos 1997), also applied the so-called doctrine of separate and unequal (Torruella 1988) to an unincorporated territory primarily inhabited by United States citizens, since defining the key contours of the relationship between Puerto Ricans and the United States.

Notwithstanding this clear history, legal actors and academics across disciplines continue to invoke an ascriptive narrative of citizenship, a second-class citizenship, to describe the status of island-born Puerto Ricans. For example, in his amicus brief for the Commonwealth of Puerto Rico submitted in the *Vaello-Madero* case, right-wing, pro-statehood Puerto Rican Attorney General Domingo Emanuelli Hernández argued that "the doctrine of incorporation established in the *Insular Cases* have placed Puerto Rican United States citizens who live in Puerto Rico in a separate, disadvantaged class—in effect, a second-class citizenship—on the sole basis of race and/or alienage, and that Congress may maintain this inequality indefinitely" (2021, 13). Or take, for example, the words of decolonial anthropologist Yarimar Bonilla: "But the fact is that Puerto Ricans are actually second-class *colonial* citizens, and their citizenship is working just as intended" (Jobson 2020). Or consider anarchist historian Jorell Meléndez-Badillo's claim: "To this day, they (Puerto Ricans) carry a second-class citizenship" (Meléndez-Badillo 2021). Ironically, all share a common political interpretation, namely an ahistorical liberal narrative of citizenship to describe the status of Puerto Rican-born citizens. This narrative not only misrepresents the actual nature of the U.S. citizenship acquired by island-born Puerto Ricans, but also reproduces a liberal paradigm that obscures the structural dimensions of the power that the U.S. empire exercises over Puerto Rico.

This is not to say that the residents of Puerto Rico do not experience a separate and unequal life. In fact, *any* citizen, regardless of race or any identity, who resides in Puerto Rico will share separate and unequal experiences, some caused by the anti-democratic nature of U.S. federalism, and some caused by territorial status ascribed to Puerto Rico. But the point that matters here is that the inequalities experienced by the residents of Puerto Rico are not determined by their citizenship; they are determined by Puerto Rico's territorial status within the U.S. empire. *Balzac* and other Supreme Court rulings that affirm the doctrine of separate and unequal, also known as the doctrine of territorial incorporation, have since shaped the contours of the unequal economic, political, and to some degree social, experiences of all U.S. citizens residing in Puerto Rico.

Drawing on the principles established in *Balzac v. People of Porto Rico* (1922), this article demonstrates that persons born in Puerto Rico hold a citizenship equal to that available to a person born in a state or the District of Columbia. More precisely, this article establishes that the Citizenship Clause of the Fourteenth Amendment is the Constitutional source of the *jus soli* or birthright citizenship available to persons born in Puerto Rico. To this extent, the citizenship statute extended to Puerto Rico does not confer a "colonial," "territorial," or second-class status. This essay also explains how the second-class citizenship narrative is premised on a liberal narrative. Specifically, I argue that the use of a second-class citizenship narrative to describe the residents of Puerto Rico reproduces a liberal narrative of citizenship that obscures the structural dimensions of U.S. hegemony over Puerto Rico.

This article is divided into four parts. Drawing on the liberal political theory of Alexander Bickel and Rogers M. Smith, Part I presents a liberal narrative of citizenship. Part II explains what the constitutional status of Puerto Rico is and why it matters. Part III provides a simple overview of the history of the extension of citizenship to Puerto Rico and documents the constitutional source of the *jus soli* or birthright citizenship available to island-born persons today. Part IV addresses the claim that the statutory nature of the citizenship legislation extended to Puerto Rico is not constitutional. The article concludes by explaining why the citizenship available to persons born in Puerto Rico confers the same constitutional status to its bearers and how the use of an ascriptive second-class citizenship reproduces an ahistorical liberal narrative of citizenship.

Part I: What is a Liberal Narrative of Citizenship?

There is a tendency among jurists, legal actors, scholars, and academics to rely on liberal narratives of membership to describe the citizenship status of Puerto Ricans. In recent years, jurists and legal actors have invoked a language of civil rights to challenge the separate and unequal (Torruella 1988) laws and policies applied to the residents of Puerto Rico. Alternatively, decolonial academics across the ideological spectrum invoke the liberal language of ascriptive citizenship to represent Puerto Ricans. This focus on citizenship individualizes what are general problems of an anti-democratic (Dahl 2003) and federalist polity. The danger, of course, is that the structural problems of a federal empire are described as problems of a second-class citizenship.

The footnotes and commentary of the more serious writers who describe the citizenship status of Puerto Ricans are generally anchored on both Alexander Bickel's rendition of liberal citizenship and Rogers Smith's iteration of ascriptive citizenships. Bickel described liberal citizenship in the following manner:

In the view of both the ancients and modern liberal political theorists, the relationship between the individual and the state is largely defined by the concept

of citizenship. It is by virtue of his citizenship that the individual is a member of the political community, *and by virtue of it that he has rights.* (1973, 369; 1975, 33—emphasis added)

Bickel's interpretation highlights two dimensions of liberal citizenship. First, a liberal vision of citizenship is premised on the idea that the status of the individual within the polity is determined by his or her citizenship. Both the subject's membership within the polity and her access to rights, or rather the application of rights to the subject, are contingent on the subject's citizenship status, or so liberal political theory posits. Of course, as Bickel also notes, in the U.S. constitutional scheme, citizenship is not the only guarantor of access to rights; aliens and citizens are also entitled to some of the civil rights afforded to citizens, including same due process rights in a court of law (1973, 382). However, unlike the citizen, the alien is not guaranteed the same political rights. Liberal theory focuses on the individual's unmediated relationship to the state.

More important, liberal iterations of citizenship ignore the role that the doctrine of territorial incorporation plays in shaping the relationships between citizens residing in Puerto Rico and the United States.

A second dimension of Bickel's interpretation contends that citizens in the polity are entitled to equality. The assumption is that the polity is a unitary space devoid of spatial hierarchies within it. The Constitution applies equality within its sovereign domain. The liberal citizen's relationship to the state is direct and unmediated by the status of the space/territory that she inhabits. This interpretation ignores the anti-democratic dimensions of federalism and the constitutional hierarchies that define the contours of the United States. More important, liberal iterations of citizenship ignore the role that the doctrine of territorial incorporation plays in shaping the relationships between citizens residing in Puerto Rico and the United States.

The United States is a federal system governed by an anti-democratic Constitution. Examples of the undemocratic nature of the Constitution abound. The Constitution recognizes a hierarchy of three or perhaps four different types of spaces, namely, states, districts, territories, and perhaps federal property (i.e., parks, etc.). The United States is a union of states, whose capital is housed in Washington, D.C. The Constitution grants states and Washington, D.C., the ability to establish rules to enable an Electoral College to select the President of the United States. Citizens in the United States do not possess the right to select the President through an electoral process. The President is selected by Electors from the states and the District of Columbia. Territories lack the constitutional power to possess Electors. Citizens living in territories, by definition, have always lacked the political power to participate in the presidential selection process. A liberal interpretation would argue that citizens residing in a territory are entitled to a right to vote in presidential elections, a claim that is constitutionally incoherent. No territory has ever been granted a power greater than that of a state. The liberal claim that citizens residing in Puerto Rico should be entitled to a right to vote in presidential elections is an example of how liberal political ideologies obscure the anti-democratic nature of U.S. federalism.

In the case of Puerto Rico, as I will explain in more detail below, the United States developed a new territorial doctrine that established a difference between incorporated and unincorporated territories. Whereas incorporated territories were treated as states in the making, unincorporated territories were not meant to become states. Federal jurisprudence established that incorporated territories are a part of the United States, and therefore the bill of rights applies within these spaces. In contrast, unincorporated territories are selectively ruled as foreign possessions in a domestic or constitutional sense, and only fundamental rights are guaranteed in these types of territories. In *Balzac v. People of Porto Rico* (1922), the Supreme Court further established that the status of the locality of the territories, not the status of the citizen, determined the application of the Constitution. To be sure, whereas citizens residing in a state or district who relocate to Puerto Rico lose civil and political rights, Puerto Rican-born citizens who move from Puerto Rico to a state or district acquire the same rights as their fellow citizens by simply residing *in* a state or district. Liberal narratives obscure or gloss over this distinction and the anti-democratic dimensions of this interpretation.

In his classic *Citizenship and the American Empire*, Judge José A. Cabranes invoked Bickel's argument to describe the case of the Puerto Rican-born U.S. citizen. Citing Bickel's work, Cabranes noted that the

notion of citizenship as the source of rights emerged in the *Dred Scott Case...* in which the Supreme Court held that rights and privileges under the Constitution were accorded to *citizens,* that citizenship and membership in the political community were synonymous, and that the concept of citizenship could not include "a negro of African descent, whose ancestors were of pure African blood, and who were brought to this country and sold as slaves." (1979, 5, n. 12)

"Citizenship," Cabranes further argued, "suggested equality of rights and privileges and full membership in the American political community" (1979, 6). However, in the case of Puerto Rico, the extension of a "second-class" citizenship served to obscure "the colonial relationship between" the U.S. empire and the Puerto Rican "dependency" (1979, 6–7). Because citizenship did not guarantee equality for Puerto Ricans within the "American political community," Cabranes' argument suggests, the extension of citizenship to Puerto Ricans had the effect of "perpetuating the colonial status of Puerto Rico" (1979, 7). In Cabranes' liberal interpretation, citizenship is not only a source of rights and equality, but in the case of Puerto Rico, a source of colonial subordination.

Of course, Cabranes' argument is confusing and vague. Perhaps that is the only way he can use a liberal interpretation to make political sense of the particularity of Puerto Rico's status within the U.S. empire. To be sure, although Cabranes used the term "second-class citizenship" to describe the status of Puerto Ricans, he never states whether the citizenship provision of the *Jones Act of 1917* was actually a different type of citizenship, perhaps a territorial citizenship or, more accurately, a collective naturalization provision conferring on its bearer an inferior type of citizenship, a naturalized citizenship. Moreover, while Cabranes rightly notes that U.S. law and policymakers decoupled the idea of citizenship from a change of Puerto Rico's territorial status (1979, 5), he seems to suggest that liberal equality, perhaps in the form of a "first class" citizenship, or rather a citizenship that guarantees equal rights to its bearers, can only be achieved by granting statehood to Puerto Rico (1979, 100–1). In the latter case, putting aside the question of whether an anti-democratic Constitution can guarantee equality to its bearers, Cabranes' arguments suggest that citizenship is a mere political or rhetorical device contingent on Puerto Rico's territorial status, not a source of equal rights or membership in itself.

More progressive liberal arguments contend that the United States has relied on ascriptive hierarchies of citizenship, or even semi-citizenships (Cohen 2009), to curtail the access to equal rights of various populations, including women, non-whites, and LGBTQ groups. In *Civic Ideals,* Rogers M. Smith, an unapologetic liberal scholar, provides the core argument for understanding the idea of an ascriptive citizenship (1997, 2). Smith argues that inegalitarian traditions and ideologies

assigned political identities—including full citizenship with eligibility for voting rights and the highest political offices—on the basis of such ascribed charac- teristics as race, gender, and the usually unaltered nationality and religion in which people were born. According to such outlooks, these traits assigned people to places in hereditary hierarchical orders that citizenship laws should reflect. (1997, 3)

In other words, ascriptive visions of citizenship led to the creation of a hierarchy of memberships within the United States polity premised on a hierarchy of identities such as race, gender, and ethnicity. Under this logic, groups of people have been ascribed different citizenship statuses, including a second-class citizenship status, based on their race, ethnicity, gender, and other ascriptive identities. Progressive liberal theory argues that ascriptive citizenships, not the status of the space that the individual inhabits, become the source of inequalities and other hierarchies within the polity.

Smith's reliance on the notion of ascriptive citizenship has led him to describe Puerto Ricans as second-class citizens. Following the United States annexation of Puerto Rico in 1898, Smith argues, federal law and policymak- ers thought that Puerto Ricans should be ascribed a "second-class citizen- ship" similar to that "of blacks and Native Americans, as well as women" (1997, 430). Smith's liberal argument contends that the U.S. government ascribed to Puerto Ricans a racialized second-class citizenship status. He posits that the ascription of this inferior citizenship can explain the unequal treatment of Puerto Ricans within the United States polity. Smith's argument sidelines the role that the particularities of the federal hierarchy of spaces, as well as the new U.S. territorial law and policy, played in shaping the hierarchies and inequalities affecting the residents of Puerto Rico. In this narrative, citizenship, not the status of the Puerto Rican space or territorial status, becomes the source of the differentiated citizenship status of Puerto Ricans within the U.S. polity.

Ironically, like Judge Cabranes, the late Judge Juan R. Torruella often coined the liberal narrative of a "second-class citizenship" to criticize Puerto Rico's "colonial" condition. Judge Torruella cited Smith's notion of the ascriptive citizenship and Cabranes' reading of Bickel (2017, 110) to describe the "second-class" or "colonial" citizenship used to rule Puerto Ricans (2017, 120). Like Cabranes, Torruella often invoked the idea of a hierarchy of citizenships without explaining what made the citizenship ascribed to Puerto Ricans different in its own terms (2017, 117–8). To be sure, as *Balzac* affirmed, Puerto Rican-born citizens acquire the same rights as any mainland-born citizen upon migrating to a state, district, or incorporated territory.

My suspicion is that like Cabranes, Torruella invoked the notion of a "second-class" or "colonial" citizenship as a rhetorical or political device to appeal or mobilize liberal sensibilities against the "injustice" of Puerto Rico's separate and unequal status.

Also, like Cabranes, Torruella acknowledged that "geography" played a role in shaping the unequal status of Puerto Ricans (2017, 124). The problem, of course, is that Torruella selectively neglected to contextualize the question of geography. To be sure, as I explained above, disenfranchising or depriving U.S. citizens residing in Puerto Rico of the right to vote in presidential election has nothing to do with their citizenship and everything to do with federalism. In the United States, as I noted above, the Electoral College selects the President and only states and the District of Columbia (by constitutional amendment) possess electors. Puerto Rican-born citizens who migrate to a state or the District of Columbia acquire the right to participate in presidential elections when they establish a residence in a place that has an electoral college. Stated differently, citizenship has nothing to do with the unequal status of the residents of Puerto Rico because state-born citizens who migrate to Puerto Rico are disenfranchised, and Puerto Rican-born citizens who migrate to a state or the District of Columbia are enfranchised. But Torruella knew this constitutional fact. Like Cabranes, Torruella understood that the solution to the problem of the unequal experience of the residents of Puerto Rico rested in granting statehood to Puerto Rico. My suspicion is that like Cabranes, Torruella invoked the notion of a "second-class" or "colonial" citizenship as a rhetorical or political device to appeal or mobilize liberal sensibilities against the "injustice" of Puerto Rico's separate and unequal status.

Although legal scholars have typically monopolized the debates over the citizenship status of Puerto Ricans, mainstream scholars who write about Puerto Rico also embrace the liberal interpretation of the status of Puerto Rican-born citizens. Take, for example, Nicholas De Genova and Ana Y. Ramos-Zayas's *Latino Crossings*, a book that offers a progressive, albeit liberal, critique of Puerto Ricans and the politics of race and citizenship. Drawing or rather citing Smith's notion of ascriptive citizenship, De Genova and Ramos-Zayas set out to explore how the "politics of citizenship in the U.S." have generated inequalities for Puerto Ricans (2003, 15). Central to their claim is that Congress enacted legislation, the *Jones Act of 1917* (39 Stat. 951), which granted Puerto Ricans a "distinctly subordinate U.S. citizenship to Puerto Ricans" (2003, 15). Of course, like most scholars who invoke the narrative of "citizenship" to explain the subordination of Puerto Ricans, they offer no evidence to substantiate their interpretation of the type of citizenship conferred by the *Jones Act of 1917*, nor do they consider that the type of citizenship that this law conferred on Puerto Ricans only lasted until 1940. For De Genova and Ramos-Zayas, the subordinate citizenship ascribed to Puerto Ricans explains the inequalities that Puerto Ricans residing in the island experience.

Decolonial academics across the ideological spectrum also embrace the liberal narrative of citizenship. For example, Frances Negrón-Muntaner, an advocate of statehood for Puerto Rico, has not only invoked the narrative of "exclusionary" "second-class citizenship" (1997, 23) to describe the status of Puerto Ricans, but more recently describes Puerto Ricans as "colonial subjects" who are not "equal citizens of the United States but *territorial* citizens with limited rights" (2018, 118; Ruiz 2019, 9). Other decolonial academics like Yarimar Bonilla (her position can be described as non-sovereign/anti-independence) (2015; Younis 2017) invoke confusing jargon to describe the "second class citizenship" that Puerto Ricans experience as a legal category "in which they have been purposefully placed through technologies of racio-colonial governance" (2020, 2). Ileana I. Diaz goes even further and claims that the citizenship conferred on Puerto Ricans is a source of "malignancy" "and directly shapes the spaces, experiences and possibilities of Puerto Ricans and the island itself" (2021, 3–4). All rely on decolonial jargon to claim progressive political possibilities while simultaneously invoking a liberal narrative of citizenship to interpret relations between Puerto Ricans and the U.S. empire.

Decolonial and other academics who write about Puerto Rico continue to rely on ahistorical and conceptually incoherent narratives of liberal citizenship.[1] Decolonial academics invoke words like "coloniality" and colonialism to contextualize the status of Puerto Rico while ignoring the particularity of the "Third View," a new type of territorial expansionism invented during the War of 1898 to rule Puerto Rico and the other ultramarine territories annexed during the War of 1898. They still use the idea of a territorial or colonial citizenship, a citizenship created by the *Jones Act of 1917* (a law that lasted between 1917 and 1940) to describe the contemporary citizenship status of persons born or residing in the Puerto Rican islands. They ignore the centrality of the structural interpretation introduced in *Balzac v. People of Porto Rico* (1922), perhaps the most consequential Supreme Court opinion after *Downes v. Bidwell* (1901), in favor of explanations that rely on individual experiences. In the pages that follow I offer an alternative reading that relies on empirical evidence to substantiate my claims. My hope is that a more honest interpretation of the citizenship status of persons born in Puerto Rico will move the debates to a more historically grounded place.

Part II: Defining Puerto Rico's Territorial Status for Citizenship Purposes

Between 1898 and 1901, United States law and policymakers invented a new tradition of territorial expansionism, with a corresponding territorial status, to rule Puerto Rico and all territories acquired since (Van Dyne 1904 [1980], 143; Gettys 1934, 145; López Baralt, 1999, 108–10). Scholars who have studied the legal and political debates of the period generally agree that, at the time, debates over what territorial status to ascribe Puerto Rico were divided in three camps: anti-imperialist or colonial, imperialist, or the Third View (Torruella 1988, 24–32; Sparrow 2006, 44–55). Central to these debates was the question of where to locate Puerto Rico within the U.S. empire for constitutional purposes. Puerto Rico's constitutional location would in turn determine what citizenship and corresponding constitutional rights could apply to the islands' residents. In the end, law and policymakers embraced the Third View, a new tradition that both rejected the colonialist and imperialist interpretations and simultaneously enabled the federal government to combine elements from the latter traditions to craft a third or new constitutional interpretation to legitimate the subsequent rule of Puerto Rico and other unincorporated territories. Each territorial status carried consequences for the nature of the citizenship, and ensuing status, conferred to the residents of these territories.

Between the founding and 1898, the federal government acquired territories for either colonialist or imperialist purposes. As both the historical record and the corresponding debates clearly show, both traditions were different (Venator-Santiago 2013; 2015). United States colonialism was premised on the idea that territories could be annexed for the purposes of creating new states. Throughout the 19th century, the United States annexed sufficient territory to create thirty-seven new states (Grupo 1984; Sheridan 1985). All territories annexed prior to 1898 were subsequently admitted as states on an equal footing with the original thirteen. While ruled as colonial territories, they were treated as a part of the United States for constitutional purposes. Stated differently, colonial territories were located *inside* or *within* the U.S. empire for constitutional purposes. It followed that all constitutional provisions not locally inapplicable applied to the territories [*American Insurance v. Canter* (1928); *Dred Scott v. Sandford* (1856)]. More important, because colonial territories were located within the U.S., by 1898 anti-imperialists or colonialists generally agreed that for citizenship purposes birth in a territory was tantamount or equivalent to birth in the United States (Torruella 1988, 24–30; Baldwin 1899, 406; Rodríguez Suárez 1986, 640). Although there were different anti-imperialist or colonialist perspectives, all agreed that the U.S. was bound to treat Puerto Rico as a part of the United States for purposes of recognizing the right to a Fourteenth Amendment birthright citizenship for persons born in Puerto Rico following its annexation.

In contrast, U.S. imperialism was premised on the strategic *occupation* of territories for economic and/or military purposes. Examples of the U.S. imperialism abound and include the occupation of Native American territories (Getches et al. 1998), the Guano Islands (Skaggs 1994), and policies such as the Monroe Doctrine and the Doctrine of Manifest Destiny (Horsman 1981). With rare exceptions (for example, Hawai'i and Oklahoma), U.S. imperialism has never been premised on the acquisition of territories for the purposes of creating new states. Territories subject to imperialist occupation have been situated *outside* of the United States for constitutional purposes.[2] This of course did not mean that Congress could not extend constitutional provisions to occupied territories, but federal lawmakers were required to do so by enacting legislation (*Fleming v. Page* 1850; Gardiner 1899, 181–2). Again, it followed that because occupied territories were located outside of the United States, for citizenship purposes birth in these territories was equivalent to birth in a sovereign nation (Torruella 1988, 24–30; Langdell 1899) or tribe (*Elk v. Wilkins* 1884). Suffice it to say that in 1898, racially eligible (Haney López 1996) persons born in an occupied territory could only acquire a U.S. citizenship via a naturalization process, which included derivative forms of paternal or *jus sanguinis* citizenship. Imperialists sought to treat Puerto Rico as an occupied territory to bar its residents from becoming citizens and demanding constitutional rights that could challenge the U.S. hegemony in Puerto Rico.

Again, as noted above, scholars generally agree that the U.S. government drew on Abbott Lawrence Lowell's Third View to craft a new territorial doctrine with a corresponding status to rule Puerto Rico and the other territories annexed in the aftermath of the War of 1898.[3] Simply put, Lowell's argument sought an alternative constitutional interpretation to the colonialist or anti-imperialist and imperialist traditions (Lowell 1899, 156–7). Lowell argued that the United States could acquire or annex two types of territories, namely, those that would become a part of the United States (colonies) and those that could be held as possessions (1899, 176). Constitutional provisions not locally inapplicable applied to those territories that were a part of the United States. Alternatively, some constitutional provisions could be withheld from territorial possessions until Congress incorporated or made these types of territories a part of the United States (1899, 176). Stated differently, the Congress could enact legislation that did not bind it to past colonialist or imperialist precedents and selectively apply or withhold constitutional provisions not locally inapplicable to Puerto Rico. Unlike the prevailing view articulated by legal scholars who argue that the ensuing territorial doctrine was developed in a Supreme Court ruling, my contention is that the new territorial doctrine resulted from political process that began with the annexation of Puerto Rico in 1898, was normalized by congressional legislation in 1900, and was institutionalized or given a constitutional garb in 1901 by the Supreme Court. But let me explain.

For the first time in its history, the United States annexed a territory without intending to incorporate its inhabitants into the Anglo-American polity.

The treaty of annexation for Puerto Rico departed from prior U.S. territorial annexation treaties (Secret Proceedings 1899, 209; Cabranes 1979, 20). Spain ceded Puerto Rico to the United States under the terms of Article Two of the *Treaty of Paris of 1898*. Formal annexation, following the Senate's ratification of the treaty on April 11, 1899, made Puerto Rico a *part* of the United States until Congress enacted organic or territorial legislation to rule Puerto Rico (*DeLima v. Bidwell* 1901). Notwithstanding, the ninth article of treaty contained two important clauses that departed from prior precedents. Whereas all prior U.S. treaties of territorial annexation contained a collective naturalization clause or promised to do so at a future time (Thorpe 1909), the first clause of the *Treaty of Paris* created an insular or in this case a Puerto Rican nationality, which barred island-born Spanish citizens from either retaining their Spanish citizenship or acquiring a U.S. citizenship. For the first time in its history, the United States annexed a territory without intending to incorporate its inhabitants into the Anglo-American polity. In addition, whereas prior colonialist jurisprudence established that the Constitution's bill of rights applied to an annexed territory *ex propio vigore* or on its own force (*American Insurance v. Canter* 1828, 542–3), Article Nine's second clause established that Congress would be responsible for enacting legislation that extended civil and political rights to Puerto Rico. Or as I have argued elsewhere, the *Treaty of Paris* annexed Puerto Rico to the U.S. global empire, while at the same time excluding Puerto Ricans from membership in the polity (Venator-Santiago 2013; 2015a; 2015b).

Simultaneously, President William McKinley imposed a military dictatorship on Puerto Rico to enable a transition from the Spanish regime to the U.S. empire.[4] The military dictatorship lasted two years, between the initial occupation of Puerto Rico on July 25, 1898, and the enactment of the *Foraker Act* on April 12, 1900. President McKinley not only tasked the military with determining what Spanish public institutions could be retained or replaced with U.S. institutions, but also to help create a new insular or territorial law and policy (Root 1970 [1916], xiv). Of the five military dictators that ruled Puerto Rico during this period, Brigadier General George Davis was the most influential. In his last report on the civil affairs of Puerto Rico, Brigadier General George W. Davis summarized the role and impact of the military dictatorship in the following words:

The scope of these orders was very wide. Almost every branch of administration—political, civil, financial, and judicial—was affected by their provisions. It may be that the military governors exceeded their authority when they changed the codes, the provisions of which were not in conflict with the political character, institutions, and Constitution of the United States; but in the absence of instructions to the contrary, it was conceived to be the privilege and duty of the military commanders to make use of such means with a view to adapting the system of local laws and administration to the one which, judging from precedents, Congress might be expected to enact for the island, thus preparing the latter for a territorial régime when Congress should be ready to authorize it. *It has been pointed out that the course adopted is understood to have been, tacitly at least, approved by Congress, for with two slight exceptions, specified in the [Foraker Act of 1900], every order promulgated by the military governors has been confirmed by Congressional enactment, has become part of the supreme law of the land, and will so remain until abrogated or changed by Congress or by the legislative assembly of the island.* (U.S. Congress 1902, 47—emphasis added)

On the question of the territorial status of Puerto Rico, Brigadier General Davis wrote, in an 1899 report on the civil affairs of Puerto Rico, that it was his understanding that Puerto Rico was "held" as a territorial "possession" and therefore treated as a "dependency" rather than a territory (U.S. War Department 1899, 73). More important, he further noted that the United States treated Puerto Rico as a foreign country for purposes of collecting tariffs and duties on merchandise trafficked between United States ports (including Hawai'i) and the island, as well as goods arriving from else-where (U.S. War Department 1899, 73). Ensuing funds collected by these tariffs were returned to the Puerto Rican treasury to subsidize local projects (Argüelles 1996, 30). Simply put, the military adopted a tariff policy that treated Puerto Rico, an annexed territory, as a foreign territorial possession.

On April 12, 1900, Congress replaced the military dictatorship with a civil government under the terms of the *Foraker Act*.[5] Central to the *Foraker Act* was the continued use of the military tariff or rather the imposition of a 15 percent *Dingley Act of 1897* tariff on merchandise trafficked between Puerto Rico and the United States. During the *Foraker Act* congressional debates, Senator John C. Spooner (R-WI) explained that the *Foraker Act* would establish that "territory belonging to the United States, as I think Puerto Rico and the Philippine Archipelago do, become a part of the United States in the *international sense,* while not being a part of the United States in the *constitutional sense*" (Senator Spooner 1900, 3629—emphasis added). Simply put, the *Foraker Act* sought to rule Puerto Rico, an annexed territory, as a foreign territorial possession selectively located *outside* of the United States for domestic or constitutional purposes.

Soon after, the Supreme Court began to rule on the constitutionality of the new territorial law and policy in a series of opinions generally known as the *Insular Cases*. Central to these court opinions were questions about the departures from past colonialist precedents, or rather the differentiated treatment of the territories annexed in the aftermath of the War of 1898. The core principles of the constitutional interpretation or doctrine that would since guide the Supreme Court's territorial jurisprudence were laid out in the concurring opinion written by Justice Edward D. White in *Downes v. Bidwell* (1901). For purposes of this article, however, I will limit my comments to clarifying the impact of the ensuing doctrine of territorial incorporation on the two questions that I am addressing in this section and in the article more generally. Namely, what is the ensuing territorial status that this opinion ascribes to Puerto Rico? And how does the ensuing doctrine of territorial incorporation shape the contours of my argument?

In *Downes* the Court addressed the constitutionality of Section Three or the *Foraker* tariff. The prevailing interpretation of the Uniformity Clause (U.S. Const. art I, §8, cl. 1) essentially established a uniform taxation on merchandise trafficked between ports within the United States and barred the imposition of discriminatory tariffs on the latter goods. The *Foraker* tariff imposed a discriminatory tax on goods trafficked between a port from an annexed territory and a state port (New York). Thus, the central question in *Downes* was whether the *Foraker* act's tariff violated the Uniformity Clause. This question was essential given that an hour earlier the Supreme Court had ruled in *DeLima* that the annexation clause of the *Treaty of Paris* made Puerto Rico *a part* of the United States. In a plurality opinion (5-4), with eight of the nine justices disagreeing with the rationale offered by the author of the majority opinion, Justice Henry B. Brown, writing for a plural majority affirmed the constitutionality of the *Foraker* tariff. In other words, a plural majority of the Court agreed that Congress could selectively treat Puerto Rico, an annexed territory, as a foreign territorial possession located *outside* of the United States for constitutional purposes. However, the rationales embraced by the judges echoed the three academic debates of the period.

Justice Brown's majority opinion reproduced the imperialist argument. Simply put, Justice Brown argued that the Constitution is a compact among states and territories and not part of the definition of the United States. Territories were not a part of or located in the United States (182 U.S. 244, 250–1). Thus, persons born in Puerto Rico were not born in the United States for purposes of the Citizenship Clause of the Fourteenth Amendment (182 U.S. 244, 251). It followed that racially eligible persons born in Puerto Rico could only acquire a U.S. citizenship via naturalization, the only constitutional type of U.S. citizenship available to persons born outside the United States.

The dissenting arguments written by Chief Justice Melville Fuller and Justice John Marshall Harlan embraced the anti-imperialist or colonialist view. Like Justice Fuller, Justice Harlan's opinion primarily focused on a critique of the "occult" nature of Justice White's thesis on territorial "incorporation." Nonetheless, Justice Harlan's interpretation was clear:

In my opinion Porto Rico [sic] became, at least after the ratification of the treaty with Spain, a *part* of and subject to the jurisdiction of the United States in respect of all its territory and people, and Congress could not thereafter impose any duty, impost or excise with respect to that island and its inhabitants, which departed from the rule of uniformity established by the Constitution. (182 U.S. 244, 391—emphasis added)

Simply put, Justice Harlan and the other dissenting Judges agreed that once the United States annexed Puerto Rico, the archipelago became a part of the United States for constitutional purposes. It followed that birth in Puerto Rico, after the ratification of the *Treaty of Paris,* would have been tantamount to birth in the United States for purposes of the Fourteenth Amendment and the Constitution more generally. Racially eligible Puerto Ricans would have acquired birthright citizenship under this interpretation after April 11, 1899, or when the Senate ratified the *Treaty of Paris.*

Justice White rejected both Justice Brown's imperialist rationale and the dissenting anti-imperialist interpretations (182 U.S. 244, 315). Instead, he embraced Lowell's Third View. To be sure, Justice White argued that the Constitutional definition of the United States included states *and* territories (182 U.S. 244, 320). There are several elements of Justice White's concurring opinion that merit special emphasis. Justice White recognized a distinction between territories that were *incorporated* and thus a *part* of the United States destined to become states of the Union, and territories that were *not* incorporated or territories that could be ruled as possessions belonging to, but not being a part of, the United States. The latter, unincorporated territories, could be selectively ruled as "foreign" possessions in a domestic or constitutional sense (182 U.S. 244, 341–2). This interpretation rejected Justice Brown's assertion that territories were located outside of the scope of the Constitution and the dissenting argument establishing that the territories were a part of the United States.

Second, Justice White argued that while Puerto Rico remained in an unincorporated status, only fundamental rights and other constitutional provisions not locally inapplicable would apply in the archipelago. In the case at hand, Justice White concluded, neither the *Treaty of Paris* nor the *Foraker Act* contained provisions that incorporated or made Puerto Rico a part of the United States. The question that followed was not whether Puerto Rico was located outside of the United States for constitutional purposes, for Justice White clearly wrote that it was not, but rather what constitutional provisions were applicable (182 U.S. 244, 292). To this extent, Puerto Rico remained a foreign (in a domestic sense) territorial possession until Congress either enacted legislation explicitly incorporating the archipelago or enacted legislation that implicitly incorporated Puerto Rico, for example, by collectively naturalizing the residents of Puerto Rico (182 U.S. 244, 329). Justice White's opinion rejected Justice Brown's imperialist interpretation argument that all territories, regardless of whether they were incorporated or not, were located outside of the U.S. for constitutional purposes, as well as the dissent's claim that territories were a part of the U.S. for constitutional purposes. This of course did not mean that Congress and the Courts could not determine that Puerto Rico was located outside of the U.S. for a *particular* constitutional provision, but this interpretation would be determined on a case-by-case basis.

He just warned that granting citizenship to Puerto Ricans would cause various other constitutional problems should Puerto Rico cease to be a part of the United States.

It is important to note, however, that like his brethren in the Court, Justice White opposed granting citizenship to "alien races" "absolutely unfit to receive it" (182 U.S. 244, 306). Justice White's opinion rejected both Justice Brown's and the dissenting judges' opinions. In the case of Justice Brown, he flat out rejected the idea that the Citizenship Clause of the Fourteenth Amendment could not apply to territories located outside of the United States. In contrast, while the dissenting judges shared the prevailing racist opinions of Puerto Ricans, their argument suggests that once a territory is annexed, the Citizenship Clause, and the Constitution more generally, applied to Puerto Rico on its own force. The point that I want to emphasize is that while Justice White opposed granting citizenship to the inhabitants of Puerto Rico, his interpretation did not bar Congress from enacting any type of citizenship legislation for Puerto Rico. Nor did his interpretation reject the possibility of applying the Citizenship Clause to the archipelago. He just warned that granting citizenship to Puerto Ricans would cause various other constitutional problems should Puerto Rico cease to be a part of the United States.

More than two decades later, in *Balzac v. People of Porto Rico* (1922), the Supreme Court both modified Justice White's interpretation of the doctrine of territorial incorporation *and applied it* to an unincorporated territory now primarily inhabited by U.S. citizens. This opinion addressed the claim by Jesús M. Balsac that he was entitled to a Sixth Amendment right to trial by jury (Ortiz Santini 2019). On appeal, the Court held that this right did not apply to Puerto Rico, an unincorporated territory. Central to the Court's rationale were two key arguments. First, the court grappled with the question of whether the collective naturalization of Puerto Ricans or any other part of the *Jones Act of 1917* had "implicitly" incorporated Puerto Rico. In both *Downes* and later in *Rassmussen v. United States* (1905), Justice White argued that the collective naturalization of the inhabitants of a territory, in the former case Puerto Rico and in the latter Alaska, was an example of Congress welcoming the inhabitants of a territory to the "American family," or an implicit form of incorporating a territory (Rivera Ramos 1997, 84; *Rasmussen v. U.S.* 1905, 197 U.S. 516). However, in *Balzac*, Chief Justice William H. Taft rejected Justice White's interpretation and tempered the doctrine of territorial incorporation. He wrote "but in these latter days, incorporation is not to be assumed without *expressed* declaration, or an implication so strong as to exclude any other view" (*Balzac* 1922, 306—emphasis added). Stated differently, until Congress explicitly enacts legislation that incorporates Puerto Rico, the archipelago will remain an unincorporated territory. The Chief Justice's opinion essentially removed the idea that Congress could enact legislation that implicitly incorporated Puerto Rico or any other unincorporated territory for that matter. Congress has never enacted legislation providing for the incorporation of Puerto Rico. Puerto Rico has remained an unincorporated territory since the enactment of the *Foraker Act of 1900*. That is, Puerto Rico remained a foreign territorial possession or locality for purposes of the Sixth Amendment.

Second, because Puerto Rico remained an unincorporated territory, Chief Justice Taft also argued that the Sixth Amendment, or the Constitution more generally, did not apply to the archipelago *ex propio vigore* or on its own force. Central to his interpretation was the following argument:

In Porto Rico, however, the Porto Rican cannot insist upon the right of trial by jury, except as his own representatives in his legislature shall confer it on him. *The citizen of the United States* living in Porto Rico cannot there enjoy a right of trial by jury under the Federal Constitution, *any more than the Porto Rican. It is locality that is determinative of the application of the Constitution, in such matters as judicial procedure, and not the status of the people who live in it.* (*Balzac* 1922, 309—emphasis added)

Stated differently, the unincorporated status of Puerto Rico *and the federalist constitutional system*, not the citizenship status of the resident of Puerto Rico, determines whether those parts of the Constitution that are not locally inapplicable can apply or not.

Two points need to be emphasized. First, since *Balzac*, the Court has embraced an interpretation of the doctrine of territorial incorporation that requires Congress to enact legislation that explicitly incorporates Puerto Rico before it can treat the island as a constitutional part of the United States. For more than a century, liberals and conservatives, Democrats and Republicans, have refused to enact legislation providing for the territorial incorporation of Puerto Rico. Second, because Puerto Rico remains an unincorporated territory, prevailing doctrinal interpretations of the status of Puerto Rico contend that birth in the island is tantamount to birth outside of the United States for citizenship purposes.

In sum, during the War of 1898, the U.S. started a new tradition of territorial expansionism, known as the doctrine of territorial incorporation, with a corresponding territorial status, the unincorporated territory. This tradition and corresponding status departed from prior U.S. traditions of territorial expansionism in large measure to avoid binding Congress and the Federal government more generally to either the colonialist or imperialist precedents. The new tradition established that annexed territories could be selectively ruled as unincorporated territories that belonged to but were not a part of the United States for domestic or constitutional purposes. To this extent, Puerto Rico could selectively remain as a foreign territorial possession for constitutional purposes. Constitutional provisions did not apply to Puerto Rico unless they were deemed fundamental or were expressly applied to Puerto Rico. Congress has never enacted legislation expressly providing for the territorial incorporation of Puerto Rico. To this extent, the Third View interpretation by the Supreme Court suggests that Puerto Rico is located *outside* or not *in* the United States for citizenship and some constitutional purposes more generally.

Part III: What Is the Constitutional Source of Citizenship for Puerto Rico Today?

Simultaneously, throughout this period Congress enacted a series of citizenship laws for Puerto Rico culminating in the extension of birthright or *jus soli* citizenship to the islands. The latter was anchored on the Citizenship Clause of the Fourteenth Amendment. Since 1898, Congress has debated upwards of 130 bills containing citizenship provisions for Puerto Rico (Venator-Santiago 2015b). Between 1898 and 1952, the Senate also ratified one treaty with a citizenship provision, and Congress enacted eleven citizenship laws for Puerto Rico.[6] Over time, these citizenship laws conferred at least four types of citizenship on persons born and/or residing in Puerto Rico, including: (1) a Puerto Rican citizenship or non-citizen nationality (1899-1934); (2) a naturalized (individual and collective) citizenship (1899-1940); and (3) birthright or *jus soli* citizenship (since 1940). Throughout this period, Congress also enacted several citizenship laws that conferred a fourth, anomalous, territorial citizenship status. Notwithstanding, since 1940, citizenship legislation for Puerto Rico confers the *same* citizenship available to any eligible person born in the United States. Stated differently, since 1940, Puerto Rican-born citizens acquire the same citizenship as persons born in the United States.

Simultaneously, since 1940 Congress has treated Puerto Rico as a part of the United States for the purpose of extending birthright or jus soli citizenship to the island without changing territorial status or incorporation.

Central to understanding the constitutional sources of the citizenships extended to Puerto Rico is the relationship between Puerto Rico's location within the United States and the types of citizenship extended to the Puerto Rican islands. Of course, as I have noted earlier, this relationship is also complicated by the antinomic relationship between the Court and Congress's legal actions towards Puerto Rico. To be sure, on the one hand, the Supreme Court has refused to rule on the constitutionality of any citizenship legislation for Puerto Rico and has affirmed the principle that unincorporated territories can be selectively ruled as foreign possessions in a domestic or constitutional sense, since they are located outside of the United States. Simultaneously, since 1940, Congress has treated Puerto Rico as a part of the United States for the purpose of extending birthright or *jus soli* citizenship to the island without changing territorial status or incorporation. Stated differently, prior to 1940, Congress enacted citizenship legislation that treated Puerto Rico as a foreign locality, but in 1940 Congress began enacting legislation that made birth in Puerto Rico tantamount to birth in the United States without changing Puerto Rico's territorial status. The legislative histories of the citizenship legislation for Puerto Rico clarify the implications.

A. Constitutional Sources of United States Citizenship in 1898

The United States Constitution only contains two clauses or sources of citizenship conferring two types of citizenship, the Naturalization Clause (U.S. Const., Art. I, §8, cl. 4), and the Fourteenth Amendment's Citizenship Clause (U.S. Const., 14th Amend., cl. 1). The Naturalization Clause authorizes Congress to enact legislation enabling persons born and naturalized outside of the United States to acquire a U.S. citizenship via various types (individual and collective) of naturalization processes. In contrast, the Citizenship Clause contains two provisions. The first provision established that with some exceptions (Native Americans and the children of foreign dignitaries), persons born in the United States acquire a birthright or jus soli citizenship. The second provision authorizes Congress to enact domestic naturalization laws for persons naturalized in the United States. Between 1898 and 1940, the period that concerns me in this article, as I will explain below, U.S. law recognized important differences between naturalized and birthright citizens, depriving the former of some constitutional protections and rights automatically available to native-born of birthright citizenship.

In 1898, persons inhabiting a U.S. territory could acquire citizenship in various ways. Because occupied territories were both located outside of the United States and parts of sovereign nations, persons inhabiting these territories could only acquire a U.S. citizenship via a special naturalization act (*Inglis v. Trustees of Sailor's Snug Harbour* 1830, 155–6). In contrast, in 1898, racially eligible inhabitants of an annexed territory could acquire U.S. citizenship in at least five ways. Frederick Van Dyne argued that citizenship was extended to a U.S. territory in four ways (Van Dyne 1907, 266–332). First, Van Dyne wrote, the U.S. government could enact special legislation to determine the citizenship status of the inhabitants of a conquered or ceded territory (Van Dyne 1907, 267). Second, a treaty of acquisition could contain language providing for the immediate or future collective naturalization of the acquired territory (ibid., 275-276). Third, Congress could enact special legislation, including organic or territorial acts, providing for the collective naturalization of the racially eligible inhabitants.[7] Finally, the racially eligible inhabitants of a territory, Van Dyne noted, were collectively naturalized once a territory became a state of the Union under the terms of the precedent established by the Supreme Court in *Boyd v. Nebraska* (1892) (Van Dyne 1907, 331–2). In addition, following the collective naturalization of the racially eligible inhabitants of the territory, Luella Gettys further contended, the Citizenship Clause of the Fourteenth Amendment became operative in the territory and automatically conferred birthright citizenship on racially eligible persons born in these territories (1934, 146–7).[8] In sum, once Congress enacted legislation (or treaty) *extending* citizenship to a territory, birth in the territory became tantamount to birth in the United States for purposes of the Citizenship Clause.

B. Non-Citizen Nationality or Puerto Rican Citizenship 1898-1934

The United States invented a non-citizen nationality or local citizenship to rule the inhabitants of Puerto Rico and the other annexed Spanish ultramarine territories during the War of 1898. As I noted before, the *Treaty of Paris* was the first U.S. treaty of territorial annexation that did not provide for the collective naturalization of the inhabitants of an annexed territory (Secret Proceedings, 209). The first clause of Article Nine in the *Treaty of Paris* established that

Spanish subjects, natives of the Peninsula, residing in the territory over which Spain by the present treaty relinquishes or cedes her sovereignty, may remain in such territory or may remove therefrom, retaining in either event all their rights of property, including the right to sell or dispose of such property or of its proceeds; and they shall also have the right to carry on, their industry, commerce and professions, being subject in respect thereof to such laws as are applicable to other foreigners. In case they remain in the territory they may preserve their allegiance to the Crown of Spain by making, before a court of record, within a year from the date of the exchange of ratifications of this treaty, a declaration of their decision to preserve such allegiance; *in default of which declaration they shall be held to have renounced it and to have adopted the nationality of the territory in which they may reside.* (30 Stat. 1754, 1759—emphasis added)

Stated differently, peninsular-born citizens residing in Puerto Rico at the time of the annexation were given the option of either retaining their citizenship or adopting a local or Puerto Rican nationality. In contrast, insular or island-born Spanish citizens were barred from retaining their allegiance to Spain and ascribed a "nationality of the territory" or local nationality. The second clause in Article Nine established that Congress would subsequently enact legislation providing for the civil and political rights of the inhabitants of Puerto Rico. The Senate ratified the *Treaty of Paris* on April 11, 1899.

A year after the ratification of the *Treaty of Paris*, Congress codified Article Nine under the terms of Section Seven of the *Foraker Act of 1900*, an organic or territorial act, which now described Puerto Rican non-citizen nationals as Puerto Rican citizens (McGovney 1934, 604–5). The language of Section Seven describing the Puerto Rican citizenship was clear:

That all inhabitants continuing to reside therein who were Spanish subjects on the eleventh day of April, eighteen hundred and ninety-nine, and then resided in Porto Rico, and their children born subsequent thereto, shall be deemed and held to be citizens of Porto Rico, and as such entitled to the protection of the United States, except such as shall have elected to preserve their allegiance to the Crown of Spain on or before the eleventh day of April, nineteen hundred, in accordance with the provisions of the treaty of peace between the United States and Spain entered into on the eleventh day of April, eighteen hundred

and ninety-nine; and they, together with such citizens of the United States as may reside in Porto Rico, shall constitute a body politic under the name of The People of Porto Rico, with governmental powers as hereinafter conferred, and with power to sue and be sued as such. (31 Stat. 77, 79)

Eligible persons subsequently born in the Puerto Rican islands would acquire a Puerto Rican citizenship at birth.

The invention of the non-citizen nationality or Puerto Rican citizenship created several antinomies or contradictions. For example, even though the United States annexed Puerto Rico and at least initially made this insular area a part of the United States,[9] it simultaneously excluded Puerto Ricans from membership (citizenship) in the polity. Neither the *Treaty of Paris* nor the *Foraker Act* contained a clause providing for the collective naturalization of Puerto Ricans. More important, the notion of a non-citizen national or Puerto Rican citizenship created a procedural problem that barred most Puerto Rican citizens from acquiring a U.S. citizenship via naturalization. To be sure, the prevailing naturalization laws required a potential citizen born outside of the United States to renounce their allegiance to a sovereign to begin the naturalization process. For Puerto Rican citizens this meant renouncing their allegiance to the United States to acquire U.S. citizenship! These contradictions were further exacerbated by the *Foraker Act* and the ensuing doctrine of territorial incorporation's treatment of Puerto Rico, an annexed territory, as a foreign possession for domestic or constitutional purposes.

The non-citizen nationality or Puerto Rican citizenship invented a separate and unequal status for insular or island–born Puerto Ricans. As I have previously explained (Venator-Santiago 2013; 2015a), this is an example of what Adi Ophir and others have described as a form of inclusive exclusion (Ophir et al. 2009). On the one hand, the United States annexed Puerto Rico and made it a part of its empire for international purposes. The annexation affirmed the inclusion of Puerto Rico within its empire. Simultaneously, the *Foraker* citizenship established the exclusion of Puerto Ricans from the U.S. polity. Again, as I will explain below, the Puerto Rican citizenship would remain until 1934, when Congress enacted a "territorial" citizenship law providing for the retroactive naturalization of Puerto Rican citizens born after April 11, 1899.

C. Naturalized Citizenship, 1898-1940

Between 1898 and 1940, Puerto Rican citizens and other persons born in Puerto Rico could acquire a U.S. citizenship via two types of naturalization. This period can be divided in two. Between 1899 and 1917, the ability to acquire a U.S. citizenship was limited to individuals.[10] In 1917, however, Congress enacted legislation providing for the collective naturalization of persons residing in Puerto Rico. Although individuals retained the ability to naturalize through an individual process, most of the legislation enacted by Congress until 1938 provided for the collective naturalization of Puerto Rican citizens and other residents of the Puerto Rican islands. Yet, while Congress enacted legislation providing for the naturalization of Puerto Ricans, it neglected to incorporate or change Puerto Rico's territorial status. That meant that birth in Puerto Rico during this period was tantamount or equivalent to birth outside of the United States. More important, Puerto Ricans could only acquire a naturalized form of citizenship, a citizenship that, at the time, was constitutionally inferior to that of a native-born citizen.

Prior to 1917, individual Puerto Ricans could acquire U.S. citizenship in one of three ways. First, individual Puerto Rican women who married U.S. citizens acquired U.S. citizenship because of coverture (Venator-Santiago 2012). The doctrine of coverture stipulated that marriage was tantamount to an individual form of naturalization, that is, women automatically acquired the citizenship status of their spouse through marriage (*Mackenzie v. Hare* 1915; Gettys 1934, 111–41). As I will explain below, the doctrine of coverture was applied in Puerto Rico until 1934, when Congress enacted legislation extending the *Cable Act of 1922* to Puerto Rico.[11]

Second, in 1906, Congress enacted legislation enabling individual Puerto Rican citizens to acquire U.S. citizenship through the prevailing individual naturalization process. The *Bureau of Immigration and Naturalization Act (BINA) of 1906* enabled persons born in Puerto Rico to be naturalized. Section Thirty of this act established the following:

That all the applicable provisions of the naturalization laws of the United States shall apply to and be held to authorize admission to citizenship of all persons not citizens who owe permanent allegiance to the United States, and who may become residents of any State or organized Territory of the United States, with

the following modifications: *The applicant shall not be required to renounce allegiance to any foreign sovereignty; he shall make his declaration of intention to become a citizen of the United States at least two years prior to his admission; and residence within the jurisdiction of the United States, owing such permanent allegiance, shall be regarded as residence within the United States within the meaning of the five years' residence clause of the existing law. (34 Stat. 596, 606–7—emphasis added)*

In other words, Puerto Rican citizens were no longer required to renounce an allegiance to a sovereign to comply with the naturalization requirements. In addition, unlike aliens residing in Puerto Rico who could naturalize in Puerto Rico, Puerto Rican citizens could not count their residence in Puerto Rico as residence in the United States but were required to travel to the mainland to undergo the naturalization process. For the purposes of the *BINA of 1906,* Puerto Ricans were treated as white aliens, eligible to naturalize under special circumstances (*In re Giralde* 1915).

Third, in 1914, Congress amended the *BINA of 1906* and provided Puerto Rican soldiers serving in the U.S. Revenue Cutter Service (Coast Guard), Navy, and Marines the ability to treat their years of service as a form of residence in the United States for naturalization purposes. Soldiers serving in the U.S. armed forces were not required to be citizens, and Puerto Ricans had been enlisting in large numbers since 1898. According to the *Naval Service Appropriations Act of 1914 (NSAA):*

Any alien of the age of twenty-one years and upward who may, under existing law, become a citizen of the United States, who has served or may hereafter serve, for one enlistment of not less than four years in the United States Navy or Marine Corps, and who has received therefrom an honorable discharge or an ordinary discharge, with recommendation for reenlistment, or who has completed four years in the Revenue-Cutter Service and received therefrom an honorable discharge or an ordinary discharge with recommendation for re-enlistment, or who has completed four years of-honorable service in the naval auxiliary service, shall be admitted to become a citizen of the United States upon his petition without any previous declaration of his intention to become such, and without proof of residence on shore, and the court admitting such

**alien shall, in addition to proof of good moral character, be satisfied by compe-
tent proof from naval or revenue-cutter sources of such service:** *Provided,* **That
an honorable discharge from the Navy, Marine Corps, Revenue-Cutter Service,
or the naval auxiliary service or an ordinary discharge with recommendation
for reenlistment, shall be accepted as proof of good moral character:** *Provided
further,* **That any court which now has or may hereafter be given jurisdiction
to naturalize aliens as citizens of the United States may immediately naturalize
any alien applying under and furnishing the proof prescribed by the foregoing
provisions. (38 Stat. 392, 395)**

This provision treated Puerto Ricans and other insular-born soldiers as
aliens for naturalization purposes. The new amendment made it possible for
Puerto Rican soldiers to use their military service as a vehicle to acquire U.S.
citizenship via naturalization.[12]

It is important to note that in 1915 a Federal District Court in Maryland
affirmed the ability of Puerto Rican soldiers to use their service as a vehicle
to naturalize. Socorro Giralde, born in Fajardo, Puerto Rico, and recently
honorably discharged from the U.S. Revenue Cutter Service, submitted a petition for naturalization in a U.S. District Court for the District of Maryland.
Subsequently, in *In re Giralde* (1915) the Federal government challenged his
petition, arguing that Puerto Ricans were not aliens for the purposes of the
NSAA of 1914. Writing for the Court, Judge John C. Rose rejected this challenge on four grounds. First, Judge Rose argued for a loose interpretation of
the word alien that could include Puerto Ricans. Second, Judge Rose argued
that the Supreme Court established in *Gonzales* that Puerto Ricans were
racially eligible to naturalize and acquire a U.S. citizenship. Third, while
he acknowledged that the U.S. military did not have a general citizenship
requirement, Judge Rose argued that the intent of the law was to enable the
naturalization of non-citizens who both "faithfully served the flag" and were
qualified to become citizens. Citizenship, Judge Rose noted, was also a pre-
condition for "increased pay." Finally, Judge Rose concluded that if the *BINA
of 1906* enabled Puerto Ricans to acquire U.S. citizenship, why would the
NSAA of 1914 bar Puerto Rican soldiers from naturalization?

On March 2, 1917, Congress enacted legislation providing for the collective naturalization of the residents of Puerto Rico without incorporat-

ing or changing the islands' territorial status established by Section Five of the *Jones Act of 1917*:

That all citizens of Porto Rico, as defined by section seven of the Act of April twelfth, nineteen hundred, "temporarily to provide revenues and a civil government for Porto Rico, and for other purposes," and all natives of' Porto Rico who were temporarily absent from that island on April eleventh, eighteen hundred and ninety-nine, and have since returned and are permanently residing in that island, and are not citizens of any foreign country, are hereby declared, and shall be deemed and held to be, citizens of the United States: Provided, That any person hereinbefore described may retain his present political status by making a declaration, under oath, of his decision to do so within six months of the taking effect of this Act before the district court in the district in which he resides... In the case of any such person who may be absent from the island during said six months the term of this proviso may be availed of by transmitting a declaration, under oath, in the form herein provided within six months of the taking effect of this Act to the executive secretary of Porto Rico: And provided further, that any person who is born in Porto Rico of an alien parent and is permanently residing in that island may, if of full age, within six months of the taking effect of this Act, or if a minor, upon reaching his majority or within one year thereafter, make a sworn declaration of allegiance to the United States before the United States District Court for Porto Rico, setting forth therein all the facts connected with his or her birth and residence in Porto Rico and accompanying proof thereof, and from and after the making of such declaration shall be considered to be a citizen of the United States. (39 Stat. 951, 953)

Stated differently, the collective naturalization clause of the *Jones Act* contained five citizenship clauses. The first three clauses applied to Puerto Rican citizens residing in the island. First, Puerto Rican citizens were given a choice between acquiring a U.S. citizenship and retaining their Puerto Rican citizenship. If they did nothing, they were automatically naturalized. Second, if Puerto Rican citizens chose to reject the collective naturalization, they were required to make a declaration in a district court within six months of the enactment of the *Jones Act*. Publicly available documents show that only 288 persons chose to retain their Puerto Rican citizenship (*Ex parte Morales* 1918,

10 PR Fed. 395, 397; Bothwell-Gonzalez 1979, 310–3). Third, Puerto Rican citizens temporarily absent from Puerto Rico, but permanently residing in the island, were given up to six months to make a declaration of their intention to acquire a *Jones Act* citizenship. Two additional clauses permitted alien residents of Puerto Rico and their children to naturalize. Alien residents were given six months and alien children were granted a one-year period after they reached the age of majority to decide whether to retain their parental citizenship or to acquire U.S. citizenship. What is important to emphasize, however, is that Puerto Ricans *residing* in Puerto Rico were given a choice to reject the U.S. citizenship and retain a non-citizen national status. The majority of Puerto Ricans chose to acquire a U.S. citizenship.

Puerto Rico retained its status as a U.S. territorial possession, located outside of the United States and primarily populated by naturalized citizens.

Following the enactment of the *Jones Act*, the Supreme Court addressed the implications of the collective naturalization provision on Puerto Rico's territorial status. In *Downes,* Justice White had previously argued that Congress could implicitly incorporate Puerto Rico by collectively naturalizing the residents of the islands (*Downes* 1901, 312). Subsequently, as Efrén Rivera Ramos has noted, writing for the majority, Chief Justice White established in *Rassmussen v. United States* (1905) that Congress's enactment of legislation providing for the collective naturalization of the inhabitants of a territory could be interpreted as an implicit form of territorial incorporation (Rivera Ramos 1997, 84; *Rassmussen v. U.S.* 1905). In Puerto Rico, local judges assumed that the collective naturalization provision of the *Jones Act* implicitly incorporated Puerto Rico.[13] However, in *People of Porto Rico v. Muratti* (1918) and *People of Porto Rico v. Tapia* (1918) the Supreme Court rejected this interpretation without providing an explanation (245 U.S. 639 1918). Four years later, a unanimous Supreme Court again rejected the theory of implicit incorporation in *Balzac v. People of Porto Rico* (1922), establishing that "incorporation is not to be assumed without express declaration, *or an implication so strong as to exclude any other view*" (*Balzac* 1922,

306—emphasis added). Nowhere in the *Jones Act of 1917* was any explicit language incorporating or changing Puerto Rico's territorial status.

Because the *Jones Act of 1917* did not incorporate Puerto Rico, birth in the islands was treated as birth outside of the United States for citizenship purposes. This meant that persons born in Puerto Rico could only acquire a U.S. citizenship via a derivative form of paternal or *jus sanguinis* (blood right) process. Only the children of male U.S. citizens could transfer their citizenship. More important, the ensuing citizenship available to Puerto Rican-born subjects ascribed a naturalized citizenship status on its bearers. Puerto Rico retained its status as a U.S. territorial possession, located outside of the United States and primarily populated by naturalized citizens. The ensuing administrative anomalies created by this antinomy motivated Congress to subsequently enact at least three corrective amendments to the citizenship provision of the *Jones Act* prior to 1940. These amendments sought to correct problems created by both the scope of Section Five and the challenge of transmitting U.S. citizenship in an unincorporated territory.

Congress first amended the citizenship provision of the *Jones Act* in 1927. Section Five(a) established:

That all citizens of the United States who have resided or who shall hereafter reside in the island for one year shall be citizens of Porto Rico: Provided, That persons born in Porto Rico of alien parents, referred to in the last paragraph of section 5, who did not avail themselves of the privilege granted to them of becoming citizens of the United States, shall have a period of one year from the approval of this Act to make the declaration provided for in the aforesaid section: And provided further, That persons who elected to retain the political status of citizens of Porto Rico may within one year after the passage of this Act become citizens of the United States upon the same terms and in the same manner as is provided for the naturalization of native Porto Ricans born of foreign parents. (44 Stat. 1418)

Stated differently, the 1927 Amendment made it possible for two types of Puerto Rican residents to acquire U.S. citizenship. The children of aliens residing in Puerto Rico who missed the deadlines established by the *Jones Act* were now granted a 1-year period to naturalize and acquire a U.S.

citizenship. In addition, Section Five(a) also granted the 288 Puerto Ricans, who in 1917 chose to retain their Puerto Rican citizenship, a new opportunity to naturalize and acquire a U.S. citizenship.

Congress subsequently amended Section Five in 1934. Also, known as Section Five(b), the 1934 amendment established that:

All persons born in Puerto Rico on or after April 11, 1899 (whether before or after the effective date of this Act) and not citizens subjects, or nationals of any foreign power are hereby declared to be citizens of the United States: Provided, That this Act, shall not be construed as depriving any person native of Puerto Rico, of his or her American citizenship hereto or otherwise lawfully acquired by such person; or to extend such citizenship to persons who shall have renounced or lost it under the treaties and/or laws of the United States or who are now residing permanently abroad and are citizens or subjects of a foreign country: And provided further, That any woman, native of Puerto Rico and permanently residing therein, who, prior to March 2, 1917, had lost her American nationality by reason of her marriage to an alien eligible to citizenship, or by reason of the loss of the United States citizenship by her husband, may be naturalized under the provisions of section 4 of the Act of September 22, 1922, entitled 'An Act relative to the naturalization and citizenship of married women,' as amended. (48 Stat. 1245)

Unlike the 1927 Amendment, which merely granted aliens and Puerto Rican citizens a one-year period to naturalize, the 1934 Amendment began to address the substantive limitations of the scope of the *Jones Act* by creating a territorial form of citizenship at birth and abolishing the doctrine of coverture in Puerto Rico without changing the islands' territorial status.

The 1934 Amendment contained clauses. The first clause provided for the retroactive naturalization of Puerto Ricans born in Puerto Rico between April 11, 1899, the date of the ratification of the *Treaty of Paris,* and the enactment of the Section Five(b) Amendment. This clause effectively created a territorial form of citizenship at birth limited to Puerto Ricans born in Puerto Rico. The second clause expressly abolished the doctrine of coverture in Puerto Rico by extending the *Cable Act of 1922* to the islands. According to Representative John McDuffie (D-AL), the 1934 amendment enabled "a native woman of Puerto Rico who is permanently residing in Puerto Rico, and who has lost her citizenship by marriage to an alien, to be naturalized under the provisions of" Section Four of the *Cable Act* (H. Rept. 73-1277). Again, it is important to emphasize, as Resident Commissioner Santiago Iglesias Pantín noted at the time, the law granted "Puerto Rico women equality of rights of naturalization with—continental—American-born women" (78 Cong. Rec. 10297, 10467). What is important to underscore, however, is that the 1934 amendment granted Puerto Rican-born women the ability to re-acquire a naturalized rather than a native-born citizenship status. Like both the 1927 and the subsequent 1938 amendments to the *Jones Act*, the 1934 amendment recognized that the collective naturalization of Puerto Ricans did not change the island's territorial status and Puerto Rican-born citizens retained a naturalized status.

On May 16, 1938, Congress amended the citizenship provision of the *Jones Act* a third time. Also, known as Section Five(c), the new amendment established:

That any person of good character, attached to the principles of the Constitution of the United States, and well-disposed to the good order and happiness of the United States, and born in Puerto Rico on or after April 11, 1899, who has continued to reside within the jurisdiction of the United States, whose father elected on or before April 11, 1900, to preserve his allegiance to the Crown of Spain in accordance with the provisions of the treaty of peace between the United States and Spain entered into on April 11, 1899, and who, by reason of misinformation regarding his or her own citizenship status failed within the time limits prescribed by section 5 or section 5a, hereof to exercise the privilege of establishing United States citizenship and has heretofore erroneously but in good faith exercised the rights and privileges and performed the duties of a citizen of the United States, and has not personally sworn allegiance to any foreign government or ruler upon or after attainment of majority, may make a sworn declaration of allegiance to the United States before any United States district court. Such declaration shall set forth facts concerning his or her birth in Puerto Rico, good character, attachment to the principles of the Constitution of the United States and being well disposed to the good order and happiness of the United States, residence within the jurisdiction of the United States, and

misinformation regarding United States citizenship status, and shall be accompanied by proof thereof satisfactory to the court. After making such declaration and submitting such proofs, such person shall be admitted taking the oath of allegiance before the court, and thereupon shall be considered a citizen of the United States. (52 Stat. 377)

Stated differently, the children of Spanish citizens born and residing in Puerto Rico since April 11, 1899, who did not take advantage of prior naturalization statutes, were allowed to naturalize by making a simple declaration and oath of allegiance to the United States. Again, this amendment made it possible for Puerto Ricans to acquire a naturalized citizenship.

Excepting the 1934 amendment, all citizenship laws enacted during this period (1899-1940) ascribed to Puerto Ricans a naturalized citizenship status. In the words of Edward J. Shaughnessy, Deputy Commissioner of the Immigration and Naturalization Service, "Strange as it may seem, although being born in a United States possession, (Puerto Ricans) had the classification of a naturalized citizen" (1942, 77ᵗʰ Cong. 4-5). Both Congress and the Supreme Court continued to treat Puerto Rico as an unincorporated territory, a foreign possession or locality for constitutional purposes. That is, between 1899 and 1940, birth in Puerto Rico was equivalent to birth outside of the United States and Puerto Ricans acquired U.S. citizenship via naturalization. At the time, the constitutional differences between a naturalized and a native-born citizenship were substantive. Unlike native-born citizens, naturalized citizens were vulnerable to expatriation or denaturalization and possessed fewer constitutional protections. At the time, naturalized citizens were given an unequal constitutional citizenship status.

According to the legislative history of the *Nationality Act of 1940*, Congress conceived the *Jones Act* amendment of 1934 as a territorial form of birthright citizenship, limited to Puerto Ricans born in Puerto Rico. According to a 1938 Report from a special Presidential Committee (hereafter President's Committee) designed to codify all citizenship, immigration, and naturalization laws, the 1934 amendment did not extend the rule of *jus soli* based on the Citizenship Clause of the Fourteenth Amendment to Puerto Rico, but rather retroactively described Puerto Ricans born in Puerto Rico between April 11, 1899 and 1934 as citizens at birth (1938, Part 1, 11-14).

The historical record is vague on the question of the constitutional source of this type of territorial citizenship at birth. Unlike the Puerto Rican citizenship, which grew out of the annexation of a territory amidst a war with a sovereign nation, the 1934 amendment was part of a process of amending a U.S. naturalization law. Although I am reluctant to recognize the power of Congress to anchor a citizenship on the Territories Clause, former jurist Raúl Serrano Geyls (2004, 63) argued that this clause can be a source of a statutory citizenship for Puerto Rico.

D. *Jus Soli* or Birthright Citizenship, 1940 to the Present

Between 1940 and 1952, Congress began to replace the *Jones Act of 1917* with three laws that treated Puerto Rico as a part of the United States for the purpose of extending *jus soli* or birthright citizenship to the islands and conferring a "native-born" status on Puerto Rican-born citizens. The *Nationality Act of 1940*, the basis for the subsequent laws, treated Puerto Rico as a *part* of the United States for citizenship purposes and established that all persons subsequently born in the islands acquired a "native-born" citizenship status. The *Pagán/Fernós-Isern Amendment of 1948* retroactively extended a native-born citizenship status on persons who acquired their citizenship in Puerto Rico prior to the enactment of the *Nationality Act*. This amendment to the *Nationality Act* protected Puerto Rican-born citizens from automatic denaturalization for, among other things, residing outside of the United States and Puerto Rico for a period of five years or longer. The *Immigration and Nationality Act of 1952*, the current source of citizenship for persons born in Puerto Rico, merely reproduced the provisions of the *Nationality Act* and its 1948 amendment. The legislative history of the *Nationality Act of 1940* unequivocally established that the Citizenship Clause of the Fourteenth Amendment was the source of the *jus soli* citizenship extended to Puerto Rico.

On April 25, 1933, President Franklin D. Roosevelt issued an executive order creating a presidential committee comprised of six representatives from the Departments of State, Labor, and Justice "to review the nationality laws of the United States, to recommend revisions, and to codify the laws into one comprehensive nationality law for submission to the Congress" (President's Committee Report 1938, v). The ensuing

President's Committee drafted a comprehensive code that was subsequently enacted by Congress as the *Nationality Act of 1940*. This national law included provisions to address the administrative problems created by the *Jones Act* citizenship and Puerto Rico's unincorporated territorial status more generally. The President's Committee recommendations for Puerto Rico were accepted with little debate and no substantive modifications. The *Nationality Act*, a statute, extended the rule of *jus soli* or birthright citizenship to Puerto Rico.

The President's Committee submitted a draft of the *Nationality Act* to President Roosevelt on June 1, 1938. In the accompanying letter of submittal, Secretary of State Cordell Hull, Attorney General Homer Cummings, and Secretary of Labor Frances Perkins wrote:

Since the citizenship status of persons born in the United States and the incorporated territories is determined by the fourteenth amendment to the Constitution, the proposed changes in the law governing acquisition of nationality at birth relate to birth in unincorporated territories and birth in foreign countries to parents one or both of whom have American nationality. (President's Committee Report 1938, v)

Stated differently, while the President's Committee believed that the Citizenship Clause was the constitutional source of *jus soli* citizenship legislation in the states and *incorporated territories*, it also recognized unincorporated territories were not located *in* the United States for purposes of the first sentence of the Fourteenth Amendment. The President's Committee believed that the Fourteenth Amendment was the only constitutional source of *jus soli* citizenship and that incorporated territories were located within the United Sates for purposes of the Citizenship Clause.

The *Nationality Act* began by establishing that Puerto Rico became a *part* of the United States for the purposes of this law only (1940, 4).[14] Section 101(d) of the *Nationality Act of 1940* established that the "term 'United States' when used in a geographical sense means the continental United States, Alaska, Hawaii, *Puerto Rico*, and the Virgin Islands of the United States" (54 Stat. 1137, 1138). The President's Committee Report explained the intent of this provision in the following terms:

In bringing the Virgin Islands within the term "United States" for purposes of acquisition of nationality, and for such purposes *treating them as if they were incorporated with the continental United States*, this code follows the act of March 2, 1917 (39 Stat 953, 965), and it extends the same advantages to Puerto Rico, where, considering the express provisions of the act of June 27, 1934, it seems clear that the common law rule of acquisition of nationality through the fact of birth within the territory and jurisdiction of the United States (*jus soli*) does not apply. According to the act mentioned, persons born in Puerto Rico acquire citizenship of the United States at birth only in case they are "not citizens, subjects, or nationals of any foreign power. *In the proposed new law this condition is eliminated, and birth in Puerto Rico will have the same effect as birth in the continental United States.* (President's Committee Report 1938, 4—emphasis added)

To become a part of the United States, the authors of Section 101(d) reasoned, Puerto Rico needed to be selectively treated as an incorporated territory. In addition, Section 102(a) unequivocally described Puerto Rico as a "State" for the sole purpose of defining the island as a part of the United States (54 Stat. 1137). This interpretation was affirmed by Representative Edward H. Rees (R-KS) during the congressional hearings for the *Nationality Act* (76th Cong. 38).

Whereas Guam and American Samoa were defined as unincorporated territories, Puerto Rico and the U.S. Virgin Islands were treated as incorporated territories, albeit for the sole purpose of extending jus soli or birthright citizenship.

When crafting Section 101(d) the President's Committee also invoked the precedent established by the U.S. Virgin Islands (U.S.V.I.). The United States purchased and annexed the U.S. Virgin Islands in 1916. In 1927, Congress enacted a citizenship statute both providing for the retroactive collective naturalization of all persons born in the U.S. Virgin Islands since January 17, 1917, and establishing the extension of *jus soli* citizenship (44 Stat. 1234). The accompanying House Report explained that Section Three of the U.S. Virgin Islands' citizenship statute of 1927 "provides for persons hereafter born in the Virgin Islands of the United States [sic] the rule of citizenship *already provided in the fourteenth amendment to the Constitution of the United States"* (H. Rep. No. 69-2093, 3—emphasis added). Stated differently, according to Representative Edgar R. Kiess (R-PA), the author of the report, the Citizenship Clause of the Fourteenth Amendment was the constitutional source of Section Three, the birthright citizenship provision of the U.S. Virgin Islands' citizenship statute of 1927. It also means that Congress began to enact birthright citizenship legislation anchored on the Citizenship Clause of the Fourteenth Amendment to unincorporated territories in 1927.

The *Nationality Act* also differentiated Puerto Rico from the other "outlying possession" or unincorporated territories for citizenship purposes. To be sure, Section 101(e) defined the term "outlying possessions" as "all territory, other than as specified in subsection(d), over which the United States exercises right of sovereignty, except the Canal Zone" (§101(e), 54 Stat. 1137). Whereas Guam and American Samoa were defined as unincorporated territories, Puerto Rico and the U.S. Virgin Islands were treated as incorporated territories, albeit for the sole purpose of extending *jus soli* or birthright citizenship. Congress could have treated Puerto Rico as an unincorporated territory, but it chose not to do so.

The *Nationality Act* contained separate provisions granting different types of birthright citizenship to persons born in the United States, as well as in its "outlying" or unincorporated territories. Persons born in the United States, and subject to its jurisdiction, acquired a *jus soli* citizenship under the terms of Section 201(a) (54 Stat. 1137, 1138). According to the President's Committee Report,

Subsection (a), which it is to replace, is in effect a statement of the common-law rule, which has been in effect in the United States from the beginning of its existence as a sovereign state, having previously been in effect in the colonies. It accords with the provision in the fourteenth amendment to the Constitution of the United States. (President's Committee Report 1938, 7)

During the congressional hearings, testifying on behalf of the President's Committee, Richard W. Flournoy, an assistant legal adviser for the State

Department, noted that the language and logic of Section 201(a) was "taken of course from the fourteenth amendment to the Constitution" (H.R. 9980 Hearings, 38). Federal lawmakers did not object to this interpretation. In sum, the Citizenship Clause of the Fourteenth Amendment was the constitutional source for Section 201(a) of the *Nationality Act of 1940*.

The *Nationality Act* also included what may be described as a territorial birthright citizenship provision. More precisely, Section 201(e) conferred a territorial citizenship at birth to persons born in an "outlying" or unincorporated territory to at least one U.S. citizen parent who had previously resided in the United States or an unincorporated territory (54 Stat. 1137, 1138). The President's Committee Report explained that,

this provision is not based solely upon either *jus soli* or *jus sanguinis* but contains elements of both. While, as indicated above, it does not seem desirable to confer citizenship of the United States at birth upon a child born outside of the United States and its outlying possessions if only one parent is a citizen of the United States and the other is an alien, unless this is made subject to strict limitations, the case is materially different when the child is born in outlying territory of the United States. It seems reasonable in such cases to confer upon the child at birth the status of a "citizen of the United States" if the citizen parent has previously resided in the United States or one of its outlying possessions. (President's Committee Report 1938, 11)

It is important to note that Section 201(e) created a territorial citizenship at birth that required at least one parent to be a U.S. citizen resident (*jus sanguinis*) and was limited to persons born in an "outlying" or unincorporated territory. Whereas Section 201(a) *jus soli* citizenship provision granted birthright citizenship to almost anyone born in U.S. soil, regardless of the citizenship status of the parent, only the children of U.S. citizens born in an unincorporated territory could claim citizenship at birth under the terms of Section 201(e). Moreover, whereas the President's Committee Report established that the Fourteenth Amendment was the constitutional source for Section 201(a), it also established that other organic acts, such as the 1934 amendment to the *Jones Act* [Section Five(b)], provided the legal precedent or source for the creation of Section 201(e) (President's Committee Report

1938, 13). Yet, while the corresponding congressional debates on this provision are a bit vague and scattered, Congress ultimately approved the section.

In sum, as of January 12, 1941, persons born in Puerto Rico acquire *jus soli* or birthright citizenship under the terms of Section 201(a), the provision enacted for persons born *in* the United States, not under the terms of Section 201(e), the provision enacted for the children of citizens born in an outlying or unincorporated territory. Whereas the Citizenship Clause of the Fourteenth Amendment was the constitutional source of Section 201(a), special naturalization statutes provided the precedents for Section 201(e). For purposes of the *Nationality Act's* birthright citizenship provisions, birth in Puerto Rico was tantamount to birth in the United States. This difference is explicit in the law. Stated differently, since 1940, persons born in Puerto Rico acquired the same citizenship as native-born U.S. citizens.

The *Nationality Act* contained an additional citizenship provision for persons born in Puerto Rico following the U.S. annexation and the enactment of the laws. In other words, Section 202 both retroactively naturalized all persons born in Puerto Rico between April 11, 1899, and January 12, 1941, and granted these persons a territorial citizenship at birth.[15] Again, the President's Committee Report summarized the intent of the law in the following manner:

> This section is designed to do what is believed to have been intended by those who sponsored the bill which became the existing law concerning nationality in Puerto Rico, that is, the act of Congress of June 27, 1934. The latter does not apply the *jus soli* to persons born in Puerto Rico, since it expressly excepts children born in the island of parents who are citizens or subjects of a foreign state. The proposed new provision will remedy this. In other words, this section will in effect apply the rule of *jus soli* to Puerto Rico as of the date of its annexation to the United States, *treating Puerto Rico for such purposes as an incorporated territory of the United States*. (President's Committee Report 1938, 11—emphasis added)

This provision was designed to correct or perhaps clarify the 1934 amendment to the *Jones Act* and was applied to previously naturalized Puerto Ricans. Naturalized Puerto Ricans were retroactively granted a birthright citizenship status, albeit via a special statute. Again, no clear objections to this provision were raised during the relevant congressional hearings.

On December 3, 1941, Puerto Rican Resident Commissioner Bolívar Pagán (S-PR) began to introduce legislation seeking to protect Puerto Ricans who had acquired their U.S. citizenship prior to 1940 and were residing outside of the United States (including Puerto Rico) from being de-naturalized or expatriated (H.R. 6165, 77th Cong. 1942). Whereas persons born in Puerto Rico who acquired a U.S. citizenship prior to the enactment of the *Nationality Act* were considered naturalized citizens, persons born after were conferred a native-born status for the prevailing immigration and naturalization laws. At the time, Section 404(c) of the *Nationality Act* established the automatic denaturalization of naturalized citizens continuously residing outside of the United States (including Puerto Rico) for a period of five years (§404(c), 54 Stat. 1137, 1170). Historically, many Puerto Ricans worked and lived in the Dominican Republic, Cuba, Venezuela, Mexico, and other countries throughout the Western Hemisphere. Although the bill(s) did not become law until 1948 (62 Stat. 1015), in large measure due to the delays caused by World War II, the legislative record demonstrates that most federal lawmakers supported Resident Commissioner Pagán's amendment to both Section Five(b) of the *Jones Act* and 404(c) of the *Nationality Act* (Venator-Santiago 2013b; 2017).

The legislative history of the *Pagán/Fernós-Isern Amendment of 1948* further reveals the prevailing interpretation of the citizenship status of Puerto Ricans among law and policymakers in Washington. I draw on two dimensions of this legislative history to substantiate my own interpretation. First, the legislative record of this amendment shows that throughout the years, namely between 1941 and 1948, there was a consensus among law and policymakers that persons born in Puerto Rico after the enactment of the *Nationality Act* became "native-born" citizens. For example, as previously noted, during the initial hearings on *H.R. 6165* on June 17, 1942, Edward J. Shaughnessy, the Deputy Commissioner of the Immigration and Naturalization Service, explained both the prevailing problem and status of Puerto Ricans to members of the House Subcommittee on Immigration and Naturalization in the following terms,

A peculiar thing is not until 1941 by virtue of the Nationality Code was Puerto Rico, for citizenship purposes, considered a part of the United States. So, since January 12, 1941, persons born in Puerto Rico *are native born citizens*, although persons born in Puerto Rico prior to that time, strange as it may seem, although being born in a United States possession, had the classification of a naturalized citizen. (77ᵗʰ Cong. 4–5—emphasis added)

United States Attorney General Francis B. Biddle amplified this interpretation in an often-cited letter to Representative Samuel Dickstein (D-NY) and embraced by the federal lawmakers that subsequently reintroduced this bill (H. Rep. 1942, No. 77-2373, 2; H. Rep. No. 1943, 78-182, 2). Second, the enactment of the *Pagán-Fernós Isern Amendment of 1948* confirmed the interpretation that the *Nationality Act of 1940* had in fact granted persons born in Puerto Rico a native or natural born citizenship status. The point that I want to continue to make is that Congress and policymakers in Washington, D.C., reached a consensus that persons born in Puerto Rico after January 12, 1941, became native-born U.S. citizens, a status that could only be conferred to constitutional citizens. More important, as I will explain below, the enactment of this law/amendment sought to protect persons born in Puerto Rico from arbitrary denaturalization/expatriation due to their prior, vulnerable, *naturalized* citizenship status.

The *Immigration and Nationality Act (INA) of 1952* is the current source of citizenship for persons born in Puerto Rico. The accompanying House Report to the law unequivocally notes that the relevant citizenship provisions of the *INA of 1952* were copied or "carried forward" from the *Nationality Act of 1952* (H. Rep. No. 82-1365 [1952], 76 [(2d Sess. 1952]). Prevailing interpretations of the *INA* suggest that Congress limited the source of U.S. citizenship for persons born in Puerto Rico to Section 302 (8 U.S.C. 1402), which was based on Section 201(a) of the *Nationality Act*. However, in the 1999 brief submitted by the Federal government in the *Lozada Colón v. Department of State* case addressing the ability of Puerto Ricans to renounce their U.S. citizenship and acquire a Puerto Rican citizenship, the Department of State, and the federal government more generally, argued that persons born in Puerto Rico acquired a U.S. citizenship under the terms of Sections 1101(a)(38) and 1401(a) or the equivalent of Section 101(a)(38) of the *INA* (Brief for Respondent in Opposition, *Lozada Colón v. Department of State* 1999, 1–2). Moreover, Section 101(a)(36) describes Puerto Rico as a "State" for purposes of the *INA* [66 Stat. 236, §101(a) (36)]. It followed that persons born in Puerto Rico were born (and therefore resided) *in* the United States for citizenship purposes. The point is that the *INA of 1952* adopted the language, rationale, and intent of the *Nationality Act of 1940*.

It is important to make a pause here and offer some clarifications to the implications of the latter argument. The President and Congress's decision to treat Puerto Rico as a "part" of the United States for citizenship purposes raises important questions. First, this is an example of an antinomy. On the one hand the Supreme Court, exercising its powers under judicial review (*Marbury v. Madison* 1803), declared that Puerto Rico is an unincorporated territory for constitutional purposes, selectively situated outside of the United States, while on the other hand Congress, exercising its constitutional powers specifically enumerated in the Territories Clause, also declared that the Puerto Rican islands were a part of the United States, albeit solely for the purposes of this citizenship legislation. Second, if McGovney is right, the Citizenship Clause does not grant or place any limitations on the powers of Congress (1911, 338). In addition, he further argued, the Citizenship Clause is a self-executing clause (1911, 339). And that Congress's declaration that Puerto Rico is a part of the United States should be sufficient to apply the Citizenship Clause to Puerto Rico. Notwithstanding, the legislative history of the *Nationality Act of 1940* suggests that Congress was applying the Citizenship Clause via statute. More important, given the Supreme Court's historical refusal to challenge Congress's power to enact citizenship statutes for Puerto Rico, as I explain elsewhere in more detail, I believe that Congress's decision to enact this citizenship legislation was consistent with the underlying logic of the doctrine of territorial incorporation.[16]

In sum, I want to highlight five dimensions of these legislative histories. First is that the President and Congress agreed that the only constitutional source of birthright or *jus soli* citizenship is the Citizenship Clause of the Fourteenth Amendment. Second is the agreement that the Citizenship Clause applies to incorporated territories or territories that can be selectively treated as incorporated. Third, in 1940, at the behest of the Roosevelt Administration, Congress extended birthright or *jus soli* citizenship anchored on the Fourteenth Amendment to Puerto Rico. Fourth, the *Pagán/Fernós-Isern Amendment of 1948* re-affirmed that Puerto Rican-born citizens, especially those born after the enactment of the *Nationality Act of 1940*, acquired a native-born citizenship status and were protected from arbitrary de-naturalization under prevailing immigration and naturalization laws. Fifth, the *Immigration and Nationality Act of 1952*, the current source of citizenship for Puerto Rican-born citizens, copies or carries forward the *Nationality Act's* provisions for Puerto Rico and persons born in these islands. Since 1940, Congress began to treat Puerto Rico as a part of the United States for the sole purpose of extending birthright citizenship without incorporating the islands! Despite this contradiction, the Supreme Court has consistently neglected to challenge Congress's power to do this or ruled on the constitutionality of the *jus soli* or birthright citizenship legislation ascribed to Puerto Rico.

Part IV: A Note on the Statutory Nature of the Citizenship Legislation for Puerto Rico

The constitutional nature of the citizenships extended to Puerto Rico has been a subject of multiple debates since 1898. Many of these debates are linked to the question of Puerto Rico's territorial status (i.e., Muñoz Morales 1936; Martínez Acosta 1938; Serrano Geyls 2004 [1945]; Rodríguez Suárez 1986; Killian 1989). Underlying these debates is whether a United States citizenship extended to Puerto Rico via statute or legislation grants Puerto Rican-born citizens the same constitutional protections afforded to persons who are born or naturalized in a state, an incorporated territory or, more precisely, *in* the United States. Alternatively, the question is whether the statutory U.S. citizenships extended to Puerto Rico ascribe a second-class citizenship status to Puerto Rican-born citizens. Stated differently, there is a tendency among scholars to argue that the citizenship extended to Puerto Rico is "legislated, not constitutional" (Álvarez González 1990, 330; Román 2005, 138–9; Smith 2015, 115–6). While it is beyond the scope of this article to provide a direct and comprehensive response to these questions, and I have done so elsewhere,[17] I do feel compelled to offer a brief overview of key arguments that refute the claim that the statutory nature of the citizenship extended to Puerto Rico ascribes a second-class status to island-born citizens.

A related question is whether Congress can enact citizenship legislation without a constitutional source or anchor. Reflecting on the Supreme Court's ruling in *Downes*, Frederic R. Coudert argued that Justice White's opinion rejected the imperialist premise of Justice Brown and other imperialists (1926, 830). As noted before, Justice Brown and other imperialists argued that territories were located outside of the United States and therefore outside of the limits of the Constitution. They argued that Congress, a creature of the Constitution, possessed a power outside of the Constitution to rule territories. As previously noted, Justice White's opinion established that the question was not whether the Constitution applied to Puerto Rico—there was no question that it did—but rather which provisions applied. The ensuing doctrine of separate and unequal, also known as the doctrine of territorial incorporation, required that Congress anchor its citizenship legislation in a constitutional source.

The question then is not whether the citizenship legislation for Puerto Rico has a constitutional source, but rather which? In a section of his 1945 MA thesis addressing the power of Congress to unilaterally denaturalize Puerto Rican-born citizens should Puerto Rico become a sovereign nation under the Tydings status bills, eminent judge and legal scholar Raúl Serrano Geyls suggested that the *Jones Act* citizenship of 1917 could have two potential constitutional sources conferring two different types of statuses (2004 [1945], 58–63). To be sure, Serrano Geyls reasoned, if the constitutional source of the *Jones Act* was the Naturalization Clause, then Puerto Rican-born citizens, like other citizens naturalized under a naturalization statute, "are in the same footing as all other naturalized citizens of the United States and they cannot be deprived arbitrarily of their citizenship" (2004 [1945], 63). But Serrano Geyls further concluded, "if Congress acted under Article IV, citizenship in Puerto Rico is just another 'rule' or 'regulation' which Congress can revoke when it pleases for it is not a fundamental right" (2004 [1945], 63). In other words, Serrano Geyls recognized a clear constitutional difference between a citizenship that was a product of a naturalization statute and a statutory citizenship that was a mere "rule" or "regulation" invented by federal lawmakers as part of their power to govern an unincorporated territory. Stated differently, some citizenship statutes have a constitutional source and others do not. The problem, of course, is that in 1945 Puerto Rican-born citizens acquired a different type of citizenship, a *jus soli* citizenship unequivocally anchored on the Citizenship Clause of the Fourteenth Amendment!

One of the fundamental problems afflicting legal scholars, political actors, and academics and scholars alike is a fetishism or fixation with the *Jones Act of 1917* citizenship, whom many believe is the first and last citizenship law enacted for Puerto Rico. To date, I am the only scholar who has written about the historical process of enacting laws between 1940 and 1952 that replaced the *Jones Act* citizenship and extended a "native-born" citizenship status to persons born in Puerto Rico. As I documented in the previous section, in 1940 Congress replaced the *Jones Act* citizenship, a law that ascribed a "naturalized" citizenship status on its bearers, with the birthright citizenship provision of the *Nationality Act* which imposed a "native-born" status on island-born citizens. In 1948, Congress amended the *Nationality Act* with the *Pagán/Fernós-Isern* law in order to further protect Puerto Rican-born citizens from the involuntary denaturalization of the prevailing immigration and naturalization laws. The legislative histories of the birthright citizenship laws and bills enacted and debated between 1940 and 1952 unequivocally demonstrate that Congress treated Puerto Rico as a part of the United States for the sole purpose of conferring a native-born status that would protect Puerto Rican-born citizens from involuntary and discriminatory denaturalization laws. Although anchored on the Citizenship Clause of the Fourteenth Amendment, these were laws conferring a statutory citizenship on all eligible persons born in Puerto Rico since 1940. Persons born in Puerto Rico acquire a statutory citizenship that confers the same native-born citizenship status that is conferred on persons born in a state or incorporated territory.

Part V: Conclusions

At the time of this writing, Puerto Rican-born citizens acquire the same citizenship status as persons born in a state or Washington, D.C. Since 1940, Congress has anchored the *jus soli* or birthright citizenship laws for Puerto Rico in the Citizenship Clause of the Fourteenth Amendment. Island-born citizens do not acquire a different, "colonial," "territorial," or second-class citizenship. To make this claim today is to neglect and ignore the historical evidence.

Balzac affirmed two basic constitutional interpretations that challenge the prevailing liberal narrative of citizenship. First, the Court affirmed the application of the doctrine of separate and unequal to a territory inhabited by citizens. This doctrine enabled the Court to selectively apply or withhold civil rights (i.e., the Sixth Amendment right to trial by jury) in Puerto Rico. Only fundamental, albeit undefined, rights were guaranteed in Puerto Rico. This interpretation departed from prior precedents, which guaranteed the application of the Bill of Rights and all constitutional rights not locally inapplicable. Second, *Balzac* affirmed a basic principle of U.S. federalism, namely, that the status of the locality determines the application of rights and the Constitution more generally. As Justice Clarence Thomas recently reminded Hermann Ferré, the attorney arguing Puerto Rico's case in *United States v. Vaello-Madero*, any citizen, regardless of race, ethnicity, or nationality, who moves to Puerto Rico will lose constitutional rights and any citizen who moves from Puerto Rico to a state will gain rights (Oral Argument in *U.S. v. Vaello-Madero* 2021, 44). Today, the membership status of Puerto Rican-born citizens is not determined by their citizenship, it is determined by their residence within the U.S. empire.

ACKNOWLEDGMENTS

This paper would not have been possible without the critiques, encouragement, and support of many colleagues and friends. I am grateful to Edwin Meléndez, Blanca Silverstrini, José Javier Colón Morera, César Ayala, Carlos Vargas Ramos, Diego Ayala-McCormick, Lydia E. Santiago, and Xavier Totti, who have endured my rants over the years and challenged me to flesh out my arguments.

NOTES

[1] I have placed all citizenship laws, bills, and key documents relating to the history of the extension of US citizenship to Puerto Rico in a publicly accessible website titled the *Puerto Rico Citizenship Archives Project* (<https://scholarscollaborative. org/PuertoRico/>). Anyone interested in reading the actual citizenship laws, legislation, and other materials can access these documents in the public archive.

[2] *U.S. v. Rice*, 17 U.S. 246 (1819) (establishing that US territory occupied by a foreign power remained foreign while under occupation); *Fleming v. Page* (1850) (establishing that the Port of Tampico remained a foreign territory while under US occupation); *New Orleans v. The Steamship Company* (1874) (establishing that the port of New Orleans could be treated as a foreign territory during the US military occupation).

[3] While it is beyond the scope of this article to address the ahistorical use of the term "coloniality," a popular modality among Puerto Rican academics to describe the US annexation of, and subsequent rule over Puerto Rico, I am compelled to start addressing this nonsensical claim in this article. Simply put, there is no historical evidence to substantiate the claim that the United States annexation of Puerto Rico can be read as an undifferentiated continuation of a Eurocentric or even "modern" imperial project. The particularity of the US territorial expansionist theory developed to rule Puerto Rico should be enough to discourage the use of the term "coloniality" to describe the relationship between Puerto Rico and the US. Even the cultural dimensions of the Anglo-American exceptionalism employed to legitimate the Third View should be enough to reject this academic jargon or modality. For examples of the misuse of the notion of coloniality to describe the case of Puerto Rico, see Negrón-Muntaner and Grosfoguel, eds. (1997); Bonilla and Lebrón, eds. (2019); and Bonilla (2020). For a more substantive alternative critique of this modality, see generally Vázquez-Arroyo (2018) and Makaran and Gaussens (2020).

[4] I use the term "dictatorship" to situate the case of Puerto Rico within a broader discussion of what Clinton Rossiter has described as a constitutional dictatorship.

Legal scholars use this term to describe the authoritarian interpretation of the US Constitution to suspend constitutional provisions and impose an anti-democratic regime within the polity (Rossiter 2004 [1948]; Trías Monge 1991).

[5] Decolonial academics tend to invent historical narratives that fit their conceptual representations of the relationship between Puerto Rico and the United States. Take, for example, Bonilla's claim that the U.S. military government in Puerto Rico lasted from 1898 to 1917 (2020, 6). This type of strategic use of "alternative facts" or "invented histories" makes it difficult to incorporate decolonial claims into substantive debates about the status of Puerto Rico within the U.S. empire.

[6] See for example *Treaty of Paris of 1898* (1899); *Foraker Act of 1900* (1900, ch. 191, 31 Stat. 77, §7; *Bureau of Immigration and Naturalization Act of 1906* (1906); *Naval Service Appropriations Act of 1914, Pub, L. No. 63-121* (1914, ch. 130, 38 Stat. 392); *Jones Act of 1917* (1917); *Naturalization of Resident Aliens of 1918* (1918); *Porto Rico Civil Revenues Act of 1927* (1927); *Puerto Rico Civil Government Act of 1934* (1934); *Puerto Rico Civil Government Act of 1938* (1938); *Nationality Act of 1940* (1940); *To Amend the Organic Act of Puerto Rico, Pub. L. No. 80-776* (1948); *Immigration and Nationality Act of 1952* (1952). For copies of these laws, see the *Puerto Rico Citizenship Archives Project.*

[7] Scholars generally allude to the Revised Statutes to explain how Congress extended citizenship to the territories. For example, Revised Statutes §1891 made the Constitution (including the 14th Amendment) and federal laws applicable to all territories. Likewise, Revised Statutes §1995 declared that "(a)ll persons born in the district of the country formerly known as the Territory of Oregon, and subject to the jurisdiction of the United States on 18th May 1872, are citizens in the same manner as if born elsewhere in the United States." See generally Revised Statutes of the United States (1878).

[8] However, while the legislative history of the Fourteenth Amendment language of the *Slaughterhouse Cases* (1872) as well as that of *U.S. v. Wong Kim Ark* clearly suggests that the Citizenship Clause treated the territories as a constitutional part of the Union, the question of whether the Fourteenth Amendment applied *ex propio vigore* or on its own force in the territories became subject of some debate. Anti-imperialists or colonialists argued that once annexed, a territory became a part of the United States for constitutional purposes and therefore for purposes of the Citizenship Clause. Anti-imperialists or colonialists often drew on the precedents established in *American Insurance v. Canter* and *Dred Scott v. Sandford* to argue that citizenship, a civil right, applied to a territory on its own force upon annexation. In contrast, imperi-

alists argued that only states could become a part of the United States for constitutional purposes and therefore civil rights did not apply automatically.

[9] *DeLima v. Bidwell* (1901) (establishing that Puerto Rico became a part of the United States for tariff purposes during the military occupation and prior to the enactment of the *Foraker Act of 1900*).

[10] Again, one of the fundamental problems facing academics who write about the status of Puerto Rican-born citizens is that they lack a clear understanding of the relevant history of the extension of citizenship to Puerto Rico. This is in large measure driven by a lack of understanding of this history, as well as by an idiosyncratic fetishism with the *Jones Act of 1917*. For example, historians like Lorrin Thomas, who wrote about the *Puerto Rican Citizen*, incorrectly claim Puerto Ricans were unable to acquire a U.S. citizenship *before* the enactment of the *Jones Act of 1917* (2010, 1–2).

[11] It is important to note that throughout this period the doctrine of coverture reduced important hardships for divorced and widowed Puerto Rican women. For example, after 1906, the Department of Labor eliminated the power of the district court in Puerto Rico to grant naturalizations requiring divorced or widowed Puerto Rican-born women who were previously married to an alien and/or the children of mixed marriages permanently residing in Puerto Rico to migrate to the mainland to acquire U.S. citizenship through the naturalization process (*Re Hastrup* 1919).

[12] It is important to note that, in 1918, after the enactment of the *Jones Act of 1917*, Congress passed a further corrective amendment to the 1906, a law enabling individual Puerto Ricans to acquire US citizenship. See *Naturalization of Resident Aliens of 1918* (1918).

[13] See, for example, *In the Matter of Garffer* (1917, at 544) (arguing that the Jones Act declared "that residents in Porto Rico shall, for naturalization purposes, be considered the same as residents elsewhere in the United States, which for naturalization purposes, therefore, amounts to an incorporation of Porto Rico [sic] in the United States").

[14] For an alternative reading reaching the same conclusions, almost three decades earlier, see Dudley O. McGovney (1911).

[15] §202, 54 Stat. 1137, at 1139. §202 became §302 in the *Immigration and Nationality Act of 1952* and is presently codified as 8 U.S.C. §1402.

[16] For examples of the Supreme Court's refusal to question congressional citizenship statutes for Puerto Rico, see generally *Gonzales v. Williams*, 192 U.S. 1 (1904) (establishing that Puerto Ricans were not aliens for prevailing labor immigration laws, but refusing to rule on the constitutionality of the Puerto Rican citizenship); *Porto Rico v.*

Tapia and *Porto Rico v. Muratti* (1918) (establishing that the collective naturalization of Puerto Ricans under the *Jones Act of 1917* did not incorporate or change the island's constitutional status or the application of some civil rights to the island); *Balzac v. People of Porto Rico* (1922) (establishing that the status of the territory, not the citizenship of the inhabitants, was determinative of the application of the constitution in Puerto Rico); *Efrón v. United States* (1998) (affirming a lower court ruling barring a Puerto Rican-born citizen from naturalizing in Florida in order to acquire a constitutional citizenship that would protect her from involuntary expatriation should Puerto Rico become independent); and *Lozada Colón v. U.S. Dept. of State* (1998) (establishing Puerto Rico was a part of the United States and not a foreign country for citizenship purposes). The Supreme Court has avoided addressing this question in other cases relating to other unincorporated territories. More recently, the 10th Circuit Court of Appeals affirmed Congress's plenary power over the extension of citizenship to the territories in *Fitisemanu v. United States (2021)*.

[17] See, generally, *Statutory Citizenship: A Historical Overview of Debates About the Power of Congress to Expatriate Puerto Ricans* (forthcoming) and *¿Cuál es la fuente constitucional de la ciudadanía estadounidense en Puerto Rico?* (forthcoming).

REFERENCES

American Insurance Co. v. Canter. 1828. 26 U.S. 511.

Álvarez González, José Julián. 1990. The Empire Strikes Out: Congressional Ruminations on the Citizenship Status of Puerto Ricans. *Harvard Journal on Legislation* 27, 309–65.

Argüelles, María del Pilar. 1996. *Morality and Power: The U.S. Colonial Experience in Puerto Rico From 1898 to 1948*. Lanham, MD: University Press of America.

Baldwin, Simeon E. 1899. The Constitutional Questions Incident to the Acquisition and Government by the United States of Island Territory. *Harvard Law Review* 12(6), 393–416.

Balzac v. People of Porto Rico. 1922. 258 U.S. 298.

Bickel, Alexander M. 1973. Citizenship in the American Constitution. *Arizona Law Review* 15(2), 369–88.

_____. 1975. *The Morality of Consent*. New Haven: Yale University Press.

Bonilla, Yarimar. 2015. *Non-Soveregin Futures: French Caribbean Politics in the Wake of Disenchantment*. Chicago: The University of Chicago Press.

_____. 2020. The Coloniality of Disaster: Race, Empire and the Temporal Logics of

Emergency in Puerto Rico, USA. *Political Geography* 78(1), 102181 (1–12).

Bonilla, Yarimar and Marisol LeBrón, eds. 2019. *Aftershocks of Disaster: Puerto Rico Before and After the Storm*. Chicago: Haymarket Books.

Bothwell González, Reece B. 1971. *Trasfondo constitucional de Puerto Rico*. Río Piedras, PR: Editorial Universitaria.

_____. 1979. *Puerto Rico: cien años de lucha política*. Vol. 2. Río Piedras, PR: Editorial Universitaria.

Boyd v. Nebraska. 1892. 143 U.S. 135.

Brief for Respondent in Opposition, *Lozada Colón v. Department of State*, 170 F. 3d. 191 (D.D.C., 1999) (No. 97cv1457). <https://www.justice.gov/osg/brief/lozada-colon-v-department-state-opposition>.

Bureau of Immigration and Naturalization Act of 1906. 1906. Pub. L. No. 59-338, 34 Stat. 596.

Cable Act of 1922. 1922. Pub. L. No. 67-346, 42 Stat. 1021.

Cabranes, José A. 1979. *Citizenship and the American Empire, Notes on the Legislative History of the United States Citizenship of Puerto Ricans*. New Haven: Yale University Press.

Citizenship for Inhabitants of Virgin Islands Act of 1927. 1927. Pub. L. No. 69-640, 44 Stat. 1234.

Cohen, Elizabeth. 2009. *Semi-Citizenship in Democratic Politics*. New York: Cambridge University Press.

Congressional Research Service. 1985. *Admission of States Into the Union After the Original Thirteen: A Brief History and Analysis of the Statehood Process*. Prepared by Peter B. Sheridan, Government Division, 85-765 GOV. Washington, D.C.

Coudert, Frederic R. 1926. The Evolution of the Doctrine of Territorial Incorporation. *Columbia Law Review* 26(7), 823–50.

Dahl, Robert A. 2003. *How Democratic Is the American Constitution?* 2nd Edition. New Haven: Yale Nota Bene.

De Genova, Nicholas and Ana Y. Ramos-Zayas. 2003. *Latino Crossings: Mexicans, Puerto Ricans, and the Politics of Race and Citizenship*. New York: Routledge.

Del Moral, Solsiree. 2013. *Negotiating Empire: The Cultural Politics of Schools in Puerto Rico, 1898-1952*. Madison: The University of Wisconsin Press.

DeLima v. Bidwell. 1901. 182 U.S. 1.

Diaz, Ileana I. 2021. Malignant Citizenship: Race, Imperialism, and Puerto Rico-

United States Entanglements. *Citizenship Studies* 25(3), 1–20.

Dingley Act of 1897. 1897. ch. 11, 30 Stat. 151.

Downes v. Bidwell. 1901. 182 U.S. 244.

Dred Scott v. Sandford. 1856. 60 U.S. 393.

Efrón v. United States. 1998. 1 F. Supp. 2d 1468.

Elk v. Wilkins. 1884. 112 U.S. 94.

Ex parte Morales. 1918. 10 PR Fed. 395.

Fleming v. Page. 1850. 50 U.S. 603.

Fitisemanu v. United States. 2021. Accessed on 19 July 2021. <https://www.equalrightsnow.org/fitisemanu>.

Foraker Act of 1900. 1900. ch. 191, 31 Stat. 77.

Gardiner, Charles A. 1899. *Our Right to Acquire and Hold Foreign Territory.* An Address Delivered Before the New York State Bar Association at Its Annual Meeting at Albany, 18 January. New York: G. P. Putnam & Sons.

Getches, David H., Charles F. Wilkinson and Robert A. Williams, Jr. 1998. *Cases and Materials on Federal Indian Law.* 4th Edition. St. Paul: West Group.

Gettys, Luella. 1934. *The Law of Citizenship in the United States.* Chicago: The University of Chicago Press.

Gonzales v. Williams. 1904. 192 U.S. 1.

Grupo de Investigadores Puertorriqueños. 1984. *Breakthrough From Colonialism: An Interdisciplinary Study of Statehood.* 2 vols. Río Piedras: Editorial de la Universidad de Puerto Rico.

Haney López, Ian F. 1996. *White by Law, The Legal Construction of Race.* New York: New York University Press.

Horsman, Reginald. 1981. *Race and Manifest Destiny, The Origins of American Racial Anglo-Saxonism.* Cambridge: Harvard University Press.

Immigration and Nationality Act of 1952. 1952. Pub. L. No. 82-414, 66 Stat. 163.

Inglis v. Trustees of Sailor's Snug Harbour. 1830. 28 U.S. (3 Pet.) 99.

In re Giralde. 1915. 226 F. 826.

In the Matter of Garffer. 1917. 9 PR Fed. 544.

In the Matter of Tapia. 1917. 9 P.R. Fed. Rep. 452.

Jobson, Ryan Cecil. 2020. Public Thinker: Yarimar Bonilla on Decolonizing Decolonization. Public Books. Accessed 5 January 2022. <https://www.publicbooks.org/public-thinker-yarimar-bonilla-on-decolonizing-decolonization/ >.

Jones Act of 1917. 1917. Pub. L. No. 64-368, 39 Stat. 951.

Johnny H. Killian. 1992. Congressional Research Service Memorandum: Discretion of Congress Respecting Citizenship Status of Puerto Rico (March 9, 1989), in *Puerto Rico: Political Status Referendum, 1989-1991*. Vol. 2, 81–5. Washington, DC: Puerto Rico Federal Affairs Administration.

Langdell, C.C. 1899. The Status of Our New Territories. *Harvard Law Review* 12(6), 365–92.

Lowell, Abbott Lawrence. 1899. The Status of Our New Possessions–A Third View. *Harvard Law Review* 13(3), 155–76.

López Baralt, José. 1999. *The Policy of The United States Towards its Territories with Special Reference to Puerto Rico*. San Juan: Editorial de la Universidad de Puerto Rico.

Lozada Colón v. U.S. Dept. of State. 1998. 2 F. Supp. 2d 43.\\

Makaran, Gaya and Pierre Gaussens, eds. 2020. *Piel blanca, máscaras negras: crítica de la razón decolonial*. México: Bajo Tierra A.C. y Centro de Investigaciones sobre América Latina y el Caribe-Universidad Nacional Autónoma de México.

Marbury v. Madison. 1803. 5 U.S. 137.

Martínez Acosta, C. 1938. *Los programas políticos de la Unión de Puerto Rico, Muñoz y la ciudadanía de los Estados Unidos*. San Juan: El Mundo. Newspaper.

Meléndez-Badillo, Jorell. 2021. Camacho-Quinn's gold medal sparked debate about Puerto Rican national identity. *The Washington Post* 5 August. Accessed 5 January 2022. <https://www.washingtonpost.com/outlook/2021/08/05/camacho-quinns-gold-medal-sparked-debate-about-puerto-rican-national-identity/>.

McGovney, Dudley O. 1911. American Citizenship. Part II. Unincorporated Peoples and Peoples Incorporated with Less than Full Privileges. *Columbia Law Review* 11(4), 326–47.

_____. 1934. Our Non-Citizen Nationals, Who are They. *California Law Review* 22, 593–635.

Mackenzie v. Hare. 1915. 239 U.S. 299.

Muñoz Morales, Luis. 1936. *Cuestiones fundamentales de la política puertorriqueña*. San Juan: El Mundo. Newspaper.

Muratti v. Foote. 1917. 25 D.P.R. 568.

Nationality Act of 1940. 1940. Pub. L. No. 76-853, 54 Stat. 1137.

Naturalization of Resident Aliens of 1918. 1918. Pub. L. No. 65-144, 40 Stat. 542.

Naval Service Appropriations Act of 1914. 1914. Pub, L. No. 63-121, ch. 130, 38 Stat. 392.

Negrón-Muntaner, Frances. 2019. Our Fellow Americans: Why Calling Puerto Ricans "Americans" Will Not Save Them. In *Aftershocks of Disaster: Puerto Rico Before and After the Storm*, eds. Yarimar Bonilla and Marisol LeBrón. 113–23. Chicago: Haymarket Books.

Negrón-Muntaner, Frances and Ramón Grosfoguel, eds. 1997. *Puerto Rican Jam: Essays on Culture and Politics*. Minneapolis: University of Minnesota Press.

New Orleans v. The Steamship Company. 1874. 87 U.S. 387.

Ophir, Adi, Michael Givoni and Sari Hanafi, eds. 2009. *The Power of Inclusive Exclusion: Anatomy of Israeli Rule in the Occupied Palestinian Territories*. New York: Zone Books.

Ortiz-Santini, Francisco. 2019. *Balsac vs El Pueblo De Puerto Rico: su historia; sus protagonistas*. n.p.: MyBookCreations.com

People of Porto Rico v. Tapia. 1918. 245 U.S. 639.

Porto Rico Civil Revenues Act of 1927. 1927. (§5a), Pub. L. No. 69-797, 44 Stat. 1418.

Puerto Rico Civil Government Act of 1934. 1934. (§5b), Pub. L. No. 73-477, 48 Stat. 1245.

Puerto Rico Civil Government Act of 1938. 1938. (§5c), Pub. L. No. 75-521, 52 Stat. 377.

Rassmussen v. United States. 1905. 187 U.S. 516.

Re Hastrup. 1919.11 PR Fed. 183.

Revised Statutes of the United States Passed at the First Session of the Forty-Third Congress, 1873-1874 (2nd ed., 1878).

Rivera Ramos, Efrén. 1997. *American Colonialism in Puerto Rico: The Judicial and Social Legacy*. Princeton: Markus Wiener Publishers.

Rodríguez Suárez, José. 1986. Congress Giveth U.S. Citizenship unto Puerto Ricans, Can Congress Take It Away? *Revista Juridica de la U.P.R.* 55, 627–41.

Román, Ediberto. 2006. *The Other American Colonies: An International And Constitutional Law Examination Of The United States' Nineteenth And Twentieth Century Island Conquests*. Durham, NC: Carolina Academic Press.

Root, Elihu. 1970 [1916]. *The Military and Colonial Policy of the United States, Addresses and Reports*, 2nd ed., Edited by Robert Bacon and James Brown Scott. Cambridge; Reprinted by New York: AMS Press.

Rossiter, Clinton. 2004 [1948]. *Constitutional Dictatorship: Crisis Government in the Modern Democracies*. New Brunswick, NJ: Transaction Publishers.

Ruiz, Sandra. 2019. *Ricanness: Enduring Time in Anticolonial Performance*. New York: New York University Press.

Secret Proceedings. 1899. *Official Verbatim Report in Spanish and English of Every Session and the Protocols and Treaty in Full Between the United States and Spain.* New York: New York Journal and Advertiser.

Serrano Geyls, Raúl. 2004 [1945]. The Territorial Status of Puerto Rico and its Effects on the Political Future of the Island. *Revista Juridica Universidad Interamericana de Puerto Rico* 39(1), 13–66.

Skaggs, Jimmy M. 1994. *The Great Guano Rush: Entrepreneurs and American Oversees Expansion.* New York: St. Martin's Press.

Slaughterhouse Cases. 1872. 83 U.S. 36.

Smith, Rogers M. 1997. *Civic Ideals: Conflicting Visions of Citizenship in U.S. History.* New Haven: Yale University Press.

_____. 2015. The Insular Cases, Differentiated Citizenship, and Territorial Statuses in the Twenty-First Century. In *Reconsidering The Insular Cases: The Past And Future Of The American Empire*, eds. Gerald L. Neuman and Tomiko Brown-Nagin. Cambridge: Harvard University Press.

Sparrow, Bartholomew H. 2006. *The Insular Cases and the Emergence of the American Empire.* Lawrence: University Press of Kansas.

Thomas, Lorrin. 2010. *Puerto Rican Citizen: History and Political Identity in Twentieth-Century New York City.* Chicago: The University of Chicago Press.

Thorpe, Francis N. ed. 1909. *The Federal and State Constitutions, Colonial Charters, and Other Organic Laws, States, Territories, and Colonies Now or Heretofore Forming the United States of America.* 7 vols. Washington, D.C.: Government Printing Office.

To Amend the Organic Act of Puerto Rico. 1948. Pub. L. No. 80-776, 62 Stat. 1015.

Torruella, Juan R. 1988. *The Supreme Court and Puerto Rico: The Doctrine of Separate and Unequal.* Río Piedras: Editorial de la Universidad de Puerto Rico.

_____. 2017. To be or Not to Be: Puerto Ricans and their Illusory U.S. Citizenship. *CENTRO: Journal of the Center Puerto Rican Studies* 29(1), 108–35.

Treaty of Paris of 1898. 1899. 30 Stat. 1754.

Trías Monge, José 1991. *El choque de dos culturas juridicas en Puerto Rico: el caso de la responsabilidad civil extracontractual.* Austin: Equity Publishing Company.

United States Congress. House of Representatives. 1902. *Annual Reports of the War Department for the Fiscal Year Ended June 30, 1900, Part 13: Report of the Military Governor of Porto Rico on Civil Affairs*, 56th Cong., 2nd sess., H.

Doc. 2, Part 13.

United States Congress. House of Representatives. 1927. *House Committee on Insular Affairs, Citizenship For Inhabitants of Virgin Islands*, H. Rep. No. 69-2093, at 3 (2d Sess).

United States Congress. House of Representatives. 1934. 78 Cong. Rec. 10297, 10467 (statement of Res. Comm. Iglesias Pantín).

United States Congress. House of Representatives. 1934. House Committee on Insular Affairs, Amend Act to Provide Civil Government for Puerto Rico, H. Rept. 73-1277 (2d Sess.).

United States Congress. House of Representatives. 1940. *To Revise and Codify the Nationality Laws of the United States into a Comprehensive Nationality Code (Nationality Act of 1940): Hearings on H.R. 6127 and H.R. 9980 Before the H. Committee on Immigration and Naturalization*, 76th Cong. 38 [statement of Representative Edward H. Rees (R-KS)].

United States Congress. House of Representatives. 1942. *Preserving the Nationality of a Person Born In Puerto Rico who Resides for Five Years in a Foreign State: Hearing on H.R. 6165 Before the House Subcomm. on Immigration and Naturalization*, 77th Cong. 4-5 (statement of Edward J. Shaughnessy, Deputy Commissioner, Immigration and Naturalization Service).

United States Congress. House of Representatives. 1942. H.R. 6165, 77th Cong. (as reported by H. Comm. on Immigration and Naturalization, July 22.

United States Congress. House of Representatives. 1942. *House Committee On Immigration And Naturalization, Preserving The Nationality Of A Person Born In Puerto Rico Who Resides For 5 Years In A Foreign States.* H. Rep. No. 77-2373 (2d Sess.).

United States Congress. House of Representatives. 1943. *House Committee On Immigration And Naturalization, Preserving The Nationality Of A Person Born In Puerto Rico Who Resides For 5 Years In A Foreign States.* H. Rep. No. 78-182 (1ST Sess.).

United States Congress. House of Representatives. 1952. *House Committee On Judiciary, Revising The Laws Relating To Immigration, Naturalization, And Nationality.* H. Rep. No. 82-1365 (2d Sess.).

United States Congress. Senate. 1900. Senator Spooner of Wisconsin, speaking for the *Foraker Act of 1900*, on 2 April, H.R. 8245, 56th Cong., 1st sess., *Congressional Record* 33, part 4: 3629.

United States v. Rice. 1819. 17 U.S. 246.

United States v. Vaello-Madero. 2021. United States Supreme Court. *Brief of the Commonwealth of Puerto Rico as Amicus Curiae in Support of Respondent*. SCOTUSblog.com. Accessed 5 January 2022. <https://www.scotusblog.com/case-files/cases/united-states-v-vaello-madero/>.

United States v. Vaello-Madero. 2021. United States Supreme Court. Transcript of Oral Argument in *U.S. v. Vaello-Madero*. Accessed 25 November 2021. <https://www.supremecourt.gov/oral_arguments/argument_transcripts/2021/20-303_n75p.pdf/>.

United States War Department. Bureau of Insular Affairs. 1899. *Report of The Insular Commission to the Secretary of War Upon the Investigations Made Into the Civil Affairs of the Island of Porto Rico, with Recommendations*. Washington: Government Printing Office.

United States v. Wong Kim Ark. 1898. 169 U.S. 649.

United States Committee to Review the Nationality Laws. 1938. 76th Congress, Report on Nationality Laws of the United States. Part 1. (Comm. Print).

Van Dyne, Frederick. 1904. *Citizenship of the United States*. New York: The Lawyer's Cooperative Publishing Co.

Vázquez-Arroyo, Antonio Y. 2018. Critical Theory, Colonialism and the Historicity of Thought. *Constellations* 25, 54–70.

Venator-Santiago, Charles R. 2012. Marriage and the Expatriation of Puerto Rican Women: A Note on the Extension of the Cable Act of 1922 to Puerto Rico. *Latino(a) Research Review* 8 (1-2), 231–46.

_____. 2013a. Extending Citizenship to Puerto Rico, The Three Traditions of Inclusive Exclusion. *CENTRO: Journal of Puerto Rican Studies* 25(1), 50–75.

_____. 2013b. Are Puerto Ricans Native-Born U.S. Citizens? The 1948 Pagán/ Fernós-Isern Amendment. *Ámbito de Encuentros* 6(2), 1–23.

_____. 2015a. *Puerto Rico and the Origins of U.S. Global Empire: The Disembodied Shade*. London: Routledge.

_____. 2015b. *Puerto Rico Citizenship Archives Project*. Accessed 17 July 2021. <https://scholarscollaborative.org/PuertoRico/>.

_____. 2017. A Note on the Puerto Rican Denaturalization Exception of 1948. *CENTRO: Journal of the Center for Puerto Rican Studies* 29(1), 224–37.

_____. Forthcoming. *Statutory Citizenship: A Historical Overview of Debates About the Power of Congress to Expatriate Puerto Ricans*.

_____. Forthcoming. *¿Cuál es la fuente constitucional de la ciudadanía estadounidense en Puerto Rico?*

Younis, Musab. 2017. Against Independence. *London Review of Books* 39(13). Accessed 19 December 2021. <https://www.lrb.co.uk/the-paper/v39/n13/musab-younis/against-independence/>.

Balzac, US Citizenship and Territorial Incorporation in Puerto Rico

EDGARDO MELÉNDEZ

ABSTRACT

This article will present a historical and analytical analysis that inserts William H. Taft's ruling in *Balzac* within the debates that US policymakers and colonial functionaries had about US citizenship and territorial incorporation in Puerto Rico in the first two decades of the 20th century. Taft reiterated the view of these officials, that granting citizenship to the inhabitants of an unincorporated territory did not imply incorporation of the territory, with all the implications that this status had regarding citizenship rights. In *Balzac*, Taft sought to clarify the nature of US citizenship in Puerto Rico and presented it as one defined by the territory's unincorporated status. Taft also presented an argument that he and other American officials had previously advanced, that the citizenship granted to Puerto Ricans was formal in nature, that it did not grant any additional rights and that it was granted only to appease their yearning for said status. The article also studies the evolution of the jury trial in Puerto Rico prior to 1922 to challenge Taft's assertions as to why this institution should not be extended to Puerto Ricans by constitutional right. [Key Words: *Balzac v. the People of Porto Rico*; US citizenship in Puerto Rico; US territorial incorporation policies; Jones Act of 1917 for Puerto Rico; US colonial policies in Puerto Rico; William H. Taft]

Edgardo Meléndez (emel@hunter.cuny.edu) is a retired Professor from the Department of Political Science at the University of Puerto Rico-Río Piedras and the Department of Africana and Puerto Rican/Latino Studies at Hunter College, CUNY. He is author of several books and multiple academic articles on the Puerto Rican experience in Puerto Rico and the United States. He is currently working on issues related to Puerto Rican migration and political incorporation in the US, and US citizenship in Puerto Rico. His forthcoming book is tentatively titled *The Puerto Rican Problem in Postwar New York City*.

The 100th anniversary of the 1922 US Supreme Court decision *Balzac v. The People of Porto Rico* will encourage many scholars to ponder the importance and consequences of this significant ruling. Considered by many as the last of the important *Insular Cases, Balzac* is best remembered today for its continued relevance regarding the political status of the US unincorporated territories and the rights of the US citizens who live there.[1] The *Balzac* ruling was written by Chief Justice William Howard Taft and was the first of the *Insular Cases* where the Territorial Incorporation Doctrine (TID) was accepted unanimously by the Court. In *Balzac,* Taft sustained the supremacy of the *Insular Cases* and the TID in dealing with the US territories and stated that Justice Edward White's opinion in *Downes v. Bidwell* (1901) had become "settled law." White had introduced the notion of territorial incorporation to the Court's jurisprudence in *Downes,* where he argued that Congress had plenary powers over the so-called unincorporated territories. In his view, the US not only had the right to conquer territory but could exclude the territory and its inhabitants from becoming part of the United States. *Balzac* sustained that view, although the territory was then inhabited by US citizens. One hundred years later, *Balzac* remains an important Supreme Court precedent with enduring consequences for the political future of Puerto Rico and the rights of its inhabitants.

For many years *Balzac* has received the attention of scholars interested in the *Insular Cases,* deservedly so. Noted Puerto Rican constitutionalist Efrén Rivera Ramos (2001, 100) argues that with *Balzac* the Supreme Court took the incorporation doctrine further by ruling that an expressed declaration of Congress was required to incorporate territory to the nation and that granting citizenship to the inhabitants of an unincorporated territory did not imply incorporation of such territory. For Bartholomew Sparrow, the idea that distinguishes *Balzac* from previous *Insular Cases* "was whether Congress's plenary power extended over persons explicitly designated as 'U.S. citizens'..." (2006, 199; 203–4 on the importance of *Balzac*). Federal judge Juan R. Torruella contends that in *Balzac* "Taft finally embedded the incorporation doctrine into the fossilized armature [of the *Insular Cases*] that has permitted it to survive unto the present" (1985, 96). Constitutionalist Carlos R. Soltero claims that by unanimously sustaining the TID in *Balzac* the Supreme Court "solidified it as part of the American legal system" and added that Taft's arguments "were simply legal rationalizations for perpetuating colonialism" (2006, quotes from 20 and 30, respectively).

This article presents a different perspective from the existing analysis of the *Balzac* case that has focused primarily on its constitutional aspects. It is a central thesis of this article that to better understand Taft's ruling in *Balzac* it is necessary to insert it into the debate regarding the grant of citizenship to Puerto Ricans and the incorporation of the territory. This deliberation had been taking place among US policymakers and colonial officials since the United States conquered Puerto Rico and the Philippines in the 1898 war against Spain. To some extent, *Balzac* is the culmination of this debate on citizenship and incorporation in Puerto Rico. As we have already mentioned, Taft used this decision to argue that TID was the supreme law in the unincorporated territories and that Puerto Rico had not been incorporated even though Puerto Ricans had been declared citizens in 1917. But in *Balzac* Taft also institutionalized a vision of US citizenship for Puerto Ricans that predominated in the discussion on this issue at that time. In this view, citizenship did not grant any additional rights to those Puerto Ricans already enjoyed, and it was granted simply to satisfy a sentimental aspiration of these people.

Balsac's defense argued that all the constitutional guarantees provided by the Bill of Rights applied to Puerto Ricans after they were declared citizens in 1917 and that Puerto Rico had been incorporated by this grant of citizenship.

To better understand Taft's ruling in *Balzac* we should ask the question: what is really new in *Balzac*? What contributions does this opinion bring to the debate on constitutional rights and citizenship in the unincorporated territories? This case arises from a libel accusation against Jesús M. Balsac [sic][2] for having published two articles very critical of Puerto Rico's governor Arthur Yager in 1918. Balsac was a leader of both the Partido Socialista (PS-Socialist Party) and the Free Federation of Labor (FLT-Federación Libre de Trabajadores), the main trade union organization on the island. Although the PS and Yager had both supported citizenship for Puerto Ricans, for several years they had sustained a very conflictive relationship regarding the rights of workers on the island and the governor's anti-labor policy. It is within this context that Yager accused Balsac of defamation for his articles. Balsac was found guilty both in a lower court and in the Supreme Court of Puerto Rico.[3]

Balsac argued that his writings against Yager were protected by the First Amendment and, more important, that his constitutional rights had been violated by not having been granted a jury trial as he had requested. Balsac's defense argued that all the constitutional guarantees provided by the Bill of Rights applied to Puerto Ricans after they were declared citizens in 1917 and that Puerto Rico had been incorporated by this grant of citizenship. PS leader Santiago Iglesias, in alliance with Samuel Gompers and the AFL in the United States, decided to take the case to the US Supreme Court. Under Iglesias' leadership the PS had been a strong supporter of the US presence in Puerto Rico and was perhaps the most enthusiastic advocate of citizenship for Puerto Ricans in Washington, with the support of Gompers and the AFL. Iglesias and Gompers saw in US citizenship a guarantee of greater rights for Puerto Rican workers and a favorable shield in their fight against the local government and the capitalists on the island. Both leaders decided to push Balsac's case to the US Supreme Court seeking an affirmation that all constitutional rights had been extended to Puerto Ricans under their new status as citizens.[4]

Balsac's case, however, addressed the same constitutional questions of two previous cases very similar to his and which had been already brought to the US Supreme Court a few years earlier: *Porto Rico v. Tapia* (1918) and *Porto Rico v. Muratti* (1918). The Tapia case was decided by Puerto Rico's Supreme Court and the case of Muratti by the federal district court on the island. Both decisions held that Puerto Rico had been incorporated into the United States with the grant of citizenship to Puerto Ricans included in the Jones Act and that, therefore, all the guarantees of the Bill of Rights—including trial by jury—had been extended to Puerto Ricans. The Attorney General of Puerto Rico, who maintained that citizenship did not imply incorporation of the territory, and that therefore the guarantee of a trial by jury in a misdemeanor case had not been extended to the island, took these two cases to the US Supreme Court. In a very brief *per curiam*, the Supreme Court, at that time with Edward White as Chief Justice, ruled against Tapia and Muratti, basically holding that Puerto Rico had not been incorporated by the Jones Act. Even so, Iglesias and Gompers decided to push Balsac's case to the US Supreme Court, believing that they could obtain a decision more favorable to Puerto Ricans with this case. The Court, now with Taft as Chief Justice, decided to hear the case.

The two main constitutional questions in Balsac's case in the Supreme Court—that of trial by jury in the unincorporated territories and whether Puerto Rico had been incorporated by the grant of citizenship to Puerto Ricans under the Jones Act—had been decided by the Court in previous cases, as Taft acknowledged in his opinion. The Chief Justice pointed out that *Dorr v. United States* (1904) had already established that it was constitutional not to extend trial by jury to the unincorporated territories. Similarly, toward the end of his ruling Taft recognized that the Supreme Court in the 1918 Tapia and Muratti per curiam had established that Puerto Rico had not been incorporated by the Jones Act.

Why then does Taft take this case for matters already resolved by the court? A possible answer might be found toward the very end of his ruling when Taft discusses the Tapia and Muratti cases. He acknowledged that the "court has passed on substantially the same questions presented here" in these two cases. After briefly elaborating on the substantive questions in each case, Taft then points out that these two cases "were disposed of by a *per curiam*. Counsel have urged us in the cases at the bar to deal with the questions raised more at length in exposition of the effect of the Organic Act of 1917 upon the issue, and we have done so" (*Balzac* 1922, 313–4). Balsac's case allowed Taft to use the constitutional question of trial by jury to sustain that the incorporation doctrine was "settled law" in the unincorporated territories and that contrary to the experience prior to 1898 such a decision now required an express declaration of Congress; it also allowed him to argue more explicitly the reasons why the citizenship granted to Puerto Ricans by Congress in 1917 had not incorporated Puerto Rico.

In *Balzac*, Taft reiterated why the right to a trial by jury had not been extended to the unincorporated territories by the Supreme Court in previous cases: not inhabited by Anglos, the racial and cultural characteristics of the peoples living in these territories made them not suitable for this type of procedure of an Anglo-Saxon tradition and character. Taft echoed the notion expressed many times by US policymakers, members of Congress and justices of the Supreme Court that the inhabitants of the territories conquered in 1898 were not capable of adjusting to or were not worthy of institutions of an Anglo-Saxon origin. That these were inferior populations to whom it should not be necessary to extend all constitutional rights is a view that has been called Teutonic constitutionalism (Weiner 2001). As an extension of this argument, Taft used this notion to characterize Puerto Ricans as unfit for incorporation or statehood.

Furthermore, the *Balzac* ruling also allowed Taft to institutionalize his vision of why US citizenship was granted to Puerto Ricans and the nature of that citizenship in Puerto Rico. The grant of citizenship to Puerto Ricans was not meant to extend equality in rights to Puerto Ricans but to satisfy their "yearning" for such status and to offer them protection by the US. It did not imply any additional rights to those they already enjoyed except for the right to move freely to the "US proper" and once there seek equal civil and political rights. In *Balzac*, Taft presented the notion of a territorial form of US citizenship, one that is defined by its "locality," i.e., by the spatial location of its citizens in the unincorporated territory.

The remainder of this article is divided into three parts. The first section reviews in detail Taft's ruling in *Balzac* in order not only to highlight his main arguments but also to go over the logic of his approach. It also frames the discussion that follows in the next sections. The second section examines the implementation and functioning of the institution of trial by jury in Puerto Rico from the point of view of the main colonial and judicial officials on the island with the purpose of questioning Taft's argument regarding why this right could not or should not be extended to Puerto Ricans. I argue that Taft's stated reasons for not extending this constitutional right to Puerto Ricans was spurious and unsustained by historical evidence. The third section looks at the debate held for decades by US officials and colonial functionaries regarding the issue of citizenship and the territorial incorporation of Puerto Rico. It advances the notion that Taft used his ruling in *Balzac* to uphold and institutionalize the ideas of these officials, that the citizenship granted to Puerto Ricans did not imply the incorporation of Puerto Rico to the United States. In effect, in *Balzac* Taft was supporting US colonial policy toward Puerto Rico. This section also discusses the perspective presented by Taft and other US colonial officials who viewed the citizenship granted to

Puerto Ricans as a formal status, given solely to satisfy their "yearning" and appease their "sentimental" aspirations for such status, and not representing any substantive concession regarding the rights of citizenship. It was a citizenship that granted them "no additional rights."

Taft's Ruling in *Balzac*

Taft begins his ruling by elaborating on the facts of Mr. Balsac's case in Puerto Rico. After Balsac was found guilty of libel in a Puerto Rican district court in 1918, he demanded a trial by jury, arguing that his Sixth Amendment right as a US citizen had been violated. Libel in Puerto Rico at that time was considered a misdemeanor and Puerto Rican legislation stipulated that misdemeanor cases on the island did not require a trial by jury. In answer to the question if the 6th Amendment applied to Puerto Rico, Taft argued that provisions for a jury trial applied to incorporated territories as had been decided by the Supreme Court in previous *Insular Cases*. On the other hand, the Court had not extended the right to a trial by jury to unincorporated territories, citing the *Hawaii v. Mankichi* (1903) and the *Dorr* rulings. He also pointed out that the Supreme Court had ruled in *Downes* and *Dorr* that Puerto Rico had not been incorporated. Taft noted that although the *Insular Cases* reveal much diversity of opinion, the Court's ruling in *Dorr* showed how the view of Justice White in *Downes* had become "settled law," that is, the supremacy of the Territorial Incorporation Doctrine in dealing with the territories. He also indicated that *Dorr* established the power of Congress to exclude trial by jury in the unincorporated territories based on the fact that it is not a fundamental right and that the Constitution does not apply *ex propio vigore* in such territories.

Taft then addressed the question of whether Puerto Rico had been incorporated, as Mr. Balsac contended. Balsac's counsel had listed a series of facts to claim that Puerto Rico had been incorporated, chiefly related to the Jones Act and its grant of citizenship to Puerto Ricans. Taft asserted that the Jones Act did not indicate by its title and did not include any clause stipulating that Puerto Rico had been incorporated, a clear indication that Congress did not intend to incorporate the island. According to Taft, few subjects were as contentious as the annexation of the Spanish territories in 1898, since the continued controversy and the differences of opinion drew attention to that issue. Had Congress intended to incorporate Puerto Rico with the Jones Act, "it is reasonable to suppose that it would have done so by the plain declaration, and would not have left it to mere inference." Before 1898,

the distinction between acquisition and incorporation was not regarded as important, or at least it was not fully understood and had not aroused great controversy. Before that, the purpose of Congress might well be a matter of mere inference from various legislative acts, but in these latter days, incorporation is not to be assumed without express declaration, or an implication so strong as to exclude any other view. (*Balzac* 1922, 306)

Taft questioned Balsac's argument that several laws and policies implemented by the US government in Puerto Rico, in addition to the grant of citizenship, had in effect incorporated the island to the US. For Taft, the fact that the Jones Act included a bill of rights section that excluded the trial by jury made clear "this substitute for incorporation and application of the Bill of Rights of the Constitution," what he considered "a conclusive argument against the contention" of Balsac's counsel (*Balzac* 1922, 307). Had Congress intended to incorporate Puerto Rico, it would not have included such a section in the Jones Act, which would have extended the Constitution's Bill of Rights *ex propio vigore* to the island.

Taft subsequently examined Balsac's contention that the grant of citizenship had, in effect, incorporated Puerto Rico. He insisted that if it were not "by the considerations already suggested," maybe Balsac's allegation that the grant of citizenship in the Jones Act "would furnish ground for [such] an inference, but under the circumstances we find it entirely consistent with non-incorporation" (*Balzac* 1922, 308). Taft elaborated on what was the meaning of US citizenship for Puerto Ricans and why it had been given to them. Puerto Ricans had lost their "protection" from Spain when they were transferred to US sovereignty and they wanted "the protection of their new sovereign," something that in "theory and in law, they had as citizens of Porto Rico." But this "was an anomalous status or seemed to be" given the fact that they were not made US citizens. For Taft, citizenship was given to Puerto Ricans to satisfy their "yearning" to be recognized as such and to provide them "protection...against foreign injustice." To him, citizenship did not give Puerto Ricans any "additional rights" but allowed them "to move into the continental United States" and once they become "residents of any State there" enjoy the "civil, social and political" rights of US citizens. "A citizen of the Philippines must be naturalized before he can settle and vote in this country. Not so the Porto Rican under the Organic Act of 1917" (*Balzac* 1922, 308). Taft viewed US citizenship in Puerto Rico as a formal status, and not a substantive citizenship. To him, as well as for many US policymakers and colonial functionaries dealing with Puerto Rico, citizenship was not granted to Puerto Ricans with the purpose of incorporating Puerto Rico or giving them any "additional rights."

Taft used the debate on trial by jury in Puerto Rico to sustain one of the main arguments of his ruling in *Balzac*: the territorial basis of the application of the Constitution and of citizenship itself. He argued that Puerto Ricans on the island can insist on trial by jury only if this right was given by Puerto Rico's legislature:

> The citizens of the United States living in Porto Rico can not there enjoy a right of trial by jury under the Federal Constitution, any more than the Porto Rican. It is *locality that is determinative of the application of the Constitution,* in such matters as judicial procedure, *and not the status of the people* who live in it. (*Balzac* 1922, 309—emphasis added)

In some cases, he continued, "in the absence of other and countervailing evidence," a law of Congress or a treaty clause could be used to interpret that a grant of citizenship to the inhabitants of a territory implied its incorporation, like Alaska, as the Supreme Court sustained in *Rassmussen*. Taft argues that the case of Alaska presented a very different situation from that of Puerto Rico:

> It was an enormous territory, very sparsely settled and offering opportunity for *immigration and settlement by American citizens.* It was on the American Continent and within easy reach of the then United States. It involved *none of the difficulties which incorporation of the Philippines and Porto Rico presents, and one of them is in the very matter of trial by jury.* (*Balzac* 1922, 309—emphasis added)

Taft asserts here that geographical location (although Puerto Rico is closer to the continental US than Alaska is) and the possibility that "American citizens" (i.e., whites) could settle in the Alaskan territory was the main difference between Alaska and Puerto Rico and the reason why the latter was not incorporated.[5]

In addition, Taft presented trial by jury as one of the problems for the incorporation of Filipinos and Puerto Ricans. Taft cited *Dorr* to indicate what those difficulties were. The cited text sustains that trial by jury is not a fundamental right that "goes wherever the jurisdiction of the United States extends" and that if Congress, in making laws for the colonial territories, "was obliged" to extend those rights there by legislation, "it would follow that, *no matter the needs or capacities of the people*, trial by jury...must be forthwith established, although the result may be to *work injustice and provoke disturbance rather than to aid the orderly administration of justice.*" Here Taft cuts the following two sentences of the *Dorr* passage, and the cited text continues by stating that if the US conquers new territory with "an established system of jurisprudence, where jury trials are unknown, but a method of fair and orderly trial prevails under an acceptable and long-established code," it would be counterproductive if

> **the preference of the people must be disregarded, their established customs ignored and they themselves coerced to accept, in advance of incorporation into the United States, a system of trial unknown to them and unsuited to their needs. We do not think it was intended, in giving power to Congress to make regulations for the territories, to hamper its exercise with this condition. (*Balzac* 1922, 309–10—emphasis added)**

It is important for our discussion to cite the part of *Dorr*'s text quoted by Taft that was cut off, which reads as follows:

> **If the United States, impelled by its duty or advantage, shall *acquire territory peopled by savages, and of which it may dispose or not hold for ultimate admission to Statehood,* if this doctrine is sound, it must establish there the trial by jury. To state such a proposition demonstrates the impossibility of carrying it into practice. (*Dorr* 1904, 148—emphasis added)**

This passage presents the notion held by the majority of the Supreme Court in that period, that the US had to be careful with the admission of those territories inhabited by people deemed as "savages," as "alien" and inferior to the US. The theory of territorial incorporation presented by White in *Downes* was based precisely on this conception: under the status of non-incorporation, the United States could acquire and control foreign territory inhabited by said "alien" and "savage" populations without having to admit them to the American union (Meléndez 2013). By supporting the supremacy of White's incorporation theory in *Balzac*, Taft reiterated that conception about keeping these territories inhabited by inferior populations out of the nation, even though one of these—Puerto Rico—is now inhabited by citizens. Whatever the reason Taft cut these lines from *Dorr*'s quoted text, this nonetheless reflects the thinking of the Supreme Court justices of why trial by jury should not be extended to new colonial possessions.

Following the lines of thought presented in *Dorr*, Taft elaborated on the problems that the institution of the trial by jury faced in the overseas territories like Puerto Rico. The jury system required citizens trained to exercise the responsibilities of jurors, he said, something that predominated in common law countries were centuries of tradition "have prepared a conception of the impartial attitude jurors must assume." The trial by jury needed the conscious participation of people in the justice system, a practice that is "hard for people not brought up in fundamentally popular government." This system gives people security that as jurors "being part of the judicial system of the country can prevent its arbitrary use or abuse." And added:

> Congress has thought that a people like the *Filipinos or the Porto Ricans*, trained to a complete judicial system which knows no juries, *living in compact and ancient communities, with definitely formed customs and political conceptions*, should be permitted themselves to determine how far they wish *to adopt this institution of Anglo-Saxon origin*, and when. (*Balzac* 1922, 310—emphasis added)[6]

Taft then argued that the US had been liberal in granting Puerto Rico and the Philippines most of the Constitutional guarantees, but has been sedulous to avoid forcing a jury system on a Spanish and civil-law country until it desired it. We cannot find any intention to depart from this policy in making Porto Ricans American citizens, explained as this is by the desire to put them as individuals on an exact equality with citizens from the American homeland, to secure them more certain protection against the world, and to give them an opportunity, should they desire, to move into the United States proper and there without any naturalization enjoy all political and other rights. (*Balzac* 1922, 311)

For a second time Taft enumerates the reasons for granting US citizenship to Puerto Ricans. Although this time he claims that it was to put them on an "exact equality" with citizens in the "American homeland," he immediately maintains that to "enjoy all political and other rights" they should move to the "United States proper." Taft also asserts that Congress had no intention of extending institutions of an Anglo-Saxon character to peoples not prepared for them. But by his reasoning, if Puerto Ricans wanted to enjoy these institutions, and of having equality in citizenship, they could simply move to the "US proper." Which begs the question, if he was not opposed to Puerto Ricans having access to the rights of citizenship in the "US proper," why not allow them to enjoy these rights in their own homeland?

In addition, Taft's reasoning is based on the idea that in 1922, after more than 20 years of US rule and Americanization, Puerto Ricans were not ready for the jury system. Although he acknowledged that trial by jury was implemented in Puerto Rico in 1902 by local legislation in felony cases, in addition to being used in the federal district court, Taft concealed the fact that—according to US colonial and judicial functionaries in Puerto Rico—this procedure had been implemented with great success and that Puerto Ricans had supported jury trials since the beginning of US rule on the island, as will be discussed later in this article. Furthermore, and he should have known this, Taft failed to acknowledge that trial by jury was not included in the bill of rights in the Jones Act, formulated by Congress with limited input from Puerto Ricans, because US policymakers and colonial functionaries excluded it from this act so they could argue that Puerto Rico had not been incorporated by the grant of citizenship, precisely what Taft affirmed in *Balzac*.

Throughout the *Balzac* ruling, Taft sustained ideas presented in the early *Insular Cases* as if nothing had changed after 24 years of US rule in Puerto Rico. Furthermore, he used the issue of trial by jury in Puerto Rico to diminish Puerto Ricans and US citizenship in Puerto Rico in order to claim that the island had not been incorporated by the grant of citizenship. It is precisely after arguing on the incapacity of Puerto Ricans to use trial by jury that Taft enunciates his opposition to statehood based on the characteristics of the Puerto Rican population.

We need not dwell on another consideration which requires us not lightly to infer, from acts thus easily explained on other grounds, *an intention to incorporate in the Union these distant ocean communities of a different origin and language from those of our continental people. Incorporation has always been a step, and an important one, leading to statehood.* Without, in the slightest degree, intimating an opinion as to the wisdom of such a policy, for that is not our province, it is reasonable to assume that *when such a step is taken it will be begun and taken by Congress deliberately and with a clear declaration of purpose*, and not left a matter of mere inference or construction. (*Balzac* 1922, 311—emphasis added)

Thus, for Taft, although Puerto Ricans living in "distant ocean communities of a different origin and language" might be granted citizenship—albeit it one diminished by its "locality" in the unincorporated territory—they are not worthy enough to receive statehood and become part of the "US proper."

Taft also questioned another contention used by Balsac's counsel to sustain that Puerto Rico had been incorporated: the existence of a US District Court on the island. He argued that this was not a true US Article III court, that the "resemblance of its jurisdiction to that of true United States courts...does not change its character as a mere territorial court." To him, it did not matter that constitutional issues arise in this court, since the US Constitution was in force in Puerto Rico as it was in force wherever the sovereign power of the US was exerted. This had been emphasized by the Court on issues arising from the *Insular Cases*, particularly in *Downes* and *Dorr*. The constitution however contains grants of power and limitations which are not applicable everywhere, "and the real issue in the *Insular Cases* was not whether the Constitution extended to the Philippines or Porto Rico when we went there, but which of its provisions were applicable by way of limitation upon the exercise of executive and legislative power in dealing with the new conditions and requirements." Certain fundamental consti-tutional rights "had from the beginning full application in the Philippines and Porto Rico..." Taft asserted that he could not find any features in the Jones Act "from which we can infer the purpose of Congress to incorporate Porto Rico into the United States with the consequences which would fol-low" (*Balzac* 1922, 312–3). He concluded his ruling by briefly reviewing the Court's Tapia and Muratti *per curiam,* as discussed earlier, and later devoted one paragraph to sustain the libel charge against Balsac.

The ramifications of Taft's ruling in *Balzac* have been examined broadly by scholars. For Sparrow, *Balzac* "settled several questions about the appli-cation of the U.S. Constitution to the territories." Puerto Ricans were US cit-izens, "but they were not necessarily full members of the American political community" and only some constitutional protections applied to residents of unincorporated territories. The US government "could exercise sover-eignty more or less indefinitely over people and areas outside the boundar-ies of the states; the United States could possess a colonial empire." Sparrow also points out the inconsistencies in Taft's rationalization for not admitting Puerto Rico as a state. Puerto Ricans, he asserts, had been living in US ter-ritory for two decades before the grant of citizenship, and their "origin and language" were "arguably no more exceptional than those of New Mexico or Hawai'i" (2006, 204). For Sparrow, *Balzac* is an example of the ambigu-ity and duality in the *Insular Cases.* While White argued in *Rassmussen* that Alaska had been incorporated even though there was no expressed language from Congress of doing so, in *Balzac* Taft decreed on the need for such lan-guage with respect to the incorporation of Puerto Rico (Sparrow 2006, 208).

Torruella makes a similar argument regarding *Balzac*, pointing to the "glaring incongruencies and inconsistencies" in Taft's ruling. For example, he shows the similarities between the treaty used by the Court in *Rassmussen* to hold that Alaska was incorporated and the Jones Act's grant of citizenship to Puerto Ricans. Furthermore, Torruella argues that the use of factors such as "distance from the United States, ease of travel, and propensity to settle-ment" to determine "whether or nor incorporation had taken place" was "never considered by the Court in this respect" and "added new elements of vagueness to an already uncertain subject matter..." (1985, 98–9).

Rivera Ramos also contends that Taft was aware that his reasoning "was at odds" with the Court's decision in *Rassmussen*, when it accepted that Alaska had been incorporated by the clause of the annexation treaty that extended citizenship to its inhabitants. (2001, 96). He points out to the "circular reasoning" in Taft's argument in *Balzac* that it is "locality" and not the status of the people what determines the constitutional guarantees. Before *Balzac*, the status of the territory—i.e., incorporation—followed from the nature of rights extended; but after *Balzac*, the "determination of the status of the territory" was based on "the nature of the rights to be enjoyed by the inhabitants" (Rivera Ramos 2001, 98–9). Rivera Ramos also maintains that the *Balzac* ruling, like that of previous *Insular Cases* dealing with criminal justice in the territories, showed the "flexibility" that this jurisprudence offered to the US government in the administration of its colonial territories. The withholding of certain constitutional rights like trial by jury would assure "the governability of foreign peoples" under US jurisdiction and "not always acquiescent to its rule" (Rivera Ramos 2001, 139).

As he said, it is "locality" that is determinative of which rights are extended to these territories.

Soltero calls "ironic and hypocritical" the arguments used by Taft for not recognizing the constitutional right to a jury trial in Puerto Rico. He suggests that if efficiency in the administration of justice was a main worry for Taft, the same concerns could be applied to the 50 states regarding the creation of grand juries and the implementation of jury trials. Furthermore, he indicates that other territories inhabited by peoples of Spanish and French descent, like Florida, Louisiana, Texas, and California used civil code systems before becoming states. Soltero points out to the circular thinking that Taft presented in *Balzac* regarding the relationship between jury trials and self-government, since the Chief Justice argued "that jury duty requires participation in self-governance and since the territories are unfit for self-government, the jury system does not really fit either" (2006, 28). This is, of course, a form of blaming the victim since self-government—an aspiration of all major parties in Puerto Rico since the beginning of US rule—had been denied to Puerto Ricans by the US government.

In *Balzac*, Taft reiterated the Court's distinction between fundamental and non-fundamental or procedural rights and that the latter—like trial by jury—are not guaranteed in the unincorporated territories even though these are now inhabited by US citizens. As he said, it is "locality" that is determinative of which rights are extended to these territories. Alan Tauber finds this distinction between fundamental and non-fundamental rights "highly strained and arbitrary," particularly when considering that trial by jury was included among the ten amendments of the Constitution by the Founding Fathers. He argues that racism by the Court seems to be the only underlying reason to deny this right to the inhabitants of the unincorporated territories, particularly when they are citizens. For Tauber, "the Justices tried to cloak some of this racist language in the guise of pushing 'self-determination' for these areas." (2006, 167–8).

Robert A. Katz suggests something similar in this regard. He argues that the Court tried to square some dominant constitutional and political American principles with the events of 1898, albeit in a contradictory way. In the *Insular Cases* the Court declared that although it is true that the Constitution applied to the new territories, there were exclusions, and it did not do so completely. While some rights declared as fundamental were extended to these territories, others that were classified as non-fundamental—such as trial by jury—were not. But more contradictory yet was "the Court's attempt to recast its denial of constitutional rights to territorial inhabitants as consistent with democratic theory." To hide the anti-democratic character of colonial governance "the Court felt compelled to package unincorporated status as vehicle for limited, local self-determination." Such is the case with the argument that the inhabitants of the territories would not be willing to use Anglo-Saxon institutions such as trial by jury. Supposedly, excluding them from this procedure would not only facilitate colonial governance but also, as Taft argued in *Balzac*, would adjust these foreign institutions to local customs and traditions (Katz 1992, 796). The next section will discuss how historically inadequate and incorrect the application of this premise was to the experience in Puerto Rico.

Trial by jury in Puerto Rico before *Balzac*

In his extensive and deeply researched analysis of the trial by jury in the United States and its territories at the turn of the twentieth century, Andrew Kent argues that, although racism was also a causal factor, US policymakers and colonial functionaries like Taft and Root and many Supreme Court justices supported not extending jury trial to the territories because of their belief that even in the US the jury system was not working adequately and because they claimed that respect for local customs and traditions was the basis for good government in the new colonial territories. He closes his analysis precisely with a review of *Balzac* and cites Taft on how Puerto Ricans "should be permitted themselves to determine how far they wish to adopt this institution of Anglo-Saxon origin." Kent concludes as follows:

Taft was expressing, somewhat allusively, views that were second nature to him and other elite lawyers who came to the bar during the era of classical legal orthodoxy and became disenchanted with the jury. Law and legal institutions must "spring from the soil" and conform to people's habits and customs if they are to work well. Making the jury work well was actually quite difficult, even in the mainland United States, where it had existed for centuries. (Kent 2018, 451)

Despite his extensive analysis, Kent's argument is not adequate to understand the Puerto Rican experience with jury trials. It tends to support Taft's view that Puerto Ricans were not prepared to use trial by jury even after several decades of US rule on the island. Furthermore, Kent's assertion that Taft and other US policymakers, as well as Supreme Court justices, supported excluding the territories from trial by jury because they believed that Congress wanted to respect local customs in the new territories conquered in 1898 does not really fit with the historical experience of Puerto Rico.

    The 1900 Foraker Act imposed a colonial government structure like that of the US, with executive, legislative, and judicial branches. The judicial system was like that of the United States, with a Supreme Court and local district courts, in addition to a US federal district court. Trial by jury was used in the federal district court and was also in practice in certain felony cases in local courts. Trial by jury in Puerto Rican courts was allowed by the local legislature. Under the Foraker Act, the governor, the Cabinet members, and the Executive Council (which functioned as the upper house of the legislature), as well as the supreme court justices, were appointed by the US president. The House of Delegates was the only legislative chamber with elected members until 1917 (when the Jones Act created the Senate). The Executive Council—where cabinet members comprised the majority of its 11 members—had a veto over the lower house, as did the governor. This colonial system gave local political forces very limited autonomous power over the colonial state.

Similarly, the US imposed its "applicable" laws on the island, the US currency, and a centralized public education system created to promote the Americanization of the country. For many decades, English was an official language in Puerto Rico as well as the language of instruction in public schools. For the majority of US policymakers and colonial functionaries, the judicial and the public education systems were seen as means to advance the Americanization of the population and thus as instruments in maintaining the US colonial system in Puerto Rico. Throughout this process, the US government imposed its institutions and laws without having much regard for local customs and institutions. Why then the exclusion of trial by jury if other US institutions had been imposed on the island?

A more obvious reason, reflected in the positions presented by US colonial functionaries in the territories and in US Supreme Court decisions regarding trial by jury in the colonies, was the belief that these new colonial subjects were not prepared for institutions of an Anglo-Saxon character. Also, many feared that the colonial subjects could use these institutions to subvert the colonial order that the United States maintained in these territories. Furthermore, as shall be discussed later, by leaving the right of trial by jury out of the Jones Act, US policymakers and colonial functionaries were later able to claim that the Constitution had not been extended fully to Puerto Rico with the grant of citizenship and that the island had not been incorporated to the United States, a reasoning sustained by Taft in *Balzac*.

Several scholars have questioned Taft's arguments for rejecting the right to a trial by jury in Puerto Rico based, correctly, on the fact that jury trials had been in use on the island since the beginning of US rule (Soltero 2006, 28–9; Rivera Ramos 2001, 99–100; and Torruella 1985, 99–100). One argument proposed by Taft to deny this constitutional right to Puerto

Ricans, already presented in previous cases like *Dorr*, was that Congress was adapting its colonial system to the customs and traditions of the newly conquered populations. But Taft presented another argument, also laid out in *Dorr*, that the new colonial subjects, characterized by different customs, cultures and traditions, living before conquest under a different system of justice and jurisprudence, were not only not accustomed to jury trials but were not capable of using this institution or of employing it correctly. As cited in previous cases, US officials feared that the orderly system of justice in the new colonial territories might be subverted by these colonial subjects.

I would like to focus on the idea advanced by Taft in *Balzac* that Puerto Ricans were not prepared to use the trial by jury or that they would not utilize it wisely or abuse it to subvert the US justice system and colonial rule in Puerto Rico. These are notions central to his objective of denying Puerto Ricans the extension of the right to trial by jury of the federal constitution. To accomplish this, I will use the reports by US colonial functionaries in Puerto Rico, the ones in charge of implementing US laws and institutions there and more directly in contact with US government on the island. At the beginning of US rule, some colonial functionaries believed that the institution of trial by jury could not be properly implemented on the island due, among other things, to the unfitness of Puerto Ricans to serve as jurors or to understand the procedure well (Governor of Porto Rico 1903, 80–3). But as years passed by, many others viewed jury trial as a way to promote the Americanization of the island and, therefore, maintain the colonial regime. Throughout the first two decades of US rule in Puerto Rico, these US colonial functionaries concluded that not only did the jury system work well here, but also that the population was inclined to use the jury system and were able to exercise the function of jurors effectively.

In his annual report to the President in 1904, Governor William H. Hunt stated that the "jury system is still an experiment, not having given very satisfactory results." He based his statement on the difficulty of finding jurors for capital punishment cases because "so great a majority of people are opposed to capital punishment, or have conscientious scruples in regard to inflicting the death penalty for crime." Hunt mentioned the numerous bills submitted in the House of Delegates to abolish the death penalty on the island, only to be stopped by the presidentially appointed Executive

Council. Nevertheless, he acknowledged the "adaptability of the people generally to new conditions" regarding the changes implemented by the US on the island, including the judicial system, and added that he anticipated no difficulty for Puerto Ricans to fall "into the new order of things." He concluded that there is "no more practical method of Americanizing our new possessions than by the enactment and enforcement of American laws, and the introduction and practice of American jurisprudence" (Governor of Porto Rico 1904, 25–6). In that same report, the island's Attorney General, Willis Sweet, argued that although many people "believed trial by jury to be premature in this country...the practice had come to stay. Trial by jury is now as much a feature of the legal procedure in Porto Rico as any other phase of its judicial life." He added that "the successful operation of the jury system by the people of Porto Rico is but another illustration of the readiness with which they adjust themselves to the new laws and practices..." (Governor of Porto Rico 1904, 55–6).

In his 1911 report, Attorney General Foster V. Brown contended that "exact justice" can be found in the courts in Puerto Rico "as can be found in the courts of the most enlightened States of the American Union," and added: "Considering the fact that the right of trial by jury was first introduced into Porto Rico in 1902, and was not really put in force until several years afterwards, and that trial by jury was introduced among a people heretofore entirely unaccustomed to sitting on juries and weighing evidence (as the people of the United States and other English-speaking countries have been in the habit of doing for years and years), I think the result attained in jury trials in Porto Rico is a most remarkable showing." He claimed that, based on his "experience in Porto Rico," "juries are as much disposed to enforce the law in Porto Rico, and are just as likely to convict a defendant when he ought to be convicted as juries ordinarily are found to be in the States." Refusal to convict alleged criminals was one of the reasons used by critics of jury trials in the US like Root and Taft, as Kent argued in his previously cited analysis. Brown pointed out that in Puerto Rico there were 187 convictions and 93 acquittals out of 280 jury trials held that year, "showing 67 per cent of convictions and 33 percent of acquittals." He concluded that Puerto Ricans were willing to convict in major criminal cases as much as the jurors in New York and that "when you consider that the people of New

York City have been accustomed to jury trials since the settlement of that city, and that the people here have not been so accustomed, that trial by jury is an innovation in Porto Rico and a mere experiment so far, the showing is very decidedly favorable to Porto Rico." (Governor of Porto Rico 1911, 255).

The reports of colonial officials closer to the year 1922, when Taft issued his *Balzac* ruling, are even more forceful in refuting his allegations regarding the inability of Puerto Ricans to use the jury system effectively. One significant example is provided by the particular circumstances created in the aftermath of the *Tapia* and *Muratti* decisions in 1917, when both the federal district court on the island and the Puerto Rican Supreme Court declared that the grant of citizenship to Puerto Ricans in the Jones Act had incorporated Puerto Rico. This prompted the island's Attorney General to prepare for the eventual extension of the fifth and sixth amendments of the Bill of Rights to Puerto Rico. In his 1917 report to the Governor, Attorney General Howard L. Kern acknowledged that "by far the most important question" that his office had to deal with that year was "whether Porto Rico became an incorporated Territory of the United States by virtue of the new organic act. This question has arisen in many forms and in many cases" (Governor of Porto Rico 1917, 509).

In his 1918 report to the Governor, Kern indicated that the US Supreme Court ruling in the *Muratti* and *Tapia* cases was "by far the most important and interesting matter from a legal point of view..." He pointed out that "the department of justice went through an interesting period" between the Tapia and Muratti decisions in Puerto Rico and the per curiam ruling by the US Supreme Court reverting these two cases. Because of the two decisions by the courts in Puerto Rico, it was "required a grand jury in all cases of infamous offenses, [and] it was necessary to immediately take steps for the establishment of a grand jury pending the decision of the Supreme Court of the United States." Although he maintained "that the new organic act did not require a grand jury," faced with the probability that many of the accused might be released by a request of habeas corpus, and since the Legislature was not in session at the time, the Attorney General decided "to organize grand juries in every district on common law lines. This was done and more than a hundred indictments were returned by these grand juries before the decisions of the local courts were reversed" by the US Supreme Court (Governor of Porto Rico 1918, 565).

After Puerto Rico's Supreme Court decision in the *Muratti* case, Kern sent a letter on July 20, 1917, to the "District Fiscals" (District Attorneys) with the instructions on how to proceed to create grand juries. He stated that "it seems advisable in order to avoid an entire interruption in the enforcement of the penal laws of Porto Rico in cases of capital and other infamous offenses to request the district courts having jurisdiction for the trial of such offenses to provide for the inauguration of a grand jury." He added, if the decision by Puerto Rico's Supreme Court stood and the "the fifth amendment to the Constitution of the United States is applicable to Porto Rico...the courts with jurisdiction to try cases of capital or other infamous offenses have jurisdiction to summon a grand jury, which is an indispensable requisite to the trial of such cases" (Governor of Porto Rico 1918, 615).

That same day, Kern advised the district court judges on the instructions given to the district attorneys (cited above) to create grand juries and told them that this matter "is within the inherent power of the court if it is true that Porto Rico is incorporated Territory of the United States. I believe it is preferable to have this matter done by each court in its discretion without any rule of court to that effect..." (Governor of Porto Rico 1918, 617). Kern acknowledged that the measures he implemented after the decisions by the two courts in Puerto Rico were without legal precedent on the island,

but it enabled the department of justice to carry on with scarcely any interruption the administration of the criminal laws during the period of doubt as to the probability on an entire reorganization of our judicial system. *The experience gained during this period shows that a grand jury may be successfully employed in Porto Rico...* (Governor of Porto Rico 1918, 566—emphasis added)

In his 1920 report to the Governor, Puerto Rico's Attorney General reported that the institution of the grand jury was established in Puerto Rico by the Legislature on June 18, 1919. From then on, all felonies were to be prosecuted by indictment of the grand jury. As to the capacity of Puerto Ricans to fulfil these tasks, he concluded: "The citizens called upon to discharge the delicate tasks of grand jurors have shown a quick adaptability to an institution unprecedented in Porto Rico, and have discharged their duties with honest, firm, and dispassionate judgement" (Governor of Porto Rico 1920, 468).

Incorporation and Citizenship

The *Balzac* ruling allowed Taft to use the matter of trial by jury to reiterate that the incorporation doctrine was the dominant view in the management of the US overseas territories and to argue why the grant of citizenship to Puerto Ricans had not incorporated Puerto Rico. Taft used *Balzac* to sustain that the incorporation of an unincorporated territory required an express declaration by Congress, that it could not be left to mere inference as had been the norm before 1898. In this ruling Taft was explicit in stating that the reasons why Puerto Rico was not incorporated was due to the racial and cultural characteristics of Puerto Ricans.

In this ruling, Taft also institutionalized their views on the nature of citizenship in Puerto Rico and the reasons why it was granted to Puerto Ricans.

But Taft also used *Balzac* to institutionalize views that US policymakers and colonial functionaries had put forward for decades: that granting citizenship would not incorporate Puerto Rico or imply a promise of statehood for Puerto Ricans. In this ruling, Taft also institutionalized their views on the nature of citizenship in Puerto Rico and the reasons why it was granted to Puerto Ricans. For Taft, US citizenship was granted to Puerto Ricans to satisfy their "yearning" for such status, and it only implied their allegiance to their sovereign and the protection they would receive from the metropolitan state. It was a view of citizenship where the rights of citizens were limited by the "locality" where they lived, that is, on the unincorporated territory, and one that entailed no "new additional rights" except the right to move to the "US proper" and once there seek equal rights in citizenship.

Since the United States took over the island in 1898 the issue regarding the incorporation of Puerto Rico became central to the debate on whether to grant citizenship to Puerto Ricans. The initial bill submitted in 1900 by Senator Foraker to create a civilian government in Puerto Rico included the grant of US citizenship to Puerto Ricans. There was strong opposition to this clause in the Senate, particularly by those who argued that it could imply the "incorporation" of Puerto Rico into the nation. US policymakers and colonial functionaries, particularly officials of the Bureau of Insular Affairs (BIA), argued that the traditional relationship between the grant of citizenship to the inhabitants of acquired territory and territorial incorporation had been decoupled by the decisions of the Supreme Court in the *Insular Cases*. These officials also contended that inclusion of a bill of rights in the Jones Act implied that the Bill of Rights had not been extended to Puerto Rico and, therefore, that the island had not been incorporated to the United States. But the fact that the Jones Act did not include explicit language indicating that Puerto Rico had not been incorporated by the grant of citizenship to Puerto Ricans allowed the Puerto Rican Supreme Court and the US district court on the island to affirm that Puerto Rico had been incorporated by the Jones Act based on past precedent. The *Balzac* ruling allowed Taft not only to rule that granting citizenship to the peoples in the unincorporated territories did not imply the incorporation of that territory, and the reasons why, but also to present a view of the citizenship given to Puerto Ricans as a formal status and one that was limited by the status of the territory where they lived. These views were similar to those that for decades had been advanced by US officials in charge of colonial affairs in Washington and Puerto Rico.

Existing scholarship of *Balzac* has not so far fully discussed how Taft's ruling in this case inserted itself into the then ongoing debate on US citizenship for Puerto Ricans by US policymakers and colonial functionaries. The following sections seek to provide some insights into this topic.

The Debate on Citizenship, Incorporation, and Statehood

The issue of citizenship was central to the debates regarding the status of the inhabitants of the new American possessions after the war of 1898. Under the Treaty of Paris, the *peninsulares* (born in Spain) were able to retain their Spanish citizenship and even naturalize as American citizens if they remained in Puerto Rico. Puerto Ricans and Filipinos lost their Spanish citizenship but were not granted US citizenship. This was the first US annexation treaty where the peoples of the annexed territory were not given US citizenship. Furthermore, under the Treaty of Paris Congress retained the power to determine the political and civil status of the inhabitants of the conquered territory.

The 1900 Foraker Act created a civilian government of a colonial nature for Puerto Rico. The initial bill included a clause granting US citizenship to Puerto Ricans. What was the reason for such an action and what was the character of that citizenship? According to Senator Foraker, after a careful examination of this issue the committee concluded:

that the inhabitants of that island must be either citizens or subjects or aliens. We did not want to treat our own as aliens, and we do not propose to have any subjects. Therefore, we adopted the term "citizens." In adopting the term "citizens" we did not understand, however, that we were giving to those people any rights that the American people do not want them to have. "Citizens" is a word that indicates, according to Story's work on the Constitution of the United States, allegiance on the one hand and protection on the other. (as quoted in Cabranes 1978, 428)

This notion of citizenship as a formal status to simply characterize Puerto Ricans as US subjects, that it did not grant them "any rights that the American people do not want them to have" and that it only implied allegiance by the colonial subjects and protection by the metropolitan state, was a conception that would be reproduced constantly by US officials throughout the first two decades of US rule in Puerto Rico. This was the conception that, for example, Frederick Coudert also advanced in the Supreme Court in *Downes* and in *Gonzales v. Williams* (1904), where he argued in favor of citizenship for Puerto Ricans (Meléndez 2013). It was the same view that Taft presented in *Balzac*.

The Foraker Act made Puerto Ricans "citizens of Porto Rico." Why was Foraker's initial bill rejected if, after all, the proposed citizenship status was to be devoid of any political rights and would not imply, as he later admitted, that Congress would not have "plenary powers" over the territory? According to Foraker, his initial proposal was abandoned to avoid any misapprehension "that we were incorporating [Puerto Rico] into the Union...thus putting it in a state of pupilage for statehood" (as quoted in Cabranes 1978, 433).

The debate on citizenship and incorporation was renewed when both the governor of Puerto Rico in his 1905 annual report and President Theodore Roosevelt—after his visit to the island in 1906—proposed granting citizenship to Puerto Ricans. In response to the president's proposal and to the House and Senate bills being discussed in Congress for such purpose, the *New York Tribune* declared that there should be "strong objection" if this grant was to be regarded as a "step preliminary to statehood." The newspaper thought that was not the case and that the president would present an "uncompromising resistance to any proposal for the incorporation of any of our outlying and detached possessions into this continental union of states." If Puerto Ricans were to become citizens, "it should be with no impossible aspirations for statehood ..." (Citizenship for Porto Ricans 1906, 6).

The *Chicago Daily Tribune* reported that there was strong opposition in Congress regarding the House and Senate bills granting citizenship to Puerto Ricans. An important reason for this opposition was based on race, since some argued that as much "as 90 percent of the entire population, are of mixed Spanish and negro blood. They are a tropical race..." One member of Congress commented that "the traditions" of US citizenship "involves first a territorial form of government and then statehood. It all looks toward statehood, which is and should be the aim of every piece of territory owned by the general government." He argued that opposition to statehood in Arizona and New Mexico was based on the large Spanish population and that this "objection to citizenship and ultimate statehood" should be raised to a "far greater degree in the case of Porto Rico." Puerto Ricans were characterized as having a "subtropical temperament" and largely illiterate in English. It would take generations to convert Puerto Ricans into US citizens and wipe out their Spanish language, methods, and traditions.

The time must be far distant when statehood can be even considered for a population so alien as that of Porto Rico...We must not confer citizenship from sentimentality, but it must be given only as a preparation for an ultimate union of some character with the United States. (No Citizenship for Porto Ricans 1906, quotes from 1 and 3)

The debate in Congress regarding the grant of citizenship to Puerto Ricans resumed in 1910, when bills for this purpose were introduced in the House and the Senate, supported by the Taft administration. Similar bills were submitted in the following years. It was made quite clear in these bills that the proposal to grant citizenship to Puerto Ricans did not carry a promise of statehood for Puerto Rico. For example, the February 1913 report by the Senate Committee on Pacific Islands and Porto Rico on a bill proposing citizenship for Puerto Ricans had to respond to opponents of the bill by emphatically stating that such a grant would "not in any way involve the right of suffrage [in the US] nor implicate directly or indirectly the question of statehood. Citizenship will give them certain personal legal rights and privileges both in their relations to the local government and in their status abroad," it will "increase their self-respect...and develop a larger capacity for self-government." Citizenship would also "promote contentment and satisfaction among the people with their allegiance to the United States, but does not involve the right to participate in the [US] government nor affect in any particular the question of statehood..." (Senate Committee on Pacific Islands and Porto Rico 1913, 1–2)

The idea that citizenship for Puerto Ricans did not entail the incorporation of Puerto Rico was advanced most strongly by officials of the Bureau of Insular Affairs (BIA), an agency attached to the Department of War. The BIA functioned for all purposes as the American Colonial Office, in charge of the administrative affairs of the territories in Washington, of collecting all the necessary information about them for public policy matters and worked as a liaison between the federal bureaucracy in Washington and the colonial functionaries in the territories. Puerto Rico came under the jurisdiction of the BIA in 1910, and since then the agency promoted granting citizenship to Puerto Ricans; together with members of Congress, the bureau wrote and lobbied for the approval of congressional bills for this purpose. As indicated in a BIA report years later, all the bills submitted to Congress since 1910 to reform the government of Puerto Rico and grant citizenship to Puerto Ricans were prepared by the BIA in conjunction with those members of Congress concerned with colonial affairs.[7]

One of the best summaries of this effort was presented by BIA director Frank McIntyre in his 1916 Report to the Secretary of War. The BIA chief acknowledged that ever since Puerto Rico was placed under the jurisdiction of the BIA, "there has been an effort, consistently backed by the presidents and by the department to obtain for Porto Rico a new organic act which would have made the Porto Ricans citizens of the United States and would give to them a practically autonomous government." In a similar fashion to many other US functionaries, he argued that the Foraker Act created an "anomalous" status for Puerto Ricans and fomented among them a "feeling of irritation." Like Foraker before him, McIntyre argued that since "the Supreme Court in the Insular Cases having made clear the status of Porto Rico and by inference what might be done without making such territory of the United States an incorporated Territory," it made possible the grant of citizenship to Puerto Ricans, a proposal made by all island governors and presidents since 1905. The fact that they have not been given citizenship "has become increasingly a humiliation to some Puerto Ricans and a basis for the agitation on the part of others." McIntyre argued that, since 1910, the BIA was guided by the following principles in trying to replace the Foraker Act with a new organic act by Congress: (1) that Puerto Ricans should be made US citizens "to make clear that Porto Rico is to remain permanently connected to the United States"; (2) that Puerto Rico would continue with its current fiscal system whereby it retained it own internal revenue and customs receipts; (3) "*It should be clear that Porto Rico was not made by the act an incorporated Territory of the United States, and therefore it should be made plain that the Constitution and general statutory laws of the United States were not extended to Porto Rico and that there was no direct or implied promise of statehood*"; (4) that Puerto Rico would obtain an autonomous form of government consistent with "fair efficiency" and the "extension of powers without radical change in the form of government"; and (5) that the new form of government "was to be a development from the experience of Porto Rico, and no sacrifice of efficiency was to be made to adapt its form to our theories." It concluded by saying that, since 1910, bills "varying in form, but designed, in general, to accomplish the foregoing results" had been considered at each session of Congress (Bureau of Insular Affairs 1916, 17–8—emphasis added).

The architects of these bills, including the Jones Act, had argued that there was no intention of incorporating Puerto Rico.

The idea that the Jones Act was not intended to incorporate Puerto Rico and that this was the clear objective of those who drafted this act in Congress and the executive was not self-evident, as the *Tapia* and *Muratti* court rulings indicate.[8] In reaction to these events, the BIA prepared a memorandum trying to clarify the intention of Congress and the Executive in conferring citizenship to Puerto Ricans, specifically stating that it did not incorporate Puerto Rico to the US. The memo stated that the 1917 Jones Act "was the final form of a bill which had been constantly before one or both houses of Congress since 1910." That year, President Taft had supported a bill submitted by Secretary of War Dickinson conferring citizenship to Puerto Ricans; the bill, conceived by the BIA, was submitted in the House by Congressman Olmsted. In his report to the House, after reviewing "the decisions of the Supreme Court bearing on the civil status" of Puerto Rico, Olmsted "made it clear that it was not the intent of the Committee in report-ing the bill to extend the Constitution to Porto Rico for all purposes or in all parts." The memo quoted Olmsted saying that the bill supported recom-mendations by Presidents Roosevelt and Taft, and that it did not "provide for statehood. It does not promise statehood. It does not incorporate Porto Rico into the United States" (Bureau of Insular Affairs 1917, quotes from 1, 3). The architects of these bills, including the Jones Act, had argued that there was no intention of incorporating Puerto Rico. But as discussed ear-lier, this was not explicitly stated in the Jones Act. Where in the Jones Act was Congress's intention not to incorporate Puerto Rico made clear? The memo argues that the 1910 bill included a section extending a "bill of rights" for Puerto Rico similar to the one included in the 1917 Jones Act and that in both versions "the Constitution of the United States was not followed. The bill was prepared in such a way as to make it clear that those preparing it did not intend that the Constitution of the United States should in all of its parts apply." It later added that the supporters of the 1910 bills in Congress "had no intention of changing the status of Porto Rico from that which had been defined by the Supreme Court as its then existing status. The bill was thereafter introduced at each session of Congress." The memo stated that all the reports from Congress and the Secretary of War on the Puerto Rican bills from 1910 to 1916 show "the continuity of the thought...that Porto Rico was not to be incorporated as a territory into the United States." The report concluded that the "intent of Congress" that Puerto Rico "should not be incorporated into the United States" by the Jones Act of March 2, 1917, "is evidenced by the contents of the act. It is also evidenced by the continuity of the several steps taken in Congress which led up to the passage of this act." (Bureau of Insular Affairs 1917, quotes from 4, 5, and 6)

The arguments presented by the BIA to establish that Puerto Rico had not been incorporated by the grant of citizenship in the Jones Act are the same that Taft made in *Balzac*. Taft used the inclusion of a "bill of rights" in the Jones Act to claim that this provision made clear that the Bill of Rights had not been extended to Puerto Rico with this act, a clear indication that the island had not been incorporated by this action of Congress. This is the same reasoning he advanced to rule that trial by jury had not been extended to Puerto Rico by Congress. Taft used his ruling in *Balzac* to reaffirm and institutionalize what members of Congress and the Executive had been arguing since 1910 regarding the grant of citizenship to Puerto Ricans, a notion that was not self-evident to many in Puerto Rico and the US: that citizenship in the unincorporated territories did not imply territorial incorporation.

Citizenship for Puerto Ricans as a Formal Status

Taft also used his ruling in *Balzac* to affirm and institutionalize in a Supreme Court decision some of the main notions that American officials had advanced since the beginning of the century to justify the grant of American citizenship to Puerto Ricans. None of these ideas implied extending them equality in citizenship, something that Taft made very clear in his *Balzac* ruling. He argued that granting citizenship to Puerto Ricans sought to correct their "anomalous status" within the American polity after coming under its jurisdiction and losing their Spanish citizenship. This idea was alluded to repeatedly during the debates regarding citizenship to Puerto Ricans from 1905 to the Jones Act. It was advanced by Governor Beekman Winthrop's in his 1905 annual report, the first time that citizenship for Puerto Ricans was proposed by a US official since Foraker's initial bill in 1900. He argued that citizenship had become a "most important question" for Puerto Ricans, and that the failure to make them citizens, particularly after they "enthusiastically welcomed American sovereignty," had left them in an "undefined status and without the benefits and distinction" of US citizenship. This situation "has had a very unfortunate effect upon these people. This uncertainty of their status has created very naturally a spirit of discontent and unrest which must be checked for the good of the American administration and of the island in general." Making them citizens would "improve the feeling of loyalty" and "would instill in them a healthy feeling of patriotism..." (Governor of Porto Rico 1905, 42)

The need to right this "anomalous" condition was made more strongly in a 1906 report by the Senate Committee on Pacific Islands and Porto Rico chaired by Senator Foraker. The objective of this bill was to amend precisely the Foraker Act that made Puerto Ricans "citizens of Porto Rico." This status had left them "in a worse condition" than Spaniards who had retained their allegiance to Spain and could be naturalized as US citizens while Puerto Ricans could not. "This is an anomalous situation. He owes us allegiance and we owe him protection and yet he is not entitled to the rights that belong to a citizen, nor can he become entitled, by naturalization, to those rights," a situation which has caused "much dissatisfaction" among Puerto Ricans. This "singular situation" has created two classes of citizens in Puerto Rico: US citizens and citizens of Porto Rico. The Foraker Act was adopted "before we legislated for the Philippines" and Congress was "anxious not to establish any precedent" that might have been applicable to that territory. The report added that the Supreme Court "had not then defined the relations of Porto Rico or any of our insular possessions to this country." Although Puerto Ricans owe allegiance to the US and the US owes them protection, they are not "even in a strictly international sense" US citizens. Unlike Spaniards in Puerto Rico who retained their citizenship, Puerto Ricans could not naturalize because they could not renounce their allegiance to a foreign power to become US citizens. They could not naturalize even if they lived in the US, and if visiting other countries they could not carry a US passport "or of having any definite status of citizenship that is known to or recognized by other countries." But apprehensions regarding the Philippines were now gone, "and there is no longer any such reason for further delay on that account. They have been patient and faithful in their loyalty to our Government, and thus they have show themselves worthy of the recognition proposed" (Senate Committee on Pacific Islands and Porto Rico 1906, quotes from 3 and 6).[9]

The notion that turning Puerto Ricans into US citizens would resolve their "anomalous status" was constantly emphasized during discussions on this issue in Congress. The report to the Olmsted bill in 1910 stated that its purpose was to clarify and finally settle the citizenship status of Puerto Ricans. Congressman William Jones maintained in his Minority Report to the Olmsted Act that the "civil and political status of the Porto Rican people is altogether anomalous" and that it should be "definitely settled by Congress" (House Committee on Insular Affairs 1910a, 2–3; 1910b, 2). This view was also sustained in Senator Miles Poindexter's report to his 1913 citizenship bill and by Governor Yager in a February 1914 letter to Secretary of War Lindley Garrison; it was also expressed by Samuel Gompers in 1912 during Senate hearings on this topic (Senate Committee on Pacific Islands and Porto Rico 1913, 2; Yager 1914; Gompers 1912, 12).

In addition to correcting their "anomalous status," US officials repeatedly claimed that citizenship was a way of showing Puerto Ricans gratitude and rewarding them for their loyalty, patriotism, and support for the US. This view is clearly evident in President Roosevelt's message to Congress in support of making Puerto Ricans US citizens after they visited the island in 1906.

I cannot see how any harm can possibly result from it, and its seems a matter of right and justice to the people of Porto Rico. They are loyal and are glad to be under our flag, they are making rapid progress along the path of orderly liberty. Surely we should show our appreciation of them, our pride in what they have done, and our pleasure in extending recognition for what has thus been done by granting them full American citizenship. (Roosevelt 1906, 4)

This notion that citizenship for Puerto Ricans was a means of rewarding their loyalty to the US was repeatedly expressed by American policymakers and colonial functionaries, like Governor Beekman Winthrop in 1905, Senator Foraker in his 1906 bill, Governor Regis Post in 1907, and Secretary of War Henry Stimson in 1912 (Governor of Porto Rico 1905, 42; Senate Committee on Pacific Islands and Porto Rico 1906, 3; Governor of Porto Rico 1907, 40; Stimson as quoted in House Committee on Insular Affairs 1912, 2–3).

Another justification voiced during this period was that making Puerto Ricans citizens was a "matter of justice" and of "doing right" for loyal subjects, a view expressed by President Roosevelt, Senator Foraker, Governnor Post, Secretary of War Stimson in 1912, and Governor Yager in 1915 (Roosevelt 1906, 4; Stimson 1912; Yager 1915). Granting citizenship to Puerto Ricans was also seen as a means of eliminating a source of unrest and discontent among these people, which would allow for a stable administration of the island by the United States. Such a notion was proclaimed at different times by Governors Winthrop and Colton, Senators Foraker and Poindexter, BIA's McIntyre, and Secretary of War Garrison (Colton 1912; McIntyre 1913; Yager 1915).

In *Balzac*, Taft alluded to another notion that he and other American officials had previously expressed: that citizenship was granted to satisfy a Puerto Rican "yearning" for such status. Taft and others saw citizenship as a "sentimental" aspiration for Puerto Ricans, not as a serious demand for citizenship rights. He voiced this idea as early as 1907 when he visited the island as vice president. According to *The New York Times* headline, Taft characterized the Puerto Ricans' demand for US citizenship as a "sentimental" thing. To him, the previous visits to Puerto Rico by President Roosevelt, Secretary of War Root and House Speaker Cannon indicated that "the people of the United States have a deep affection for the people of Porto Rico and feel more kindly toward them, and have a greater interest in them, than in the people of Cuba or the Philippines." The United States has given Puerto Rico "the markets and the prosperity she enjoys to-day [sic]. She has given every Porto Rican the same liberty enjoyed by the People of the United States." In response to the question why Puerto Ricans have not been granted citizenship, he replied: "I ask what is it that a Porto Rican does not enjoy that an American enjoys? You have every guarantee and security which a citizen of the United States has under the Constitution. You have the writ of habeas corpus and *the trial by jury*, and when you are in a foreign country the same flag protects you that protects a citizen of the United States." He concluded by saying that when President Roosevelt supported citizenship for Puerto Ricans, "he urges it on the ground of *gratifying the sentiment of the people of this island*. But when you come to examine the facts of what you ask, the question is whether it is not nominal rather than substantial." (Porto Rico Demand Sentimental—Taft 1907, 6—emphasis added).

Taft reiterated these views in a letter to PS leader Iglesias in 1912, where he stated that since the connection between Puerto Rico and the United

States was "regarded as permanent...both as a matter of sentiment and practical justice the Porto Ricans should be made citizens." The best interests of both the US and Puerto Rico will be best served "by affording [Puerto Ricans] the largest opportunity for the development of local traditions and habits, which are very different from our own." Taft commented that Puerto Ricans should aspire to and the US should grant "the fullest possible measure of local and fiscal self-government," which should be "the most fitting political aspirations of the island, as well as a recognition of the public opinion of the United States, that in the minds of neither people is the grant of citizenship associated with any thought of statehood" (In Senate Committee on Pacific Islands and Porto Rico 1912, 25–6).

The idea that granting citizenship to Puerto Ricans was a means of gratifying their sentimental aspirations was reiterated by Secretary of War Stimson while testifying before Congress in 1910. He stated that "the demand for American citizenship on the part of Porto Ricans is genuine and well-nigh universal." To continue denying them this ambition "will gravely wound the sensibilities of this loyal people. It is a practical as well as a sentimental matter. A Porto Rican traveling abroad is literally a man without a country." He added that their request was "just" and was "amply earned by sustained loyalty" (as quoted in House Committee on Insular Affairs 1912, 2). Stimson expressed similar views again during Senate hearings in 1912. He contended that since the beginning of US rule Puerto Ricans have "looked forward to their connection with us as permanent," but the fact that they have not been granted citizenship represented "the one badge of inferiority which one nation could put upon another." He characterized Puerto Ricans as "thoroughly Latin Americans. They have all the sensitiveness and all the spirit of that people." Regarding citizenship, Stimson added that "sentimentally it is of vital importance in removing what has become a rather deep-seated source of irritation." Asked about any practical benefits Puerto Ricans would get from citizenship, he replied: "There will be some practical benefit, but it is mainly sentimental" (Senate Committee on Pacific Islands and Porto Rico 1912, quotes from 4 and 6).

The idea that colonial subjects such as the Puerto Ricans and Filipinos were sentimental peoples was consistent with the notion presented since 1898 that justified American colonialism as a way to "civilize" these savage and alien populations, with infantile tendencies and primal instincts.

This notion that citizenship would mostly satisfy a sentimental emotion of Puerto Ricans was clearly a way of diminishing their capacity as people and vindication of their demands, as well as justifying the denial of citizenship rights to them. The idea that colonial subjects such as the Puerto Ricans and Filipinos were sentimental peoples was consistent with the notion presented since 1898 that justified American colonialism as a way to "civilize" these savage and alien populations, with infantile tendencies and primal instincts. It is an idea consistent with that put forward by Taft and most US officials that these populations were not suitable for higher institutions of Anglo-Saxon origin such as trial by jury. It is also consistent with the idea that these inferior and "alien" peoples do not deserve to be admitted to the Union as a state.

In his *Balzac* ruling, Taft upheld that the granting of citizenship to Puerto Ricans gave them "no additional rights" except the right to move to the "US proper" and once there seek equal rights. The idea that citizenship would not grant Puerto Ricans additional rights was not new. It was presented earlier when Foraker pointed out in 1900 that citizenship would not grant Puerto Ricans "any rights that the American people do not want them to have." It was advanced by US officials multiple times later. For example, Governor George R. Colton stated in his 1912 annual report that citizenship "is a concession that, while entailing no new obligation or responsibility upon the people of the United States, would be of inestimable value" to Puerto Ricans (Governor of Porto Rico 1912, 22). But Taft did add something new to this notion by stating that citizenship gave Puerto Ricans the right to freely enter the United States. He acknowledges the right of Puerto Ricans to migrate to the United States while recognizing citizenship as the only guarantee to ensure that right. Puerto Ricans and Filipinos could enter the United States freely after the Court's decision of *Gonzales v. Williams* in 1904. In *Balzac*, Taft pointed out that Filipinos—who remained as US nationals after the Jones Act for the Philippine Islands in 1917—would have to go through the naturalization process in order to become citizens. As non-citizens, migration from the Philippines to the United States was greatly limited by Congress and hundreds of thousands of Filipinos were repatriated in response to a racist and nativist anti-Filipino movement during the 1930s. For all practical purposes, citizenship became a requisite to move freely from the American colonial periphery to the "US proper."

Final Comments

What can we say about *Balzac* on the 100th anniversary of Taft's famous ruling? In many respects, the ideas issued in this ruling continue to affect the lives of Puerto Ricans. Puerto Rico remains an unincorporated territory under the plenary powers of Congress, an authority that has been repeatedly recognized by the Supreme Court to this day. Puerto Rico today is governed by a fiscal supervision board appointed by Congress under the use of its plenary powers over the territories; its legality was upheld by the Supreme Court. Congress continues to discriminate against its US citizens in Puerto Rico in the distribution of federal funds and programs with the consent of the Supreme Court, although in recent years this discriminatory policy has been questioned in the courts (without success so far) and even by sectors of the US Democratic Party. And even though most of the constitutional rights have been extended to Puerto Rico by the courts or Congress, its inhabitants continue to have limitations in their citizenship rights, such as not being able to vote for the president and not having any real representation in Congress.

Taft was emphatic in reiterating the position of US policymakers and colonial functionaries that the grant of citizenship by the Jones Act was not to be seen as a promise of statehood for Puerto Rico. However, despite this declaration, the statehood movement in Puerto Rico—with its ups and downs—has been an important political force on the island ever since. Furthermore, citizenship became the central axis of the Puerto Rican annexationist discourse. In the 1940s, statehood ideologues argued that citizenship was the "gateway to statehood," that its granting to Puerto Ricans precisely established a congressional commitment to future statehood. Since the 1970s, annexationist leaders have proclaimed that statehood is the only way to achieve equality in citizenship and to end American colonialism in Puerto Rico. In 1968, the pro-statehood New Progressive Party became a governing party and has since been dedicated to promoting statehood on the island and in the United States (Meléndez 1988). In the last decades, several bills have been introduced in Congress to incorporate Puerto Rico, without any success. Although support for statehood has shown some progress in the metropolis, the American social and political elite is very divided over Puerto Rico's statehood. Meanwhile, Puerto Rico's colonial status remains unresolved.

In *Balzac*, Taft stated twice that citizenship granted Puerto Ricans "no additional rights" except to be able to freely enter the "US proper," and that once established there they could seek "equality in citizenship" and enjoy US "civil and political" rights. It was precisely from the 1920s on, that migration from the island to the United States increased considerably. Puerto Ricans migrated not necessarily to seek greater civil and political rights as Taft claimed, but to look for jobs that did not exist on the island. Puerto Rican migration to the United States has undoubtedly been one of the great developments in Puerto Rican history in the last hundred years. This migration has certainly been based on the citizen's right to move without restriction within the American territory. Between 1945 and 1960 more than half a million Puerto Ricans moved to the big cities and agricultural fields of the Northeast to supply cheap labor to the grow-ing manufacturing industries, services, and agriculture. Although citizens, they were viewed as foreigners from a distant colonial territory inhabited by people of a different race, language, and culture. They were subjected to discrimination in their jobs and education, in their neighborhoods, and in the acquisition of their civil and political rights. They acquired the latter after long struggles and protest movements. A new wave of migration has occurred over the past two decades, this time to Florida and other southern and southwestern states. It has been triggered by the severe economic crisis that has affected the island since the beginning of the 21st century, together with the grave fiscal crisis of the colonial government; migration has also increased after recent natural disasters. Since the beginning of this century, the majority of the people of Puerto Rican origin reside in the metropolitan territory, a pattern that continues to grow and has no signs of ending.

In Puerto Rico, Puerto Ricans continue to experience limitations in their citizenship rights due to the "locality" in which they live, as Taft affirmed in *Balzac*, that is, because they lived in a territory that remains unincorporated.

In the United States, although they are supposed to have access to all civil and political rights, the vast majority of Puerto Ricans have experienced elements of second-class citizenship like other ethnic and racial minorities. Whether in Puerto Rico or in the United States, most Puerto Ricans continue to face the dilemmas and contradictions of US citizenship.

NOTES

[1] For a general review of *Balzac* see: Rivera Ramos (2001, 94–100); Torruella (1985, 93–100); Sparrow (2006, 197–204); and Soltero (2006, chapter 2). For a general background on Jesús M. Balsac and his case, including in the US Supreme Court, see Ortiz Santini (2019). There is an almost general consensus that considers *Balzac* as the last of the *Insular Cases* or at least as the last of the important cases within this category. For a brief discussion of which Supreme Court cases should be included in the *Insular Cases*, see Duffy Burnett (2001, 389–90).

[2] The surname of Jesús M. Balsac was written with an "s." It was changed to Balzac during his trial in the Supreme Court of Puerto Rico and then in the US Supreme Court (Ortiz Santini 2019, 39).

[3] For a detailed historical background to Balsac's case, particularly the conflict between Yager and the PS, see Ortiz Santini (2019, particularly chapters 2–4).

[4] For the background on the process for Balsac's cases in Puerto Rico and the US Supreme Court see Ortiz Santini (2019, particularly chapters 4–5).

[5] It is striking the similarities between the language used by Taft in *Balzac* to characterize Puerto Ricans and the reasons why they should not be incorporated into the union with that which Justice Brown used in *Downes v. Bidwell* to deny citizenship to these "alien peoples." In *Downes*, Brown made a crucial distinction between the new overseas territories and its peoples and the contiguous territories of the United States: "It is obvious that in the *annexation of outlying and distant possessions* grave questions will arise from *differences of race, habits, laws, and customs of the people*, and from differences of soil, climate, and production, which may require action of the part of Congress that would be quite unnecessary in the *annexation of contiguous territory inhabited only by people of the same race*, or by scattered bodies of native Indians" (*Downes v. Bidwell* 1901, 282—emphasis added).

[6] Although Filipinos and Puerto Ricans had shared a similar position within the US colonial periphery as unincorporated territories and their inhabitants as US nation-

als since 1898, by the time Taft wrote his *Balzac* ruling the fate of both had been altered with the two Jones Acts for the Philippine Islands and Puerto Rico passed by Congress in 1917. While both territories remained unincorporated, Puerto Ricans became US citizens while Filipinos remained as US nationals destined for future independence. However, in *Balzac* Taft repeatedly included both territories and its people in discussions about rights, the Constitution, and their ability to govern themselves as if nothing had changed in their respective status. Taft reproduces here some arguments and perspectives presented in the early *Insular Cases*—in particular *Downes* and *Dorr*—that made references to Filipinos and Puerto Ricans in a negative and racist way and as sharing the same status within the US polity. But presumably Taft should have known that the status of both territories and their people within the American empire had changed in 1917. Taft, for example, mentions twice in *Balzac* how one of the benefits of citizenship for Puerto Ricans was that they could enter the "US proper" and once there seek the social and political rights of US citizens, contrary to the Filipinos who would have to naturalize to legally remain there. Perhaps Taft sought to use the deep racism and prejudice that existed in the United States towards Filipinos to diminish the status of Puerto Ricans, as well as the type of citizenship they would obtain, and thus support his argument against the incorporation of the territory and its eventual statehood.

[7] "All details connected to the organic acts for Porto Rico and the Philippine Island, including the preparation of them in their original format prior to their passage was largely the work of the Bureau. The Bureau represented the executive department of the government in the hearings pending the passage of these bills, and supplied the committees of the Senate and the House with the information desired on all points connected with them" (Bureau of Insular Affairs 1926, 5).

[8] After the Tapia and Muratti rulings in Puerto Rico affirmed that the island had been incorporated by the grant of citizenship in the Jones Act, BIA Chief McIntyre commented to governor Yager that: "This was quite contrary to the intent of those who framed the Porto Rican law and gives to the decision an added interest." Weeks later, Yager replied to McIntyre: "Of course, you and I know that Congress or at any rate the Committee that had in charge the shaping of the Jones Bill, had not intention of making Porto Rico a regular incorporated territory." The governor hoped that "the final decision of the Supreme Court of the United States on this matter will not be long delayed" (Yager 1917; McIntyre 1917).

[9] This notion that Puerto Ricans lived in an "anomalous" status was also reproduced

in the press after President Roosevelt proposed citizenship for Puerto Ricans during his visit to the island and later when he proposed citizenship in a message to Congress. See for example, Citizenship for Porto Ricans (1906, 6), and The President Tells of His Visit to Porto Rico (1906, 4).

REFERENCES

Balzac v. The People of Porto Rico. 1922. 258 U.S. 298.

Bureau of Insular Affairs. 1916. *Report of the Chief of the Bureau of Insular Affairs to the Secretary of War 1916*. Washington, D.C.: Government Printing Office, 1916; in National Archives and Records Administration (NARA), Record Group (RG) 350, Entry 5, General Records, Box 15, File 119.

_____. 1917. The Conferring of Citizenship on Porto Ricans as Affecting the Territorial Status of Porto Rico Under the Constitution, September 1; in NARA, RG 350, box 309, file 1444, doc. 25.

_____. 1926. Memorandum Regarding Organization and Functions of Bureau of Insular Affairs, October 25; in NARA, RG 350, Entry 5, General Records, Box 16, File 119.

Cabranes, José A. 1978. Citizenship and the American Empire: Notes on the Legislative History of the United States Citizenship of Puerto Ricans. *University of Pennsylvania Law Review* 127(2), 391–492.

Citizenship for Porto Ricans. 1906. *New York Tribune* 23 November.

Colton, George. 1912. Letter to Henry Stimson, December 26; in NARA, RG 350, Entry 5, General Records, Box 180G, File 1286.

Dorr v. United States. 1904. 195 U.S. 138.

Downes v. Bidwell. 1901. 182 U.S. 244.

Duffy Burnett, Christina 2001. A Note on the *Insular Cases*. In *Foreign in a Domestic Sense: Puerto Rico, American Expansion and the Constitution*, eds. Christina Duffy Burnett and Burke Marshall. 389–92. Durham, NC: Duke University Press.

Garrison, Lindley M. 1913. Letter to President Woodrow Wilson, October 6; in NARA, RG 350, Entry 5, General Records, Box 180G, File 1286.

Gompers, Samuel. 1912. In US Senate, Committee of Pacific Islands and Porto Rico, "Citizenship of Porto Ricans," Hearings on H.R. 20048, Sixty-second Congress, Second Session, May 7, 1912. Washington, DC: Government Printing Office.

Governor of Porto Rico. 1903. *Third Annual Report of the Governor of Porto Rico,*

1902-1903. Washington, DC: Government Printing Office.

_____. 1904. *Fourth Annual Report of the Governor of Porto Rico*. Washington, DC: Government Printing Office.

_____. 1905. *Fifth Annual Report, From July 1, 1904 to June 30, 1905*. Washington, DC: Government Printing Office.

_____. 1907. *Annual Report of the Governor of Porto Rico for the Fiscal year ending June 30, 1907*. Washington, DC: Government Printing Office.

_____. 1911. *Report of the Governor of Porto Rico to the Secretary of War 1911*. Washington, DC: Government Printing Office.

_____. 1912. *Report of the Governor of Porto Rico to the Secretary of War 1912*. Washington, DC: Government Printing Office.

_____. 1917. *Report of the Governor of Porto Rico to the Secretary of War 1917*. Washington, DC: Government Printing Office.

_____. 1918. *Report of the Governor of Porto Rico to the Secretary of War 1918*. Washington, DC: Government Printing Office.

_____. 1920. *Report of the Governor of Porto Rico to the Secretary of War 1920*. Washington, DC: Government Printing Office.

Hawaii v. Mankichi. 1903. 190 U.S. 197.

Katz, Robert A. 1992. The Jurisprudence of Legitimacy: Applying the Constitution to U.S. Territories. *University of Chicago Law Review* 59(2), 779–806.

Kent, Andrew. 2018. The Jury and Empire: The *Insular Cases* and the Anti-Jury Movement in the Gilded Age and Progressive Era. *Southern California Law Review* 91, 375–465.

McIntyre, Frank. 1913. Letter to Senator James P. Clarke, January 17; in NARA, RG 350, Entry 5, General Records, Box 180G, File 1286.

_____. 1917. Letter to Governor Arthur Yager, July 27; in NARA, RG 350, box 309, file 1444.

Meléndez, Edgardo. 1988. *Puerto Rico's Statehood Movement*. Westport, CT: Greenwood Press.

_____. 2013. Citizenship and the Alien Exclusion in the *Insular Cases*: Puerto Ricans in the Periphery of American Empire. *CENTRO: Journal of the Center for Puerto Rican Studies* 15(1), 106–45.

No Citizenship for Porto Ricans. 1906. *Chicago Daily Tribune* 21 December.

Ortiz Santini, Francisco. 2019. *Balsac vs el Pueblo de Puerto Rico: su historia; sus protagonistas*. np: Editorial My Book Creations.

Porto Rico v. Muratti. 1918. 245 U.S. 639.

Porto Rico v. Tapia. 1918. 245 U.S. 639.

Rivera Ramos, Efrén 2001. *The Legal Construction of Identity: The Judicial and
    Social Legacy of American Colonialism in Puerto Rico.* Washington, DC:
    American Psychological Association.

Roosevelt, Theodore. 1906. Message of the President of the United States Relative
    to his Recent Visit to the Island of Porto Rico, Transmitting the Report of
    the Governor of Porto Rico. 59th Congress, Senate, 2nd Session, December
    11. Washington, DC: Government Printing Office.

Torruella, Juan R. 1985. *The Supreme Court and Puerto Rico: The Doctrine of Separate
    and Unequal.* Rio Piedras: Editorial de la Universidad de Puerto Rico.

Soltero, Carlos R. 2006. *Latinos and American Law: Landmark Supreme Court
    Cases.* Austin: University of Texas Press.

Sparrow, Bartholomew H. 2006. *The Insular Cases and the Emergence of American
    Empire.* Kansas City: University Press of Kansas.

Stimson, Henry L. 1912. Letter to Senator Miles Poindexter, August 10; in NARA,
    RG 350, Entry 5, General Records, Box 180G, File 1286.

Tauber, Alan. 2006. "The Empire Forgotten: The Application of the Bill of Rights to
    U.S. Territories." *Case Western Reserve Law Review* 57(1), 147–78.

The President Tells of His Visit to Porto Rico. 1906. *The Sun* 12 December.

US Congress. House of Representatives. Committee on Insular Affairs. 1910a.
    Amending Act Relating to Revenues of Civil Government of Porto Rico.
    Report no. 750, submitted by Congressman Olmsted, 61st Congress, 2nd
    Session, March 15.

_____. 1910b. Civil Government for Porto Rico. Report no. 750-part 2, Views of
    the Minority, submitted by Congressman William Jones, April 1.

_____. 1912. Citizens of Porto Rico to be Citizens of the United States. Report No.
    341 submitted by Congressman William Jones, 62nd Congress, 2nd Session.
    February 20.

US Congress. Senate. Committee of Pacific Islands and Porto Rico. 1906.
    Inhabitants of Porto Rico to be Citizens of the United States. Report to
    accompany S. 2620, 59th Congress, 1st session. Report no. 2746, April 20.

_____. 1912. Citizenship of Porto Ricans. Hearings on H.R. 20048, Sixty-second
    Congress, Second Session, May 7. Washington, DC: Government Printing
    Office.

_____. 1913. Porto Rican Citizenship. Report no. 1300, 62nd Congress, 3rd Session, submitted by Senator Miles Poindexter, February 24, 1913.

Weiner, Mark S. 2001. Teutonic Constitutionalism: The Role of Ethno-Juridical Discourse in the Spanish American War. In *Foreign in a Domestic Sense: Puerto Rico, American Expansion and the Constitution*, eds. Christina Duffy Burnett and Burke Marshall. 48–81. Durham, NC: Duke University Press.

Yager, Arthur. 1914. Letter to Secretary of War Lindley M. Garrison, February 19; in NARA, RG 350, Entry 5, General Records, Box 180G, File 1286.

_____. 1915. Letter to President Woodrow to Wilson, November 2; in Woodrow Wilson Papers, Library of Congress, reel 269, series 4, Case File 400 QQ (1913-1916).

_____. 1917. Letter to Frank McIntyre, August 7, 1917, in NARA, RG 350, box 309, file 1444.

Balzac v. Porto Rico: Dead Letter after Ramos v. Louisiana?

JOEL A. COSME MORALES

ABSTRACT

Balzac v. Porto Rico meant a before and after in the doctrine of territorial incorporation created by the Supreme Court of the United States. Their racially prejudiced legal reasoning determined that the Sixth Amendment protection does not apply to unincorporated territories. The Supreme Court concludes, ignoring its own precedents, that an affirmative expression on the part of the U.S. Congress is necessary to incorporate the territories. This essay questions both conclusions using a historical analysis of the jurisprudential development of the right to trial by jury and of Puerto Rico's relations with the United States over time. In light of that evaluation, similar to the one used in *Ramos v. Louisiana*, which revoked a legal doctrine because of its racist origins, it is proposed that *Balzac* became a dead letter. [Keywords: Puerto Rico, territorial incorporation, Sixth Amendment, de facto territorial incorporation, Balzac v. Porto Rico, Ramos v. Louisiana]

Joel A. Cosme Morales (joelcosmemorales@gmail.com) is a graduate of the Pontifical Catholic University of Puerto Rico from where he obtained a degree in Political Science and Law with a minor in Public Administration and Labor Relations, and Pre-legal Studies, *summa cum laude*. In addition, he holds a Juris Doctor from the PUCPR School of Law, *summa cum laude*, where he served as Editor-in-Chief of Volume LX of the *Revista de Derecho Puertorriqueño*.

One hundred years have passed since the United States Supreme Court decision in *Balzac v. Porto Rico*. This precedent is so vital in the jurisprudence of the territories that it still resonates on a day-to-day basis. It is even mentioned in oral arguments that apparently have nothing to do with the territories. In the oral argument of *Ramos v. Louisiana* (2020), Justice Alito asked the petitioner's attorney the following:

Since you mentioned Balzac, can I ask you a question about that? So let's imagine this case is decided in your favor, and then a defendant who has been convicted by a non-unanimous verdict in Puerto Rico comes here and he says, look, I am a citizen of the United States, and the only reason why I was able to be convicted by a non-unanimous verdict is—*are these old Insular Cases that reflect attitudes of the day in the—in the end of the—after the—the aftermath of the Spanish American war, and just as you brushed aside Apodaca, you should brush aside the Insular Cases.* (Heritage Reporting Corporation 2020, 68–9—emphasis added)

This article aims to answer that question in the affirmative. The *Insular Cases*, especially *Balzac*, must be expressly repealed by the very forum that created them: the Supreme Court of the United States of America. We even argue that after what was resolved in *Ramos v. Louisiana*, *Balzac* was highly weakened to the point of being considered, in some respects, a dead letter, specifically in the aspects related to the right to trial by jury in the territories. As a historical fact, at the time that *Ramos v. Louisiana* was pronounced, Puerto Rico went through some particular circumstances. Much had happened since *Balzac v. Porto Rico* (1922): Puerto Ricans had approved a constitution, developed industrially, and then entered an economic crisis that led to implementing a Fiscal Oversight Board in the archipelago (Díaz and Vélez 2017). However, the territorial status of Puerto Rico has been constant: Puerto Rico is "foreign to the United States in a domestic sense" (*Downes v. Bidwell* 1902, 341).

The territorial status of Puerto Rico, in legal terms, is that of an "unincorporated territory." That was the conclusion that the United States Supreme Court gave us in *Balzac*, and it is the one that remains in the Puerto Rican political and legal consciousness. This article seeks to challenge the validity of said conclusion through the jurisprudence subsequent to the *Balzac* resolution by the United States Supreme Court.

The analysis will focus on two parts. The first part consists of a discussion about the meaning and scope of *Ramos v. Louisiana* on the right to trial by jury and the racial issues surrounding it. Above all, the institution of the right to trial by jury and its impact on American constitutional history is studied. The second part examines the Supreme Court's jurisprudence on the territories before and after the Spanish-American War. This part intends to analyze the *ratio decidendi* of the Supreme Court from a legal perspective and study the coherence of the decisions with respect to their precedents. Finally, and by way of conclusion, the possible political and legal implications of repealing *Balzac* are explored. In other words, this part ponders the consequences of removing *Balzac* from the books and its effects on the lives of citizens and nationals living in the territories.

Part I. Jury as a fundamental right in the American scheme of justice

To understand *Balzac v. Porto Rico* and its relationship with *Ramos v. Louisiana*, we must comprehend the contemporary history of the right to trial by jury in the United States of America. In essence, the right to trial by jury went from being a non-fundamental right to a "'fundamental [right] to the American scheme of justice' and incorporated against the States under the Fourteenth Amendment" (*Ramos v. Louisiana* 2020, 1397—majority opinion). The right to a trial by jury is found twice in the United States Constitution: in Article III and in the Sixth Amendment (U.S. Const., Art. III, §2, cl. 3 & Amend. VI). In the pertinent provisions, the U.S. Constitution reads as follows: "The Trial of all Crimes, except in Cases of Impeachment, shall be by Jury . . ." and at the same time, the Sixth Amendment provides that "In all criminal prosecutions, the accused shall enjoy the right to a speedy and public trial . . ."

The right to trial by jury has been an institution of vital importance in American history since its time as the Thirteen Colonies. Justice Story stated the following: "[t]he trial by jury is justly dear to the American people. It has always been an object of deep interest and solicitude..." (*Parsons v. Bedford* 1830, 446). Despite this, the relationship of the right to trial by jury and the concept of due process of law was not always clear. For example, *Maxwell v. Dow*, which had an 8–1 majority of Supreme Court justices, the same court that settled the *Insular Cases*, stated that "[t]rial by jury has never been affirmed to be a necessary requisite of due process of law" (*Maxwell v. Dow*, 1900, 603). Even the Supreme Court once pointed out that the right to trial by jury should not be "ranked as fundamental" as "trial by jury may be abolished" in the states (*Snyder v. Massachusetts* 1934, 105). However, this view of the Supreme Court changed in *Duncan v. Louisiana*.

In 1968, the United States Supreme Court ruled that the right to a trial by jury in criminal proceedings is inherent to the guarantee of due process of law that permeates the entire U.S. constitutional system: "Because we believe that trial by jury in criminal cases is fundamental to the American scheme of justice, we hold that the Fourteenth Amendment guarantees a right of jury trial in all criminal cases which—were they to be tried in a federal court—would come within the Sixth Amendment's guarantee" (*Duncan v. Louisiana* 1968, 149). In *Duncan v. Louisiana*, it is explained that: "[a] right to jury trial is granted to criminal defendants in order to prevent oppression by the Government" (1968, 155). Subsequently, the Supreme Court had to decide whether the right to a unanimous jury trial is applied in all states.

In *Apodaca v. Oregon* and *Johnson v. Louisiana*, the United States Supreme Court upheld the constitutionality of several state laws that allowed guilty verdicts to be rendered by a majority vote of the jury. It appears from the facts of these cases that the state of Oregon allowed majority verdicts with ten out of twelve votes, and the state of Louisiana allowed majority verdicts with nine out of twelve votes (*Apodaca v. Oregon* 1972; *Johnson v. Louisiana* 1972, 360). Pursuant to both rulings, the Supreme Court determined that a unanimous verdict does not constitute a requirement to establish the accused's guilt beyond a reasonable doubt nor to promote the right to trial by jury, as established in the Sixth Amendment to the United States Constitution. This was the legal doctrine in force until *Ramos v. Louisiana*.

This is extremely important because the majority of the Supreme Court used a historical analysis to conclude that the segregation motives that were allowed by a non-unanimous jury were contrary to the fundamental principles of the constitution.

A. *Ramos v. Louisiana* and the racism behind the non-unanimous juries

Ramos v. Louisiana "vindicated core principles of racial justice" (*Edwards v. Vannoy* 2021, 1574—Kagan, J., dissenting). On this occasion, the Supreme Court was faced with the following controversy: is the requirement of unanimity of the jury a constitutional guarantee that binds the states? In answering in the affirmative, the majority of the Supreme Court exposed the racist reasons that gave rise to the existence of a non-unanimous jury in the states of Louisiana and Oregon. This is extremely important because the majority of the Supreme Court used a historical analysis to conclude that the segregation motives that were allowed by a non-unanimous jury were contrary to the fundamental principles of the constitution.

In this case, one defendant challenged a sentence handed down in the state of Louisiana. He was found guilty of the commission of a felony, following a guilty verdict by a majority of 10 of the 12 jurors. As a result of that verdict, he was sentenced to a life sentence without the possibility of parole. It was argued before the United States Supreme Court that unanimity was an essential requirement of the right to a criminal jury trial and that any state provision allowing non-unanimous verdicts of severe crimes was unconstitutional.

The majority of the Supreme Court begins by stating that Louisiana passed, at a constitutional convention in 1898, non-unanimous verdicts for felonies for the avowed purpose of establishing "'the supremacy of the white race,' and the resulting document included many of the trappings of the Jim Crow era" and "[w]ith a careful eye on racial demographics, the convention delegates sculpted a 'facially race-neutral' rule permitting 10-to-2 verdicts in order 'to ensure that African-American juror service would be meaningless'" (*Ramos v. Louisiana* 2020, 1394—majority opinion). Likewise, the Supreme Court traced the origins of the unanimous verdicts in Oregon with the rise of the Ku Klux Klan (*Ramos v. Louisiana* 2020, 1394—majority opinion). This fact has not been denied by the Louisiana and Oregon courts, which "have frankly acknowledged that race was a motivating factor in the adoption of their States' respective nonunanimity rules" (*Ramos v. Louisiana* 2020, 1394—majority opinion).

Focusing on the jurisprudential core of the case, Justice Gorsuch stated that since the *Apodaca* case was one of a fractional nature, it had no binding force as a precedent (*Ramos v. Louisiana* 2020, 1402–4—majority opinion). Gorsuch analyzed the quality of *Apodaca*'s opinion and mentioned that "it's just an implacable fact that the plurality [of *Apodaca*] spent almost no time grappling with the historical meaning of the Sixth Amendment's jury trial right, this Court's long-repeated statements that it demands unanimity, *or the racist origins of Louisiana's and Oregon's laws"* (*Ramos v. Louisiana* 2020, 1405; majority opinion—emphasis added). After presenting the functional- ist reasons and the cost–benefit analyses that were weighed when deciding the *Apodaca* case, a majority of the United States Supreme Court indicated that "[w]ho can profess confidence in a breezy cost–benefit analysis like that? Lost in the accounting are the racially discriminatory reasons that Louisiana and Oregon adopted their peculiar rules in the first place" (*Ramos v. Louisiana* 2020, 1401—majority opinion).

The concurring opinion of Justice Kavanaugh focused on the stare decisis doctrine. On this matter, Kavanaugh indicated that "[a] case may be egregiously wrong when decided, see, e.g., *Korematsu v. United States*, . . .; *Plessy v. Ferguson*, . . ., or may be unmasked as egregiously wrong based on later legal or factual understandings or developments" (*Ramos v. Louisiana* 2020, 1415—Kavanaugh, J., concurring in part). Additionally, Kavanaugh highlighted that "*Apodaca* is egregiously wrong. The original meaning and this Court's precedents establish that the Sixth Amendment requires a unanimous jury" (*Ramos v. Louisiana* 2020, 1416—Kavanaugh, J., concur- ring in part). To support this point, he cited the case of *Thompson v. Utah*, an important case to understand the arbitrariness of *Balzac v. Porto Rico*. Justice Thomas summarized it as follows:

The Court reasoned that Thompson, a Utah prisoner, was protected by the Sixth Amendment when Utah was still a Territory because "the right of trial by jury in suits at common law appl[ied] to the Territories of the United States." The Court then stated that this right "made it impossible to deprive him of his liberty except by [a] unanimous verdict." (*Ramos v. Louisiana* 2020, 1421— Thomas, J., concurring in judgment)

Furthermore, Justice Kavanaugh stated that *Apodaca* has negative consequences since it protects a Louisiana legislation of racist origins. He exposed the following:

But the question at this point is not whether the Constitution prohibits non-unanimous juries. It does. *Rather, the disputed question here is whether to overrule*
an erroneous constitutional precedent that allowed non-unanimous juries. And
on that question—the question whether to overrule—the Jim Crow origins and
racially discriminatory effects (and the perception thereof) of non-unanimous
juries in Louisiana and Oregon should matter and should count heavily in favor
of overruling, in my respectful view. After all, the non-unanimous jury "is today
the last of Louisiana's Jim Crow laws."... And this Court has emphasized time and
again the "imperative to purge racial prejudice from the administration of justice" generally and from the jury system in particular. (*Ramos v. Louisiana* 2020,
1418; Kavanaugh, J., concurring in part—emphasis added)

Based on this analysis, we can reach the following conclusions: (1)
Ramos v. Louisiana not only reaffirms that the right to trial by jury is a fundamental one but also decidedly in favor of unanimity and (2) the Supreme
Court, through a historical analysis, took into consideration the historical
background and racial prejudice to rule out a precedent. I consider that this
precedent informs how the lower courts should interpret the right to trial
by jury in the territories, and consequently, the scope of *Balzac v. Porto Rico*
in the current legal system.

Part II. The U.S. territorial doctrine and its evolution

The original congressional source to administer and control the territories is
the well-known Territorial Clause that states the following: "The Congress
shall have Power to dispose of and make all needful Rules and Regulations
respecting the Territory or other Property belonging to the United States"
(U.S. Const., Art. IV, §2, cl.2). However, I argue that this interpretation was
not always the case. Before the Spanish-American War, the jurisprudence
of the Supreme Court had a tendency that this clause only applied to the
territories that the United States of America had at the time of the approval
of the federal constitution (Tauber 2006, 155). This was held in *Scott v.
Sandford*, a reprehensible case for its involvement in American slavery, but
that is illustrative of the origin of the Territorial Clause. This case mentioned that the Territorial Clause "was a special provision for a known and
particular territory, and to meet a present emergency, and nothing more"

(*Scott v. Sandford* 1857, 432). In this way, *Scott* points out that the power to govern the territories after the federal constitution's ratification comes from the authority to admit new states to the union (U.S. Const., Art. IV, §1, cl. 1). It should be noted that *Scott* interpreted the Constitution in such a way that the United States Congress cannot maintain colonies indefinitely:

There is certainly no power given by the Constitution to the Federal Government to establish or maintain colonies bordering on the United States or at a distance, to be ruled and governed at its own pleasure; nor to enlarge its territorial limits in any way, except by the admission of new States. That power is plainly given; and if a new State is admitted, it needs no further legislation by Congress, because the Constitution itself defines the relative rights and powers, and duties of the State, and the citizens of the State, and the Federal Government. *But no power is given to acquire a Territory to be held and governed permanently in that character.* **(Scott v. Sandford 1857, 446—emphasis added)**

In this way, it can be inferred that at the time, "the Constitution applied in the territories of the United States," that is, "the Constitution extends to any place that Congress's power extends" (Tauber 2006, 156). After all, the United States, in the words of Chief Justice Marshall, "is composed of States and territories" (*Loughborough v. Blake* 1820, 319). The constitutional view on territories was that, once acquired, they should be integrated as a federated state: "Territories acquired by Congress, whether by deed of cession from the original States, or by treaty with a foreign country, are held with the object, as soon as their population and condition justify it, of being admitted into the Union as States, upon an equal footing with the original States in all respects" (*Shively v. Bowlby* 1894, 49).

I contend that the United States cannot have territories ad perpetuam.

Additionally, before the Spanish-American War, the Supreme Court, through the voice of Justice Brown, said that "[i]n the future growth of the nation, as heretofore, it is not impossible that Congress may see fit to annex territories whose jurisprudence is that of the civil law" because "[i]t would be a narrow construction of the Constitution to require them to abandon these, or to substitute for a system, which represented the growth of generations of inhabitants, a jurisprudence with which they had had no previous acquaintance or sympathy" (*Holden v. Hardy* 1898, 389).

Despite this, the position taken after the Spanish-American War contradicts the long jurisprudential tradition that we have reviewed. I am not arguing that the United States Congress does not have plenary powers over the territories, as it always has (*The Late Corp. of the Church of Jesus Christ of Latter-Day Saints v. United States* 1890, 42; *Murphy v. Ramsey* 1885, 44; *Nat'l Bank v. County of Yankton* 1879, 133). I contend that the United States cannot have territories *ad perpetuam.*

A. *Insular Cases*: Taxes, Duties, and Jury Trials

The *Insular Cases*, originally known as the *Insular Tariff Cases*, have been viewed with skepticism (Derieux and Weare 2020, 286; Saavedra 2011, 268). In particular, the application of the *Insular Cases* boils down to questions of duties, taxes, and rights related to jury and trial (Derieux and Weare 2020, 295–6). For this reason, the Supreme Court recently recognized how highly criticized the *Insular Cases* are at the moment, expressing that it would not attempt to evaluate them in a topic related to the appointments clause because "[t]hose cases did not reach this issue, and *whatever their continued validity* we will not extend them in these cases" (*Fin. Oversight & Mgmt. Bd. for P.R. v. Aurelius Inv., LLC* 2020, 1665—emphasis added). After all, "[t]oday, no scholar defends the Insular Cases as correctly decided; any defense is qualified by practical concerns about overturning a century-old system and precedent" (Kane 2019, 1237). In addition, "it is not clear that the reasoning of [the Insular Cases] would still be viable" (*United States v. Tiede* 1979, 249).

To be conscious of the legal juggling that the Supreme Court incurred to justify the unequal treatment of the territories, it is necessary to understand three reasons: (1) the economic relationship between the empire and its territories, (2) the skepticism of the time about the right to trial by jury, and (3) the racist view of the moment toward the inhabitants of the newly annexed territories (Díaz and Vélez 2017; Kent 2018). In addition to the obvious racial reasons that influenced the thinking of the time, coming from the perspective of the era of *Plessy v. Ferguson*, Díaz and Vélez (2017) highlighted that the economic relationship with the territory largely justified the conclusions of the Supreme Court justices. The authors stated that, "Our position is that the relationship between Puerto Rico and the United States is primarily an economic arrangement, and that is how it should be approached and managed" (Díaz and Vélez 2017, 2—author's translation).

However, Kent (2018) differs from the classical view in academia that unincorporated territories are devoid of rights. Kent explains with regards to Puerto Rico that, "[f]irst by executive order, and then by statute and judicial decisions, residents of [the territory] came to possess almost all of the same rights as the U.S. Constitution provided, except for the Second and Third Amendments and the partial exception of jury rights" (2018, 392). He argues that part of the *ratio decidendi* in the *Insular Cases* comes from a view by the judiciary against juries (2018, 412).

With this conceptual framework, it is necessary to briefly examine the constitutional development of the *Insular Cases* up to *Balzac*. The first case is *Downes v. Bidwell*, a 4-1-4 fractured decision where the only thing that existed as a consensus on the part of the majority of the justices was "to conclude that Congress could impose a tax on products from Puerto Rico in a non-uniform way concerning the rest of the tax-contributory system in force in the United States" (Díaz and Vélez 2017, 8—author's translation). In this case, the Supreme Court noted that the Uniformity Clause did not apply to Puerto Rico because it was "a territory appurtenant and belonging to the United States, but not a part of the United States within the revenue clauses of the Constitution" (*Downes v. Bidwell* 1901, 287). Saavedra explains that *Downes* "decided that the Constitution allowed the United States to conquer territories and rule them as colonies. In other words, the Court concluded that the Constitution does not follow the flag" (2011, 968—author's translation).

Downes v. Bidwell is a contradiction to the precedents already outlined and is a gross departure from American constitutional principles. As Cabán points out, "*Downes v. Bidwell* (1901) perverted legally accepted principles of territorial incorporation to create a novel territorial category in order to deny the inhabitants of the insular possessions collective naturalization" (2017, 250). Justice Brown, issuing the opinion of the Court alone, stated that the territories "are inhabited by alien races, differing from us in religion, customs, laws, methods of taxation and modes of thought, the administration of government and justice, according to Anglo-Saxon principles, may for a time be impossible" (*Downes v. Bidwell* 1901, 286). After all, Brown ruled that "[t]he Constitution was created by the people of the United States, as a union of states, to be governed solely by representatives of the states" (*Downes v. Bidwell* 1901, 251). Furthermore, he justified the United States' power to conquer and rule the territories by comparing the federation with other countries. However,

> [t]he problem with Justice Brown's analysis is that it ignores that the United States, at the time, was unlike any other sovereign country in existence, in that it drew, and continues to draw, its power from a written Constitution. Furthermore, in a system of enumerated powers such as ours, the power to legislate over territories must be explicitly granted, not explicitly limited. (Tauber 2006, 161)

On the other hand, Justice White developed a theory that distinguished the incorporated and unincorporated territories and mentioned that "the determination of what particular provision of the Constitution is applicable. . . involves an inquiry into the situation of the territory and its relations to the United States" (*Downes v. Bidwell* 1901, 293). With no basis in American constitutional law, this theory is what commentators have called a middle ground: "White's doctrine of incorporation allowed him to carve out what seemed to be a middle position between Brown's extension theory and the dissenters' insistence on fundamental republican principles embodied in the Constitution" (Thomas 2001, 87). Nevertheless, the concept of incorporated territories is "a legal category invented by a fractured U.S. Supreme Court in the widely-reviled Insular Cases a century ago" (Blocher and Gulati 2018, 229).

Chief Justice Fuller strongly dissented and pointed out that the majority of the Supreme Court widely differs in the reasoning by which the conclusion is reached and then criticized the theory of incorporated territories: "What is meant by such incorporation we are not fully informed, nor are we instructed as to the precise mode in which it is to be accomplished" (*Downes v. Bidwell* 1901, 389). Fuller mentions that the idea of incorporated territories contains an "occult meaning which my mind does not apprehend. It is enveloped in some mystery which I am unable to unravel" (*Downes v. Bidwell* 1901, 391). Justice Harlan adds,

In my opinion, Congress has no existence and can exercise no authority outside
of the Constitution. Still less is it true that Congress can deal with new territories
just as other nations have done or may do with their new territories. This nation
is under the control of a written constitution, the supreme law of the land and
the only source of the powers which our Government, or any branch or officer of
it, may exert at any time or at any place. (*Downes v. Bidwell* 1901, 380)

---

*In this 5-4 decision, a plurality opinion written by Justice Brown held that Congress had
the power to determine the criminal procedure in the territories and that Congress did
not intend to require the territory to conduct criminal trials according to the Fifth and
Sixth Amendments.*

Later came *Hawaii v. Mankichi*, a case about the grand jury and jury
trials in the new acquired territories (*Hawaii v. Mankichi* 1903). Osaki
Mankichi was convicted of the crime of murder in 1899 by a Hawaiian
court. There was no indictment through the grand jury, and a unanimous
jury did not convict him. Subsequently, Mankichi filed habeas corpus,
alleging that his judgment in the trial court violated the Fifth and Sixth
Amendments to the United States Constitution. The controversy was
simple: "whether it was intended that this practice should be instantly
changed, and the criminal procedure embodied in the Fifth and Sixth
Amendments to the Constitution be adopted as of August 12, 1898, when
the Hawaiian flag was hauled down and the American flag hoisted in its
place" (*Hawaii v. Mankichi* 1903, 212). In this 5-4 decision, a plurality
opinion written by Justice Brown held that Congress had the power to
determine the criminal procedure in the territories and that Congress did
not intend to require the territory to conduct criminal trials according to
the Fifth and Sixth Amendments. Justice White held the same conclusion
under his unincorporated territory theory:

The mere annexation not having effected the incorporation of the islands into
the United States, it is not an open question that the provisions of the Constitution as to grand and petit juries were not applicable to them. . . Nor is there

anything in the provision in the act of annexation relating to the operation of the Constitution in the annexed territory which militates against the conclusions previously expressed. (*Hawaii v. Mankichi* 1903, 220)

On the other hand, the dissenting opinion of Justice Harlan highlighted that

When the annexation of Hawaii was completed, the Constitution – without any declaration to that effect by Congress, and without any power of Congress to prevent it – became the supreme law for that country, and, therefore, it forbade the trial and conviction of the accused for murder otherwise than upon a presentment or indictment of a grand jury, and by the unanimous verdict of a petit jury. (*Hawaii v. Mankichi* 1903, 248-9)

Harlan denounced the "colonial system" as one "entirely foreign to the genius of our Government and abhorrent to the principles that underlie and pervade the Constitution" (*Hawaii v. Mankichi* 1903, 240). This colonial system creates two types of government within the federation: "one, existing under a written Constitution, creating a government with authority to exercise only powers expressly granted and such as are necessary and appropriate to carry into effect those so granted; the other, existing outside of the written Constitution, in virtue of an unwritten law to be declared from time to time by Congress, which is itself only a creature of that instrument" (*Hawaii v. Mankichi* 1903, 240). *Mankichi* validates the incorporation theory and shows the "determining criterion for concluding whether a territory had been incorporated into the United States" (Torruella 2007, 316). Despite this, and continuing with the theory of unincorporated territories, we can deduce that in *Hawaii v. Mankichi*, the Court found that the territory was incorporated after granting U.S. citizenship to the Native Hawaiians (Gelpí 2011, 23). Regarding the right to trial by jury, the Supreme Court in this case concluded that unanimity was not necessary to find a person guilty of a crime because the right to a unanimous trial by jury was not a fundamental right.

A year later, in *Dorr v. United States*, the Supreme Court ruled that the right to a trial by jury did not apply in the Philippines, a "territory peopled by savages," because the Philippines was not an incorporated territory (*Dorr v. United States* 1904, 138–43—majority opinion). After this, the Supreme Court resolved *Rassmussen v. United* States, another case related to the jury's right (*Rassmussen v. United States* 1905). In particular, this case concerns a person who was convicted by a six-member jury rather than a twelve-member jury. Given this, *Rassmussen* challenged the conviction and the opinion endorsed by Justice White stated that granting the U.S. citizenship to Alaska "is the equivalent, as pointed out in *Downes v. Bidwell*, of the formula, employed from the beginning to express the purpose to incorporate acquired territory" (*Rassmussen v. United States* 1905). That is to say, giving U.S. citizenship to a territory, as long as we accept the theory of unincorporated territories, is sufficient action to infer the incorporation into the federation. In this case, the Supreme Court concluded that a 6-person jury was unconstitutional.

Based on this reasoning, later, the Federal District Court and the Supreme Court of Puerto Rico concluded that Puerto Rico was incorporated after collectively nationalizing the Puerto Ricans. As a preamble, President Woodrow Wilson signed the Jones Act, which recognized Puerto Ricans as American citizens and created a republican form of government, thus separating the executive, legislative, and judicial branches (Cosme 2019, 11). According to the previous factual background and following the theory of incorporated and unincorporated territories exposed until 1917, the best conclusion was that Puerto Rico was incorporated after obtaining an organized government structure and American citizenship.

In The Matter of Carlos Tapia, another criminal case, Tapia was charged with attempted murder without having been indicted by a grand jury. The controversy in the case is whether, under the Jones Act of 1917, the Fifth Amendment to the Constitution applies, which requires that "no person shall be held to answer for a capital, or otherwise infamous crime, unless on a presentment or indictment of a grand jury" (*In the Matter of Tapia* 1917). In a highly illustrative opinion, beginning with the United States' genesis and the institution of the grand jury, the Court concluded that Puerto Rico was incorporated into the federation as an incorporated territory because the incorporation of territory is only for the benefit of the inhabitants, present and future:

The word "citizen" we have seen employed once in the Declaration of Independence, oftener in the Articles of Confederation, and still more frequently in the Constitution, but even in the latter "persons" and "inhabitants" are more common. "People of the United States" and "citizens" are synonymous. (*In the Matter of Tapia* 1917, 476)

The Court then pointed out that

Congress has made [Puerto] Rico a part of the geographical, commercial, and judicial system of the nation, and has by the last organic act conferred citizenship also.... [I]ncorporation and citizenship imply each other, for they are practically synonymous.... This being true, the Constitution applies to those newly made Americans in Porto Rico just as much as to the older Americans on the continent. There cannot be two kinds of Americans under a Republic... (1917, 476)

The Supreme Court of Puerto Rico also concluded the same in *Muratti v. Foote*. Muratti was charged with second-degree murder in the absence of a grand jury (*Muratti v. Foote* 1917, 569). The Supreme Court of Puerto Rico relied on the fact that the process dictated in the Fifth Amendment of the United States Constitution was not followed. After a historical analysis of the relations of the territories with the federal government, the Court concluded that Puerto Rico had become an incorporated territory:

The history of incorporating the territories of the United States has been traced in the Insular Decisions and in the Rasmussen case. It has also been made the subject of an able and elaborate opinion of Mr. Justice Hamilton in the matter of Carlos Tapia recently decided. Given the antecedents and especially the Rasmussen case it follows that, while some of the judges of the Supreme Court have held that less is sufficient, all have agreed that the acquisition of territory plus citizenship plus organized government is incorporation. In Porto Rico the only difference is that citizenship was the last concession. To hold that incorporation is not here is to say that the acquisition of territory plus organized government plus citizenship in the case of Porto Rico is not equal to the acquisition of territory plus citizenship plus organized government in the case of Alaska, the equivalent of denying the algebraic truth that a+b+c=a+c+b. (*Muratti v. Foote* 1917, 581)

In other words, at that historical moment, the determination of the Supreme Court of Puerto Rico, like the Federal District Court for Puerto Rico, was that the United States citizenship of the inhabitants of an unincorporated but organized territory has the effect of changing the territorial nature to an incorporated one. That logic can be reached by following the *Insular Cases* themselves and Justice White's theory. However, in an exercise of legal and cryptic juggling, both cases were reversed without explanation *per curiam*, citing only the same cases that the lower forums used to reach their conclusion (*Porto Rico v. Tapia* 1918).

Given this uncertainty, *Balzac v. Porto Rico* arrives to serve as an interpretation of trials by jury in the territories. Jesús M. Balsac, the editor of a newspaper, was convicted of a less serious criminal charge of libel under Puerto Rico's laws (*Pueblo v. Balzac* 1920; Santini 2019, 175–204). Before the Supreme Court of Puerto Rico, Mr. Balsac claimed that he had the right to a trial by jury under the Sixth Amendment (*Pueblo v. Balzac* 1920, 151). The Supreme Court rejected the claim and said "that part of Amendment VI to the Constitution of the United States that grants the accused in all criminal cases the right to trial by jury, is not applicable to Puerto Rico" (*Pueblo v. Balzac* 1920, 151). Balsac was tried and convicted without a jury trial and appealed his conviction, arguing that, following the Jones Act of 1917, this procedure violated the Sixth Amendment to the United States Constitution. Faced with such an issue, the United States Supreme Court in *Balzac* clarified *Tapia* and modified the territorial incorporation theory with the sole objective of not incorporating Puerto Rico (*Balzac v. Porto Rico* 1922). Arnaud (2017, 302) pointed out:

A major contention was that the Foraker Act did not give Puerto Ricans citizenship—a major provision of the Northwest Ordinance and its progeny—so the Jones Act surely manifests Congress's intention to incorporate Puerto Rico into the Union. However, the Supreme Court in another pivotal case, *Balzac v. Porto Rico*, held that the granting of citizenship through the Jones Act did not represent sufficient congressional action as to incorporate Puerto Rico.

The U.S. Supreme Court ruled that Mr. Balzac, who had been sentenced to nine months in prison for the crime of libel, was not entitled to a jury trial by dispelling any doubt that the Jones Act failed to incorporate into Puerto Rico the trial by jury clause derived from the Sixth Amendment of the Constitution. Chief Justice Taft expressed on the constitutional provisions that "it is just as clearly settled that they do not apply to territory belonging to the United States which has not been incorporated into the Union" (*Balzac v. Porto Rico* 1922, 304–5). In this case, it was determined that the Jones Act was not sufficient to incorporate the island's right to trial by jury provided in the Sixth Amendment, as that was not the purpose of Congress, by concluding that the incorporation needs an express declaration or a firm intention by Congress. Similarly, Taft decided that if Congress had wanted to incorporate the territory, it would have declared it clearly and not left it to mere inference, thus contradicting the Supreme Court pronouncement in *Rassmussen* and *Mankichi* (*Balzac v. Porto Rico* 1922, 306). Tauber explained that "mandating that Congress articulate its intent to incorporate a territory is an odd requirement for incorporation in this case" so that "it is hard to imagine a greater indication of congressional intent to extend the full protection of the Constitution to the people of Puerto Rico than granting them United States citizenship" (Tauber 2006, 165). The Supreme Court pointed out that the *Insular Cases* ruled that only the federal Constitution's fundamental rights were applicable in Puerto Rico (*Balzac v. Porto Rico* 1922, 312–3). Additionally, the Court noted, in a highly racist and unsubstantiated tone in law, the following:

The jury postulates a conscious duty of participation in the machinery of justice which it is hard for people not brought up in fundamentally popular government at once to acquire. One of its greatest benefits is in the security it gives the people that they, as jurors, actual or possible, being part of the judicial system of the country, can prevent its arbitrary use or abuse. Congress has thought that a people like the Filipinos or the Porto Ricans, trained to a complete judicial system which knows no juries, living in compact and ancient communities, with definitely formed customs and political conceptions, should be permitted themselves to determine how far they wish to adopt this institution of Anglo-Saxon origin... (*Balzac v. Porto Rico* 1922, 308-9)

Judge Gelpí highlighted that "[a]s was the case with the original *Insular Cases*, the Balzac decision made no common sense and again showed extreme racism as well as ignorance of the realities of the island at the time" (*Consejo de Salud v. Rullan* 2008, 30). Judge Torruella explained that "[The] assertion that somehow Puerto Ricans were incapable of understanding 'the responsibilities of jurors' and 'popular government' is without any basis in the record or the facts" (Torruella 2007, 326). Gelpí showed that the Supreme Court ignored the irrefutable fact that since 1899 in Puerto Rico, there had been jury trials in both the civil and criminal fields in the federal court (*Consejo de Salud v. Rullan* 2008, 30). At the same time, Gelpí indicated that since 1901, the Puerto Rican courts have carried out jury trials in cases of serious crimes (*Consejo de Salud v. Rullan* 2008, 30). Similarly, Puerto Rico was already a territory organized by Congress itself in the Foraker and Jones Acts, reflecting the political system of the federal government and the states: an executive, a bicameral legislature, a Supreme Court, and a federal district court, as well as a representative in Congress (*Consejo de Salud v. Rullan* 2008, 30).

Balzac, a unanimous opinion, is based on the house of cards of the first *Insular Cases*, a series of fragmented and inconsistent decisions.

The *Balzac* Court, somewhat surprisingly, made completely inconsistent statements concerning the citizenship status of the people of Puerto Rico. Despite holding that such citizens did not have a constitutional right under the Sixth Amendment, the Court announced that the grant of United States citizenship to the people of Puerto Rico was "to put them as individuals on an exact equality with citizens from the American homeland..." (Román 1998, 24)

Álvarez explains that

[t]he decision in *Balzac* caused some surprise at the time. The doctrine of territorial incorporation, as originally developed by Justice White in his opinion in *Downes*, clearly suggested that the granting of American citizenship to the inhabitants of a territory was an implicit way in which Congress could incorporate into that territory to the inhabitants of a U.S. territory. (1988, 139—author's translation)

Even *Balzac*, and the rest of the *Insular Cases*, was a clear break with a precedent that still lasts in jurisprudence: *Thompson v. Utah* and others. There, after citing the Sixth Amendment, the Supreme Court holds that it was "no longer an open question" that "the provisions of the Constitution of the United States relating to the right of trial by jury in suits at common law apply to the Territories of the United States" to later say that "[i]t is equally beyond question that the provisions of the National Constitution relating to trials by jury for crimes and to criminal prosecutions apply to the Territories of the United States" (*Thompson v. Utah* 1898, 346–7). Furthermore, in *Reynolds v. United States*, another criminal proceeding in the Utah Territory, the Supreme Court assumed that the Sixth Amendment applied to criminal proceedings (*Reynolds v. United States* 1878, 154). Despite this, the Supreme Court in *Balzac* ignored its prior precedents and partially consolidated the theory of incorporation of Justice White, also requiring an express mandate from Congress.

After *Balzac*, the United States Congress passed the Nationality Act of 1940, providing jus soli citizenship in Puerto Rico (8 U.S.C. § 1402), and later, Puerto Rico adopts a Constitution (48 U.S.C. §.731b et. seq). Throughout this entire process, the provision was maintained that "[t]he rights, privileges, and immunities of the citizens of the United States shall be respected in Puerto Rico to the same degree as if Puerto Rico were a State of the Union and subject to the provisions of subsection 1 of sec. 2 of Art. IV of the Constitution of the United States" (1 L.P.R.A. Const. 3, § 2). Given this de facto incorporation, it is worth asking ourselves if reality contradicts the precedent. Riley Edward Kane stated,

It seems that the territorial incorporation doctrine, resting on a century of precedent—even if steeped in folly—may continue to exist, albeit with lessened vigor. The comment about constitutional significance [in *Boumediene v. Bush*] suggests a warning for the legislature (and ultimately territorial citizens as well) that territories could someday become de facto incorporated, in direct contravention of *Balzac*. Perhaps the Supreme Court would even use *Balzac* to overturn itself by finding a century of congressional inaction serves as de facto incorporation, as *Balzac* did speak about the territories with an eye to their newly acquired and uncertain future statuses. (2019, 1245)

Despite this, after a whole process of Puerto Rican constitutional development and "thirty four years later, in *Reid v. Covert*, ... the Supreme Court again expressed itself in regards to the *Insular Cases*" (*Consejo de Salud v. Rullan* 2008, 31). In *Reid*, a woman and civilian was tried and convicted by a United States Martial Court without a jury trial. Through a writ of habeas corpus, she stated that the conviction violated her Fifth and Sixth Amendment rights (*Reid v. Covert* 1957). The Supreme Court ruled that it was unconstitutional to apply military law to civilians living in military bases in peacetime. Neuman notes that "juxtaposing *Reid v. Covert* with the *Insular Cases* produces bizarre results. For example, a U.S. citizen prosecuted by the federal government has a constitutional right to a jury trial in Japan, but not in Puerto Rico" (2001, 190). It should be noted that the Supreme Court rejected the application of the *Insular Cases* in this case:

The "Insular Cases" can be distinguished from the present cases in that they involved the power of Congress to . . . govern temporarily territories with wholly dissimilar traditions and institutions whereas here the basis for governmental power is American citizenship. None of these cases had anything to do with military trials and they cannot properly be used as vehicles to support an extension of military jurisdiction to civilians. Moreover, it is our judgment that neither the cases nor their reasoning should be given any further expansion. The concept that the Bill of Rights and other constitutional protections against arbitrary government are inoperative when they become inconvenient or when expediency dictates otherwise is a very dangerous doctrine and if allowed to flourish would destroy the benefit of a written constitution and undermine the basis of our government. If our foreign commitments became of such nature that the Government can no longer satisfactorily operate within the bounds laid down by the Constitution, that instrument can be amended by the method which it prescribes. But we have no authority, or inclination, to read exceptions into it which are not there. (*Reid v. Covert* 1957, 14—emphasis added)

However, the *Insular Cases* and their progeny have been used to discriminate against territories on countless occasions. Regarding the right to trial by jury, we must analyze how the lower courts have applied *Balzac* in the territories of American Samoa and the Northern Mariana Islands. Let's look first at the case of American Samoa. There, Jake King, a citizen of the United States and a resident of American Samoa, was denied a trial by jury because there was no legislation that enabled said right and because the *Balzac* ruling had concluded that the right to trial by jury was not fundamental. (*King v. Morton* 1975). He was found guilty and sentenced, for which King appealed to the Appellate Division of the High Court of American Samoa. Said court ruled that in 1974, despite *Duncan's* decision in force, that the right to trial by jury was not applicable in American Samoa because "the imposition of the Anglo-American jury system upon Samoa's legal structure 'would be an arbitrary, illogical, and inappropriate foreign imposition'" (*King v. Morton* 1975, 126). After a procedural analysis, the DC Circuit Court of Appeals discusses the right to a jury trial in American Samoa. *King's* argument can be reduced to a simple syllogism: (1) American Samoa is unincorporated territory; (2) the Supreme Court ruled that those fundamental rights only apply in unincorporated territories; and (3) after *Duncan*, the right to a trial by jury is fundamental, which is why it applies in American Samoa. However, the majority of the Court of Appeals stated that

Balzac, Dorr, Hawaii and the *Insular Tariff* cases all involved unincorporated territories similar to American Samoa, but at a time much earlier in our nation's history. Those cases have never been overruled; specifically, they have not been overruled by the *Duncan* and *Baldwin* cases, which dealt with the right to trial by jury in states rather than unincorporated territories. (*King v. Morton* 1975, 126)

So, the Court remanded the case to determine whether the right to trial by jury was compatible with the American Samoan culture. Judge Tamm dissented and noted that "[a]ll of the *Insular Cases* which concern the right to jury trial were decided at a period in our history when that right was not considered 'fundamental.' Obviously, *Duncan* has significantly undermined that premise, especially when *Duncan* overturned the idea that 'jury trial is not fundamental to ordered liberty' and consequently 'at least to that extent, *Dorr* and *Balzac* are no longer valid'" (*King v. Morton* 1975, 126—Tamm, J., dissenting). Subsequently, and after an analysis of the life and culture of American Samoa, the United States District Court for the District of Columbia determined that the right to trial by jury did apply in that territory (*King v. Andrus* 1977, 452 F. Supp. 11). Rosenthal and Weare (2019) point out that "the King decisions recognized that, even under the Insular Cases, restricting application of the Constitution in the Territories could only be justified by the most compelling facts on the ground" (Rosenthal and Weare 2019, 24–5).

On the other hand, in *Northern Mariana Islands v. Atalig*, the United States Court of Appeals for the Ninth Circuit, ruled that, despite *Duncan's* ruling, Northern Mariana Islands (hereinafter, NMI) was not entitled to a trial by jury under the Sixth Amendment (*Northern Mariana Islands v. Atalig* 1985). For this, the Court of Appeals stated a reasoning that, in our opinion, was intended to justify a predetermined conclusion: that the *Insular Cases* were not affected by jurisprudential development on fundamental rights. In *Atalig*, the defendant had been convicted in an NMI trial court of a crime that only involved a maximum penalty of one year in prison, a fine of $1,000, or both. At the time, NMI only granted the right to a jury in a criminal case for crimes punishable by more than five years in prison or a fine of $2,000. For this reason, Atalig did not receive a jury trial. However, the intermediate court reversed the conviction, holding that Atalig was denied his right to a jury trial guaranteed by the Sixth and Fourteenth amendments to the United States Constitution. The Ninth Circuit reversed this again, using as justification that the right to a jury trial guaranteed by the Sixth Amendment and the right to a formal indictment by a large jury guaranteed by the Fifth Amendment to the United States Constitution are not "fundamental rights" according to *Insular Cases*. The Ninth Circuit found that the intermediate court had incorrectly relied on *Duncan v. Louisiana*.

The history of incorporation of the Bill of Rights under the Due Process Clause also makes us reluctant to apply *Duncan* to the *Insular Cases*. That history reveals that the Court proceeded cautiously with this incorporation. Through this gradual process in the century following ratification of the Fourteenth Amendment, nearly all the rights guaranteed in the Bill of Rights have been found applicable to the states. We believe that a cautious approach is also appropriate in restricting the power of Congress to administer overseas territories. Were we to apply sweepingly *Duncan's* definition of "fundamental rights" to unincorporated territories, the effect would be immediately to extend almost the entire Bill of Rights to such territories. This would repudiate the *Insular Cases*. We are not prepared to do so nor do we think we are required to do so. (*Northern Mariana Islands v. Atalig* 1984, 690—emphasis added)

I consider this reasoning, of trying to avoid a conclusion, to be legal cherry-picking. In essence, the Ninth Circuit rejects *Duncan*'s breadth of fundamental rights in order not to have to apply it to the territories. Is it that there are perhaps two types of fundamental rights? In my opinion, *Balzac* referred to the fundamental rights that were recognized for the citizens of the states. A right is fundamental, not because of where the depositary of that right is located, but because of who that depositary is. In this case, the depositaries are the American citizens of the states and territories.

Contemporaneously, in West Germany, which was occupied by the United States, an interesting case was resolved that demonstrates the *Balzac* doctrine's inconsistencies. In *United States v. Tiede*, the United States Court for Berlin noted that the *Insular Cases'* position about the right to trial by jury in criminal cases not being a fundamental right was authoritatively overruled in *Duncan*. The practical effect of this decision was that a German living in postwar U.S.-occupied Berlin had the right to a jury trial, while Americans living in U.S. territories did not. The judge recognized the incon-sistencies of the *Insular Cases*:

The *Insular Cases*, in the manner in which the results were reached, the incon-gruity of the results, and the variety of inconsistent views expressed by the different members of the court, are, I believe, without parallel in our judicial history. It is unfortunate that the cases could not have been determined with such a preponderance of consistent opinion as to have satisfied the profession and the country that the conclusions were likely to be adhered to by the court. Until some reasonable consistency and unanimity of opinion is reached by the court upon these questions, we can hardly expect their conclusions to be final and beyond revision. (*United States v. Tiede* 1979, 248)

Part III: *Balzac*: Notes on its validity

Balzac was the last of this series of cases to consolidate the doctrine of unincorporated territories in a modified way, by answering the question of whether the Sixth Amendment applied in Puerto Rico—nothing more and nothing less. That has been the common denominator in several *Insular Cases*. After a century of jurisprudential development, *Balzac*, in my opin-ion, was partially revoked after *Ramos v. Louisiana*. In the same way, the

Supreme Court of Puerto Rico contemplates that "[a]lmost a century after the expressions issued by the United States Supreme Court in *Balzac*, it is evident that the passage of time has been in charge of modifying the rule of law in force at that time, to the point that what is established there regarding the right to a trial by jury has become a dead letter" (*Pueblo v. Torres Rivera* 2020, 18—author's translation).

According to the Puerto Rico Supreme Court, the Sixth Amendment applies in Puerto Rico because it is a fundamental right. Álvarez mentions that notwithstanding what was resolved in *Balzac v. Porto Rico*, "since *Duncan v. Louisiana*, 391 U.S. 145 (1968) ruled that [the right to trial by jury] is 'fundamental" and, as such, applicable to the states. . . it seems reasonable to conclude that that right applies to Puerto Rico under the doctrine of territorial incorporation" (2009, 428—author's translation). Beyond that, "in the face of this modern reality, the compelling question is whether *Balzac* still controls the question of the applicability in Puerto Rico of the trial by jury clause of the Sixth Amendment of the federal Constitution" (*Pueblo v. Santana Vélez* 2009, 83—author's translation). I believe that the answer to this obligatory question is that "regarding the non-fundamental nature of the federal constitutional right to trial by jury, *Balzac* is probably no longer good law" (Álvarez 2009, 428—author's translation).

As an associate justice, Martínez Torres explained that "insisting on what was resolved in *Balzac* after *Duncan's* precedent would result in American citizens in Puerto Rico having fewer fundamental rights than those they would enjoy if they were in any of the states of the Union" (*Pueblo v. Santana Vélez* 2009, 84—author's translation). Martínez Torres adds that "keeping *Balzac* in force after *Duncan* would be to deny the equality of fundamental rights of American citizens in Puerto Rico, which would be contrary to the congressional purpose in which Puerto Rico is treated in a manner analogous to a federated state, and to our constitutional duty to guarantee justice and equality to all" (*Pueblo v. Santana Vélez* 2009, 84—author's translation).

Although after the fundamental right to trial by jury was recognized in *Duncan*, an issue that weakens *Balzac*'s precedent, the question asked by multiple people was whether there was a right to unanimous jury determinations. As we already know, in the territories, this right was not applicable.

In *Mankichi,* a non-unanimous guilty verdict of nine votes in favor and three against was validated, issued by the laws of the then-territory of Hawaii. However, it seems that after *Ramos v. Louisiana,* which ruled out non-unanimous juries on racial grounds, *Mankinchi* loses its authoritative vigor when it comes to interpreting unanimity in territorial juries and complements the thesis that *Balzac* is based on a house of cards.

A. *Balzac:* A precedent sustained by a house of cards

Muchnick stated that "[t]he *Insular Cases* are widely recognized as having contradicted precedent of their time and as having been motivated by politics and racial biases... [T]he Court's attitude in the *Insular Cases* toward 'alien races' seems anachronistic and inapposite to the current situation facing what this Note will call 'Insular Citizens'" (2016, 800). Judge Torruella specified that "[t]he *Insular Cases,* would today be labeled blatant 'judicial activism.'" Also, "[t]hey are anchored on theories of dubious legal or historical validity, contrived by academics interested in promoting an expansionist agenda" because "[t]hese theories in turn provided a platform that allowed a receptive bare plurality of Justices to reach a result unprecedented in American jurisprudence and unsupported by the text of the Constitution" (*Igartua-de la Rosa v. United States* 2005, 163—Torruella, J., dissenting).

"There is no question that the Insular Cases *are on par with the Court's infamous decision in* Plessy v. Ferguson *in licensing the downgrading of the rights of discrete minorities within the political hegemony of the United States."*

It is imperative to note that *Balzac* and the *Insular Cases* interpret the constitution and its applicability to the territories. This is vital because the stare decisis "is at its weakest when we interpret the Constitution because our interpretation can be altered only by constitutional amendment or by overruling our prior decisions" (*Agostini v. Felton* 1997, 235). This doctrine is a reiterated one throughout the American jurisprudence: "it is common wisdom that the rule of stare decisis is not an 'inexorable command,' and certainly, it is not such in every constitutional case" (*Planned Parenthood v. Casey* 1992, 854).

Additionally, as historical detail, the majority of the Supreme Court who decided that the *Insular Cases* that give basis to *Balzac* are the same people who decided the terrible case of *Plessy v. Ferguson* (*Consejo de Salud v. Rullan* 2008, 28). Judge Torruella emphasizes: "There is no question that the *Insular Cases* are on par with the Court's infamous decision in *Plessy v. Ferguson* in licensing the downgrading of the rights of discrete minorities within the political hegemony of the United States" (*Igartua-De La Rosa v. United States* 2005, 162—Torruella, J., dissenting).

Likewise, in the opinion of *Trump v. Hawaii*, the Supreme Court banished the *Korematsu* case from the books. This case dealt with the legitimacy of the forced relocation of U.S. citizens to concentration camps, solely and explicitly based on race. Chief Justice Roberts said, "The dissent's reference to *Korematsu*, however, affords this Court the opportunity to make express what is already obvious: *Korematsu* was gravely wrong the day it was decided, has been overruled in the court of history, and—to be clear—'has no place in law under the Constitution'" (*Trump v. Hawaii* 2018, 2423). Similarly, the Supreme Court should conclude that *Balzac* and the *Insular Cases* were gravely wrong the day they were decided and have no place in law under the Constitution.

Under the *Ramos v. Louisiana* reasoning of precedent, it is entirely feasible for the Supreme Court of the United States to overturn *Balzac* once and for all along with the *Insular Cases* that support it. In Puerto Rico, the aspect regarding the right to the jury that *Balzac* decided is inoperative (Alicea Matías 2020, 20). Only the doctrine that sustains it remains, used to justify colonialism on the archipelago and the territories.

After *Balzac* and *Duncan*, the incorporation of fundamental rights in Puerto Rico has been increasing. Regarding the application of fundamental rights to Puerto Rico, the United States Supreme Court itself has accepted that "[i]t is clear now, however, that the protections accorded by either the Due Process Clause of the Fifth Amendment or the Due Process and Equal Protection Clauses of the Fourteenth Amendment apply to residents of Puerto Rico" (*Examining Bd. Of Engineers, Architects and Surveyors v. Flores de Otero* 1976, 600). Later, in *Pueblo v. Santana Vélez*, the Supreme Court of Puerto Rico stated that "[t]he right to trial by jury of the Sixth Amendment is a fundamental right that applies to the states through the due process clause of the Fourteenth Amendment and, therefore, to Puerto Rico"

(*Pueblo v. Santana Vélez* 2009, 65). We can infer that the right to a jury trial, at least today, applies in its entirety to Puerto Rico.

Despite the fact that Puerto Rico does not have a substantial problem regarding trial by jury, *Balzac*'s reasoning persists. For this reason, I agree with Álvarez (1988) that there are several ways in which the precedent could be challenged again. He argues that *Balzac* would have to be revoked in an appropriate case (Álvarez 1988, 150). To do this, Álvarez (1988) proposes a process where the accused is charged with more than one misdemeanor and, therefore, consecutive prison sentences totaling more than six months can be imposed, but he would not have the right to a trial by jury. In this way, *Balzac* could be challenged, giving the Supreme Court the opportunity to reassess the precedent.

Conclusion

After one hundred years of *Balzac v. Porto Rico*, we must emphasize that it no longer has the validity that it originally had. As is evident, in the last 124 years, "the ties between the United States and any of its unincorporated Territories" have been "strengthen[ed] in ways that are of constitutional significance" (*Boumediene v. Bush* 2008, 757). After all, "the Constitution has independent force in these Territories, a force not contingent upon acts of legislative grace" (*Boumediene v. Bush* 2008, 757). Gelpí explained that "[t]he controversial *Insular Cases*, decided in the early 1900s, created the framework of incorporated and unincorporated territories,... were grounded on outdated premises" (*United States v. Vaello-Madero* 2018, 375). These premises come from colonial racial and socioeconomic doctrines that justify unequal treatment by the United States of its territories (*Segovia v. Bd. Of Election Comm'rs for Chi.* 2016, 937). Based on the above, I argue that the analysis of *Ramos v. Louisiana* on the precedent, the historical context on constitutional rights, and the right to trial by jury, should serve as a new interpretation for the lower courts that constantly grapple with the territories. The "impractical and anomalous" test must be discarded once and for all, which only serves to arbitrarily determine which rights apply to the territories.

It is a matter of time for a territory to have an adequate case that allows questioning all the centuries-old jurisprudence that violates U.S. citizens' constitutional rights who inhabit the territories. The thesis outlined in this article is that it should be the Supreme Court, the creator of these precedents, who revokes them. Although many argue that the territorial condition of Puerto Rico is a strictly political matter, we cannot deny that the said condition stems from the premises of the legal imperialism of the early twentieth century. Furthermore, "[a]bstaining from questions involving formal sovereignty and territorial governance is one thing. To hold the political branches have the power to switch the Constitution on or off at will is quite another" (*Boumediene v. Bush* 2008, 765).

Revoking *Balzac* could imply a path of no return to statehood for territories that are not classified as possessions (a distinction that is constitutionally recognized) (*Fitisemanu v. United States* 2021, 69—Bacharach, J., dissenting). Likewise, it could be criticized that the said determination by the courts would eliminate the right to self-determination of the territory. Without pretending to take a position, the political destiny of the territories must be a dignified and not a colonial one, so that in due course, Congress will have to take a position if *Balzac* is left off of the books.

At the same time, the fight for legal equality in all U.S. territories inherits the battle for legal equality for women, African Americans, the LGBTTQ+ community, and Native-American tribes. Although the political future of Puerto Rico will not be resolved by repealing *Balzac* and the *Insular Cases,* without a doubt, the dignity of all the inhabitants of the United States territories will be reaffirmed. There is no space in American jurisprudence to sustain the separate and unequal status of Puerto Rico and other territories.

REFERENCES

1 L.P.R.A. Const. 3, § 2.

48 U.S.C. §.731b et. seq.

Agostini v. Felton. 1997. 521 U.S. 203.

Alicea Matías, José. 2020. Los derechos de confrontación y juicio por jurado en tiempos de Pandemia. *Revista de Derecho Puertorriqueño* 60, 1–27.

Álvarez González, José Julián. 1988. La protección de los derechos humanos en Puerto Rico. *Revista Jurídica de la Universidad de Puerto Rico* 57, 133–69.

_____. 2009. *Derecho Constitucional de Puerto Rico y relaciones constitucionales con los Estados Unidos.* Bogotá: Editorial Temis S.A.

Apodaca v. Oregon. 1972. 406 U.S. 404.

Arnaud, Emmanuel Hiram. 2017. A License to Kill: State Sponsored Death in the Oldest Colony in the World. *Revista Jurídica de la Universidad de Puerto Rico* 86, 291–320.

Balzac v. Porto Rico. 1922. 258 U.S. 298.

Blocher, Joseph and Mitu Gulati. 2018. Puerto Rico and the Right of Accession. *The Yale Journal of International Law* 43(2), 229–68.

Boumediene v. Bush. 2008. 553 U.S. 723.

Caban, Pedro. 2017. Puerto Ricans as Contingent Citizens: Shifting Mandated Identities and Imperial Disjunctures. Latin American, Caribbean, and U.S. Latino Studies Faculty Scholarship 1–103.

Cepeda Derieux, Adriel I. and Neil C. Weare. 2020. After Aurelius: What Future for the Insular Cases? *The Yale Law Journal Forum* 130, 284–307.

Consejo de Salud v. Rullan. 2008. 586 F. Supp. 2d 22. Federal District Court of Puerto Rico.

Cosme Morales, Joel Andrews. 2019. Expulsión del Comisionado Residente de la Cámara de Representantes de los Estados Unidos. *Revista de Derecho Puertorriqueño* 59, 1–29.

Díaz Olivo, Carlos and Edwin Vélez Borrero. 2017. PROMESA incumplida, Sánchez Valle, Franklin Trust: el rol de la rama judicial federal en la relación entre Puerto Rico y los Estados Unidos. *Revista Jurídica de la Universidad de Puerto Rico* 86, 1–49.

Downes v. Bidwell. May 27, 1902. 182 U.S. 244.

Duncan v. Louisiana. 1968. 391 U.S. 145.

Examining Bd. Of Engineers, Architects and Surveyors v. Flores de Otero. 1976. 426 U.S. 572.

Fin. Oversight & Mgmt. Bd. for P.R. v. Aurelius Inv. June 1, 2020. *LLC 2.* 140 S. Ct. 1649.

Fitisemanu v. United States 2021 U.S. App. LEXIS 17819.

Gelpí, Gustavo A. 2011. The Insular Cases: A Comparative Historical Study of Puerto Rico, Hawai'i, and the Philippines. *The Federal Lawyer* March/April, 22–5, 74.

Hawaii v. Mankichi. June 1, 1903. 190 U.S. 197.

Heritage Reporting Corporation. 2020. Ramos v. Louisiana Oral Transcript. *Supreme Court Website* 22 June. Accessed 26 June 2021. <https://www.supremecourt.gov/oral_arguments/argument_transcripts/2019/18-5924_6j37.pdf/>.

Holden v. Hardy. February 28, 1898. 169 U.S. 366.

Igartua-de la Rosa v. United States. August 3, 2005. United States Court of Appeals, First Circuit, 417 F.3d 145.

In the Matter of Tapia. 1917. 9 P.R. Fed. Reports 452. Federal District Court of Puerto Rico.

Johnson v. Louisiana. 1972. 406 U.S. 356.

Kane, Riley Edward. 2019. Straining Territorial Incorporation: Unintended Consequences from Judicially Extending Constitutional Citizenship. *Ohio State Law Journal* 80(6), 1230–63.

Kent, Andrew. 2018. The Jury and Empire: The Insular Cases and the Anti-Jury Movement in the Gilded Age and Progressive Era. *91 Southern California Law Review* 91, 375–465.

King v. Morton 1975, 172 U.S. App. D.C. 126.

Loughborough v. Blake. March 10, 1820. 18 U.S. (5 Wheat.) 317.

Maxwell v. Dow, 1900. 176 U.S. 581.

Muchnick, Nathan. 2016. The Insular Citizens: America's Lost Electorate v. Stare Decisis. *Cardozo Law Review* 38(2), 798–834.

Muratti v. Foote. 1917. 25 DPR 568.

Murphy v. Ramsey. March 23, 1885. 114 U.S. 15.

Nat'l Bank v. County of Yankton. October 1, 1879. 101 U.S. 129.

Neuman, Gerald L. 2001. Constitutionalism and Individual Rights in the Territories. In *Foreign in a Domestic Sense: Puerto Rico, American Expansion, and the Constitution*, eds. Christina Duffy Burnett y Burke Marshal. 186–206. Durham: Duke University Press.

Northern Mariana Islands v. Atalig 1985, 723 F.2d 682 [9th Cir.].

Ortiz Santini, Francisco. 2018. *Balsac vs El Pueblo de Puerto Rico: Su historia; sus protagonistas*. N.p: N.p.

Oyez. *Ramos v. Louisiana*. October 7, 2019. Accessed 24 January 2021. <https://www.oyez.org/cases/2019/18-5924/>.

Parsons v. Bedford, 1830. 28 U.S. (3 Pet.) 433.

Payne v. Tennessee. 1991. 501 U.S. 808.

Planned Parenthood v. Casey. 1992. 505 U.S. 833.

Pueblo v. Balzac. 1920. 28 DPR 150.

Pueblo v. Santana Vélez. 2009. 177 DPR 61.

Pueblo v. Torres Rivera. 2020. TSPR 42.

Ramos v. Louisiana. 2020. 140 S. Ct. 1390.

Rassmussen v. United States. April 10, 1905. 197 U.S. 516.

Reid v. Covert. 1957. 354 U.S. 1.

Reynolds v. United States. 1878. 98 U.S. 145.

Román, Ediberto. 1998. The Alien-Citizen Paradox and other Consequences of U.S. Colonialism. *Florida State University Law Review 26(1)*, 1–44.

Rosenthal, Steven S., and Neil C. Weare. 2019. Brief for Amicus Curiae Equally American Legal Defense and Education. U.S. Supreme Court Web Site. Accessed 25 July 2021. <https://core.ac.uk/download/pdf/234129535.pdf/>.

Saavedra Gutiérrez, Carlos. 2011. Incorporación de jure o incorporación de facto: dos propuestas para erradicar fantasmas constitucionales. *Revista Jurídica de la Universidad de Puerto Rico 80*, 968–92.

Scott v. Sandford. 1857. 60 U.S. (19 How.) 393, 432.

Segovia v. Bd. Of Election Comm'rs for Chi. 2016. 201 F. Supp. 3d 924. United States District Court for the Northern District of Illinois.

Shively v. Bowlby. March 5, 1894. 152 U.S. 1.

Snyder v. Massachusetts, 1934. 291 U.S. 97.

Tauber, Alan. 2006. The Empire Forgotten: The Application of the Bill of Rights to U.S. Territories. *Case Western Reserve Law Review 57*, 147–78.

The Late Corp. of the Church of Jesus Christ of Latter-Day Saints v. United States. May 19, 1890. 136 U.S. 1.

Thomas, Brooke. 2001. A Constitution Led by the Flag. In *Foreign in a Domestic Sense: Puerto Rico, American Expansion, and the Constitution,* eds. Christina Duffy Burnett and Burke Marshall. 82–103. Durham, NC: Duke University Press.

Thompson v. Utah. 1898. 170 U.S. 343.

Torruella, Juan. 2007. The Insular Cases: The Establishment of a Regime of Political Apartheid. *University of Pennsylvania Journal of International Law 29(2)*, 283–347.

Trump v. Hawaii. 2018. 138 S. Ct. 2392.

United States v. Gaudin. 1995. 515 U.S. 506.

United States v. Tiede. March 14, 1979. 86 F.R.D. 227. United States Court for Berlin.

United States v. Vaello-Madero. 2018. 313 F. Supp. 3d 370. United States District Court for the District of Puerto Rico.

U.S. Const., Art. IV, §2, cl.2

The Undying Dead: Why a Century after *Balzac v. Porto Rico* the *Insular Cases* Are as Important as Ever

BARTHOLOMEW SPARROW

ABSTRACT

The centennial of *Balzac v. Porto Rico* (1922) is no cause for celebration. The U.S. government's political apartheid with respect to the people and government of Puerto Rico persists. This article reviews the *Insular Cases*. It explains the significance of *Balzac v. Puerto Rico*. And it discusses the U.S. Supreme Court's decision in *Commonwealth of Puerto Rico v. Sanchez Valle et al.* (2016). In *Sanchez Valle* the Court upheld the *Insular Cases* and reinforced the incorporation doctrine, even though Justice Kagan's opinion never cited the *Insular Cases*. This article explains why the *Sanchez Valle* ruling marks a radical departure from previous Court decisions and strengthens the incorporation doctrine, despite the fact that the Court opinion neglected relevant Supreme Court precedents, and ignored long-standing governmental and judicial practices. [Key Words: *Balzac v. Porto Rico*; *Insular Cases*; *Puerto Rico v. Sanchez Valle*; double jeopardy; incorporation doctrine; Puerto Rico]

Bartholomew Sparrow (bhs@austin.utexas.edu) is Professor of Government at The University of Texas at Austin. He studies how the United States interacts with the residents and areas lying beyond the borders of the several states. Sparrow is particularly interested in the political and constitutional dimensions of the United States' relations with its territories, dating from the late eighteenth century through the early twenty-first. He is the author of *The* Insular Cases *and the Emergence of American Empire* (University Press of Kansas, 2006) and three other books.

The fact that we remember *Balzac v. Porto Rico* 258 U.S. 298 (1922) a century after the fact is hardly a cause for celebration. A hundred years have
elapsed since the Nineteenth Amendment and the granting of women's suffrage throughout the United States. The better part of a century has passed
since the Civil Rights Era of the 1950s and 1960s. And nearly a decade has
gone by since the beginning of the Black Lives Matter movement in 2013.[1]
Nonetheless, the precedent established in *Insular Cases* and the legacy
of the "incorporation doctrine"[2] persist. More than two decades into the
twenty-first century, the United States still practices "political apartheid"
vis-à-vis Puerto Rico (Torruella 2007).[3] The "de jure *and* de facto" colonial
condition of Puerto Rico[4] as institutionalized by the Supreme Court in the
Insular Cases endures (Torruella 2007, 346–7—italics in original).

The late Judge Juan Torruella (1985; 2007; 2013) is not alone in his condem-
nation of the *Insular Cases* (also see Álvarez González 1990; González Berdecía
2019; Cabranes 1979; Cepeda Derieux and Weare 2020; Issacharoff et al. 2019;
Kent 2014; Lawson and Sloane 2009; Rivera Ramos 2001; Smith 2015). The
rulings constitute "shameful precedents" (González Berdecía 2016, 136). They
"reflect badly outdated theories of imperialism and racial inferiority" (Netter
2015, 4; also see Torruella 2013). And "[n]o one today," the Puerto Rico Bar
Association comments, "would contend that Puerto Ricans or other territorial
residents are an 'alien race' unprepared for the 'blessings of a free government,'
Downes, 182 U.S. at 287, or 'savage tribes' unworthy of inclusion in American
society. *De Lima,* 182 U.S. at 219 (McKenna, J., dissenting)" (Netter 2015, 21). "[T]
he Supreme Court's decisions in the *Insular Cases* and the 'territorial incorporation doctrine' are contrary to the text and history of the Constitution," Professor
Cuison-Villazor told members of Congress in 2021; they "rest on racial views
and stereotypes from the era of *Plessy v. Ferguson* that have long been rejected,
are contrary to the Nation's most basic constitutional principles, and should be
rejected as having no place in U.S. constitutional law" (Cuison-Villazor 2021, 1).

Yet the *Insular Cases* remain good law[5] and Puerto Ricans remain subject
to the U.S. government's plenary power over both political procedure and
policy substance (González Berdecía 2016, 140–1; Terrasa 1997). Even more
notably, the incorporation doctrine has been reaffirmed and further legitimated with the Supreme Court's pathbreaking decision in *Commonwealth of
Puerto Rico v. Sanchez Valle et al.* (2016) (also see González Berdecía 2016),[6]

despite the fact that the ruling in *Sanchez Valle* nowhere refers to the *Insular Cases* or the incorporation doctrine.[7]

"The Undying Dead" addresses each of these observations. First, the article explains why *Balzac v. Porto Rico* constitutes the capstone of the *Insular Cases* (Burnett and Marshall 2002, 20n.3; Rivera Ramos 2001, 94–100; Rivera Ramos 2015, 35–6; Torruella 1985, 93–100; Sparrow 2006, 199–204). It summarizes the main points of the *Insular Cases* and explains the significance of Chief Justice Taft's ruling in *Balzac v. Porto Rico*. Second, it discusses the Supreme Court's decision in *Sanchez Valle* and why the Court's ruling both affirmed the importance of the *Insular Cases* and further legitimated the incorporation doctrine. Third, the article explores the inconsistency between Justice Kagan's omission of the *Insular Cases* in her opinion in *Sanchez Valle* and her legitimation of the incorporation doctrine. I submit that the Court's non-citation of the *Insular Cases* reflects a broader phenomenon: that the *Insular Cases* have joined a set of infamous Court decisions jurists have chosen to ignore because the opinions in these cases express culturally unacceptable values, even as the decisions and their attendant doctrines remain good law.

I. *Balzac* as Capstone

The *Insular Cases*. The *Insular Cases* established a new constitutional status for the island groups acquired by the United States after the Spanish-American War: Puerto Rico, the Philippines, and Guam (via the 1898 Treaty of Paris), Hawai'i (May 1898) and American Samoa (1899), which were annexed at almost the same time, the U.S. Virgin Islands in 1917, and the Northern Marianas, added much later, in 1976. They invented a novel, *post hoc* distinction between the United States' "incorporated" territories and its "non-incorporated" (or "unincorporated") territories (*Downes v. Bidwell* 1901, 252–6, 278–81, 28–344, White, J., concurring). The former territories were "surely destined for statehood" and integral to the United States, hence the Constitution applied in full; the latter were "appurtenant" to, but not part of, the United States, and therefore could "be governed under the power existing in Congress to make laws for such territories, and subject to such constitutional restrictions upon the powers of that body as are applicable to the situation" (*Downes v. Bidwell* 1901, 287, 293, 341–2, White, J., concurring).

The Supreme Court's decisions in *Downes* and others of the *Insular Cases* upended the *ex proprio vigore* doctrine of Chief Justice Marshall and Chief Justice Taney. For Chief Justice Marshall, the "United States" "is the name given to our great republic, which is composed of the states *and the territories*" (*Loughborough v. Blake* 1820, 5 Wheat. 317, 319—emphasis added). "The district of Columbia, or the territory west of the Missouri, is not less within the United States, than Maryland or Pennsylvania." Accordingly, the Constitution required "uniformity in the imposition of imposts, duties, and excises" throughout the states, territories, and District of Columbia (*Loughborough v. Blake* 1820, 5 Wheat. 317, 319). Later, Chief Justice Taney similarly commented that "[t]here is no power given by the Constitution to the Federal Government to establish or maintain colonies bordering on the United States or at a distance, to be ruled and government at its own pleasure" (*Dred Scott v. Sandford* 1856, 432).[8]

With Congress's ratification of the treaty on February 6, 1899, Puerto Rico and the Philippines now belonged to United States.

For Justice White, following Lowell's "third view" (Lowell 1899), the territory clause (Art IV, Sec. 3, Cl. 2)[9] gave Congress "a free hand" in handling its new territories (Rowe 1901, 41; Torruella 2007, 290)—especially since Article IX of the 1898 Treaty of Paris let Congress determine "the civil rights and political status of the native inhabitants of the territories hereby ceded to the United States" (*De Lima v. Bidwell* 1901, 196; *Downes* 1901, 267–8, 285–6, 290–2, 315; White, J., concurring). Accordingly, "what particular provision of the Constitution is applicable, generally speaking, in all cases, involves an inquiry into the situation of the territory and its relations to the United States" (*Downes* 1901, 299; White, J., concurring). Congress, for Justice White and eventually all the justices, was to conduct that inquiry.

The exception to Congress's authority over areas of U.S. sovereignty is the president's war powers, such as those exerted over the United States' Caribbean and Philippine island possessions before the 1898 Treaty of Paris.

With Congress's ratification of the treaty on February 6, 1899, Puerto Rico and the Philippines now belonged to United States. The Supreme Court therefore denied the U.S. government's authority to tax trade and upheld the clause during that period, before the Treaty of Paris (Art. I Sec. 8, Cl. 1), per its decisions in *De Lima, Goetze v. United States* and *Crossman v. United States* (1901), *Dooley v. United States* (1901) [*Dooley I*], and *Armstrong v. United States* (1901).

But when Congress passed the Foraker Act in 1900, which imposed tariffs on goods shipped from Puerto Rico to the 45 mainland American states (among its other provisions), the uniformity clause no longer applied to Puerto Rican trade, per the Supreme Court's decisions in *Downes v Bidwell* (1901) and *Dooley v. United States* (1901) [*Dooley II*], both of which affirmed the legitimacy of the tariffs imposed on goods shipped within the United States. And because Congress had not created new U.S. wartime powers during the Philippine rebellion, the Court held that tariffs levied under the July 1898 presidential order on the war with Spain had been superseded by the Treaty of Paris and the Act of July 1, 1902, which established an organized territorial government in the Philippines (*Lincoln v. United States*; *Warner, Barnes & Co. v. United States* 1905).

When President Howard Taft insisted on a rehearing of *Lincoln* and *Warner, Barnes*, the Court again ruled against the executive branch (*Lincoln v. United States*; *Warner, Barnes & Co. v. United States* 1906). Because the Act of July 1, 1902, did not use "clear and unambiguous language" to ensure the continuation of wartime powers of taxation (*Lincoln*; *Warner, Barnes* 1906, 487), the insurrection tariffs were invalid.[10] The U.S. Congress may have *appeared* to ratify the Philippine wartime tariffs in the Act of July 1, 1902, the Chief Justice ruled, but Congress had to do so *explicitly* (*Lincoln*; *Warner, Barnes* 1906, 498–9). By the same token, when Congress responded by taxing Philippine trade with the mainland United States, and when Philippine businesses then sued to recover their confiscated taxes, the Court ruled in favor of the U.S. government. If Congress explicitly imposed a tariff on trade with the Philippines, Justice White ruled, then the uniformity clause no longer applied (*United States v. Heinszen & Co.* 1907).[11]

The same held for disputes involving criminal law and political rights: the Court could deny the residents of the new territories the protections of the Constitution (Sparrow 2006, 169, 181–5). In *Hawaii v. Mankichi* (1903) the Court refused to extend Fifth and Sixth amendment rights to a Hawaiian man charged with murder. "We place our decision...upon the ground that the two rights [trial by jury and grand jury indictment in criminal cases] are not fundamental in their nature," Justice Brown ruled. Instead, the two rights "concern merely a method of procedure which sixty years of practice had shown to be suited to the conditions of the islands and well calculated to conserve the rights of their citizens to their lives, their property, and their wellbeing" (*Hawaii v. Mankichi* 1903, 218).

The same logic applied to the right to a jury trial and indictment by grand jury; the provisions of the Fifth and Sixth amendments did not apply *ex proprio vigore* to the Philippines or any other non-incorporated U.S. territory. The rulings in "the so-called '*Insular Cases*,'" Justice Day ruled in a Philippine libel case, rendered "superfluous any attempt" to question the constitutional status of the territories (*Dorr v. United States* 1904, 143). The *Downes* decision had "settled" the matter: "[u]ntil Congress shall see fit to incorporate territory ceded by treaty into the United States," it had the authority to govern "subject to such constitutional restrictions as are applicable to the situation" (*Dorr* 1904, 143). Ten years later, Justice Pitney rejected the application of the Sixth Amendment's right to "be informed of the nature and cause of the accusation" in a Philippines case (*Ocampo v. United States* 1914, citing *Hawaii* [1903], *Dorr* [1904], and *Dowdell v. United States* [1911]).

Suffrage, citizenship, and political procedures of "Anglo-Saxon jurisprudence" were "artificial or remedial rights...peculiar to our own system of jurisprudence" (*Downes* 1901, 382, White, J., concurring). These were to be contrasted with "certain principles of natural justice inherent in the Anglo-Saxon character which need no expression" (*Downes* 1901, 381, White, J., concurring). These "natural rights" included religious freedom, "the right to personal liberty and individual property; to freedom of speech and of the press; to free access to courts of justice, to due process of law, and to an equal protection of the laws; to immunities from unreasonable searches and seizures, as well as cruel and unusual punishments" (*Downes* 1901, 382, White, J., concurring). The Court upheld these distinctions in subsequent rulings in the *Insular Cases*, which granted the extradition of criminals (*Kopel v. Bingham* 1909), per the extradition clause (Art. IV, Sec. 2, Cl. 2), due process with respect to the Fifth Amendment's takings clause (*Ochoa v. Hernandez*

1913), the Eighth Amendment's protection against "cruel and unusual punishment" (*Weems v. United States* 1910), and the Eleventh Amendment's
immunity from suits (*Porto Rico v. Rosaly* 1913).

Balzac v. Porto Rico. The Supreme Court's unanimous decision in
Balzac v. Porto Rico cemented the incorporation doctrine into place. Chief
Justice Taft established that even though Puerto Ricans were statutory U.S.
citizens per the 1917 ruling, and even though Puerto Ricans enjoyed other
rights and privileges as Americans, the Court could deny Puerto Ricans
certain constitutional protections—specifically, in *Balzac v. Porto Rico*, the
Sixth and Seventh Amendments' guarantees of a jury trial for Jesús M.
Balzac, a newspaper editor (*El Baluarte*, Arecibo) charged with libel.

Not only had Puerto Ricans been granted U.S. citizenship in 1917, per the
Jones-Shafroth Act ("Jones Act"), Puerto Rico was part of the United States
in other ways as well. Puerto Rico had a district court within the federal court
system (an Art. IV court), and the U.S. Supreme Court served as the appellate
court for the Supreme Court of Puerto Rico. Puerto Rican waters were within
the navigable waters of the United States, and Puerto Rico came within U.S.
trade and immigration laws. U.S. copyright and other laws applied to Puerto
Rico, unless it was explicitly excluded, and Puerto Ricans used U.S. postage.
Puerto Rican men could attend West Point and the Naval Academy, and they
would soon serve in the Great War (Sparrow and Lamm 2017, 303–4).

Even so, Chief Justice Taft ruled that in the absence of Congress's "express
declaration" of the territorial incorporation of Puerto Rico, the Constitution
does not fully extend to Puerto Ricans (*Balzac* 1922, 304–6).[12] The Chief
Justice (who had previously served as U.S. Solicitor General from 1890 to 1892
and as the first civilian governor of the Philippines from 1901 to 1904) rejected
Balzac's right to a jury trial. Taft pointed out that the second section of the
Jones Act "included every one of the guaranties of the Federal Constitution
except those relating to indictment by a grand jury in the case of infamous
crimes and the right of trial by jury in civil and criminal cases" (*Balzac* 1922,
306). "The power to govern territory, implied in the right to acquire it, and
given to Congress in the Constitution in Article IV, §3," the Chief Justice
quoted from *Dorr* (1904, 149), "does not require [Congress] to enact for ceded
territory, not made a part of the United States by Congressional action, a system of laws which shall include the right of trial by jury" (*Balzac* 1922, 305).

Now that Justice White's opinion in *Downes* had "become the settled law of the court," the Constitution did not "carry" into a territory "through its own force," at least not "without legislation" (*Balzac* 1922, 305).

Had Congress "intended to incorporate Porto Rico into the Union by this act" and extend the entire Bill of Rights, "why," Chief Justice Taft asked, "was it thought necessary to create for it a Bill of Rights and carefully exclude trial by jury?" (*Balzac* 1922, 307). Congress had not done so, he reasoned, because Puerto Ricans were not "citizens trained to the exercise of the responsibilities of jurors"; they had not been "brought up in fundamentally popular government" and were unaccustomed to "a conception of the impartial attitude jurors must assume" (*Balzac* 1922, 310).

The *Balzac* decision marked the victory of the incorporation doctrine in three ways. The Court's ruling underscored the breadth and flexibility of the incorporation doctrine (Burnett 2005; Erman 2019, 55; Rivera Ramos 2001, 138–9; Sparrow 2006, 208–9; Thomas 2001, 87–8). In the absence of Congress's "express declaration" of incorporation, the U.S. government could refuse the right to a jury trial (*Balzac* 1922, 305–6), notwithstanding that Puerto Ricans were statutory U.S. citizens.

Second, the ruling was unanimous. It had been only Justice White, joined by Justice Shiras and Justice McKenna in *Downes*, who had adopted Lowell's the "third view" in support of the incorporation doctrine. The crucial decisions in *Dorr* and *Rassmussen v. United States* (1905) had been accompanied by a dissenting opinion (Justice Harlan in the former case) and concurring opinions (Justice Harlan and Justice Brown in the latter). So, with the ruling in *Balzac*,[13] Justice White's position finally and fully prevailed.

The decisions in the Insular Cases *remain operative.*

Lastly, it was an almost entirely reconstituted Supreme Court that affirmed the *Insular Cases*. Except for Justice McKenna (ret. 1925),[14] none of the justices of the 1901 Fuller Court were still on the bench: not Justice White (d. 1921), not Justice Harlan (d. 1911), not Chief Justice Fuller (d. 1910), not Justice Brewer (d. 1910), not Justice Peckham (d. 1909), not Justice Brown (ret. 1906), not Justice

Shiras (ret. 1903), and not Justice Gray (d. 1902). A generation after *Downes* and the original *Insular Cases* of 1901, an essentially new Supreme Court affirmed the *Insular Cases* and the incorporation doctrine.

In short, with the *Balzac* decision the Court manifested Judge Torruella's "political apartheid." Because of the "different origin and different language" of the United States' "distant ocean communities" (*Balzac* 1922, 310–1), the Court allowed Congress and the federal government to discriminate on the basis of geography. The "foreign-ness" of Puerto Ricans' ancestry, as the Chief Justice put it—Puerto Ricans have a mixed European, indigenous Indian, and African ancestry—coincided with their Caribbean island location; "locality" was "determinative of the application of the Constitution" (*Balzac* 1922, 309).

The decisions in the *Insular Cases* remain operative. The *Insular Cases* have "never been overruled," Gerald Neuman observes, "despite the tectonic shifts in constitutional law, international law, and human rights conceptions that have intervened since 1901" (Neuman 2015, xiv).

This need not mean that the Supreme Court and federal courts have not issued decisions that address the legacy of the *Insular Cases* and incorporation doctrine.

II. *Puerto Rico v. Sanchez Valle*

Background. In 2015 the Supreme Court of Puerto Rico ruled that the Puerto Rican government was not sovereign for the purpose of the Fifth Amendment's prohibition against double jeopardy.[15] The Puerto Rican government could not separately charge Luis Sánchez Valle and Jaime Gómez Vásquez for the illegal possession and sale of firearms because the U.S. government had already indicted the two men. The Puerto Rico government appealed to the U.S. Supreme Court, arguing that Puerto Rico was effectively a "state" for the purpose of the double jeopardy carve-out allowed the American states.

The Court heard argument on *Commonwealth of Puerto Rico v. Sanchez Valle* on January 13, 2016 and issued its decision on June 9. Justice Kagan wrote the 5,700-word opinion for the Court, joined by Chief Justice Roberts, Justice Kennedy, and Justice Alito. Justice Ginsburg wrote a concurring opinion, joined by Justice Thomas. Justice Thomas also wrote a separate concurring opinion.

And Justice Breyer wrote a dissenting opinion, joined by Justice Sotomayor.[16]

The Court determined that the government of Puerto Rico was *not* sovereign with respect to the constitutional prohibition against double jeopardy (*Sanchez Valle* 2016, 1869).[17] Whereas "[a] state does not derive its powers from the United States," Justice Kagan proclaimed, "a territory does" (*Sanchez Valle* 2016, 1873). States are the "ultimate source" of their prosecutorial power by the authority of the Tenth Amendment (*Sanchez Valle* 2016, 1869, 1870, 1871, 1872, 1874, 1875), just as the Indian tribes are "self-governing sovereign political communities" (*United States* v. *Wheeler* 1978, 322–3, in *Sanchez Valle* 2016, 1872).[18] Given that both the states' and the tribes' independent sources of sovereignty precede the U.S. Constitution (*Sanchez Valle* 2016, 1873 n.5), the double jeopardy clause does not bar the federal and state governments from prosecuting the same crime. Indian tribes (the Navajo in *Wheeler*) and federal prosecutors can therefore both issue criminal indictments (*Sanchez Valle* 2016, 1872).

In contrast, Puerto Rico's prosecutorial authority is not separate from that of the federal government for the purposes of double jeopardy (*Sanchez Valle* 2016, 1874–5). Justice Kagan recognized that Public Law 600 in 1950, which granted Puerto Rico the right to convene delegates and draft a constitution, and that Public Law 447 in 1952, which approved the constitution (and which the Puerto Rican electorate ratified via referendum) (*Sanchez Valle* 2016, 1868–9, 1874–6; Lewis 1953), created "a new kind of political entity"—a commonwealth "still closely associated with the United States but governed in accordance with, and exercising self-rule through, a popularly ratified constitution" (*Sanchez Valle* 2016, 1874). But this later incarnation of Puerto Rico did not change the "ultimate source" of Puerto Rico's "prosecutorial power" (*Sanchez Valle* 2016, 1869, 1870, 1871, 1872, 1874, 1875).

"[I]n the early decades of this last century," per the Court's decision in *Puerto Rico v. Shell Co.* (1937), the Court had determined that "U.S. territories—including an earlier incarnation of Puerto Rico itself—are not sovereigns distinct from the United States" (*Sanchez Valle* 2016, 1873). The Court's decisions in *Shell Co.* (1937) and *Heath v. Alabama* (1985) had established that "the territorial and federal laws" in Puerto Rico (and earlier the Philippines) were "creations emanating from the same sovereignty" (*Sanchez Valle* 2016, 1873). Even the passage of P.L. 600, the ratification of the Constitution of Puerto Rico, and Congress's endorsement and approval of the Commonwealth of Puerto Rico—giving rise to "a new chapter of democratic self-government (*Sanchez Valle* 2016, 1876)—did "not break the chain" of Congress's ultimate authority over the territories, according to Justice Kagan and the Court (2016, 1875-6). Puerto Rico, as a U.S. territory, was *ipso facto* the creation of the U.S. government. The fact that Congress had not previously chosen to exercise its power to veto Puerto Rican laws did not mean that it had relinquished the authority to do so. Congress could not "airbrush...erase or otherwise rewrite its own foundational role in conferring political authority" (*Sanchez Valle* 2016, 1876).

The Radicalism of *Puerto Rico v. Sanchez Valle*. With the ruling, the Court took the unprecedented step of disregarding the U.S. Congress's and national government's own policies with respect to the political status of the citizens and government of Puerto Rico and of asserting its own prerogative instead.

The hallmark of the *Insular Cases* was the Supreme Court's deference to Congress, given that the territory clause conferred Congress with the authority over the territories and possessions of the United States. In none of the *Insular Cases* or in subsequent disputes over the extraterritorial application of the Constitution (e.g., *Reid v. Covert* [1956]; *United States v. Verdugo-Urquidez* [1990]) had the Supreme Court ignored or rejected duly enacted congressional legislation. If Congress were explicit on how particular constitutional provisions extended to territories, as Chief Justice Taft argued in *Balzac*, then the Court followed Congress's lead. Only if Congress were ambiguous or silent on incorporation could the Court use its discretion as to how the U.S. Constitution applied to territorial disputes.

The Court's acceptance of Congress's guidance was evident in its decisions in *Downes* (1901), *Dooley II* (1901), and *Heinszen* (1907), which (as we have seen) followed the Foraker Act, the Act of July 1, 1902, and the Act of June 30, 1906 (34 Stat. 636), respectively. Other *Insular Cases* also manifested the Court's reliance on congressional policy. The plaintiff in *Kopel v. Bingham* (1909), who was to be extradited to Puerto Rico, sued the New York police commissioner on the grounds that the extradition clause (Art. IV, Sec. 2, Cl. 2) applied only to the states. Chief Justice Fuller denied Kopel's suit for habeas corpus, finding that it was "long" established that the "power to extradite fugitive criminals, as between State and Territory is as complete as between one State and another." Congress in 1793 had already "made provision for the demand and surrender of fugitives by the governors of the territories as well as of the states" (*Kopel v. Bingham* 1909, 474); thus, the plaintiff could be extradited to Puerto Rico.

So, too, with the Court's unanimous decision in *Board of Public Utility Commissioners v. Ynchausti & Co.* (1920), when Philippine coastal shippers charged that their uncompensated carriage of the mail was tantamount to the "taking of property." In his ruling, Chief Justice White allowed that the Bill of Rights applied to the Philippines, but he noted that Congress in 1904 had institutionalized the long-standing custom of the Philippines' regulation of coastwise trade. Because of Congress's delegation of power to the Philippines territorial government, there was no taking of property. Chief Justice White wrote that "if the Philippine government possessed the plenary power, under the sanction of Congress, to limit the right to engage in the coastwise trade to those who agree to carry the mails free," then "it is impossible to conceive how either the guaranty by the Bill of Rights of due process or its prohibition against the taking of private property for public use without compensation can have the slightest application to the case" (*Board v. Ynchausti* 1920, 404).

The same logic obtained in cases of double jeopardy. When Congress extended the Bill of Rights to the Philippines in 1902 and explicitly granted Philippine residents protection against being put twice in jeopardy,[19] the Court upheld the law of the organized territorial government and disallowed double jeopardy (*Kepner v. United States* 1904; *Mendezona v. United States* 1904).[20] It also did so in *Grafton v. United States* (1907), a case in which a unanimous Court again upheld the prohibition against double jeopardy.[21] The decision did not "require determination of the question whether the jeopardy clause became the law of the islands after the ratification of the treaty without Congressional action, as the *act of Congress made it the law of these possessions* when the accused was tried and convicted," Justice Harlan wrote, quoting from *Kepner* (*Grafton* 1907, 345—emphasis added).[22]

Conversely, because Congress had *not* explicitly extended constitutional guarantees to Hawaiian residents in the 1898 Newlands Resolution, the Court denied the plaintiff's right to a twelve-person jury (*Hawaii v. Mankichi* 1903). For Justice Brown the answer was self-evident. The Newlands Resolution stated that the "municipal legislation of the Hawaiian Islands, not enacted for the fulfillment of the treaties so extinguished and not inconsistent with this joint resolution nor contrary to the Constitution of the United States nor to any existing treaty of the United States, shall remain in force *until the Congress of the United States shall otherwise determine*" (*Hawaii v. Mankichi* 1903, 209— emphasis added). And Congress had not done anything to change Hawaiian law. Chief Justice Taft used identical reasoning in *Balzac*.

"Puerto Rico has a relationship to the United States" without "parallel in our history."

In *Rassmussen v. United States* (1905), the Court held that Alaska was incorporated, consistent with Article III of the 1867 treaty with Russia,[23] which stated that "the inhabitants of the ceded territory" were to "be admitted to the enjoyment of all the rights, advantages, and immunities of citizens of the United States, and shall be maintained and protected in the free enjoyment of their liberty, property and religion."[24] Given that Congress had not passed legislation specifying the incorporation of Alaska and its residents, Justice White could have easily used the Court's discretion *not* to incorporate Alaska. But Justice White and the Court proclaimed the sparsely populated and remote Alaska to be an incorporated territory. Six years later, Congress officially "extended" the "Constitution...and all the laws thereof which are not locally inapplicable...[to] the said Territory as elsewhere in the United States" to organize a territorial government and establish the Territory of Alaska (Public Law No. 334, 1912).

Two late twentieth-century cases continued the pattern set in the *Insular Cases*. In *Califano v. Torres* (1978), the Burger Court refused to extend Supplemental Security Income payments to a U.S. citizen travelling to Puerto Rico. The SSI program explicitly defined the "United States" as "the 50 States and the District of Columbia" (*Califano v. Torres* 1978, 2), whereas "Puerto Rico has a relationship to the United States" without "parallel in our history," the Court declared in the per curiam decision, citing *Balzac, Dorr,* and *Downes* (*Califano v. Torres* 1978, 3fn 4). Travel to Puerto Rico did not interfere with Congress's authority to distinguish Puerto Rico from the states, as long as there were sound reasons for doing so; "the problems of the poor and the needy are not subject to a constitutional strait-jacket" (*Califano v. Torres* 1978, 5).

The Court argued the same in *Harris v. Rosario* (1980), a dispute over the extension of Aid to Families with Dependent Children (and another per curiam decision). Congress could "treat Puerto Rico differently from States so long as there is a rational basis for its actions" (*Harris v. Rosario* 1980, 651–2).[25] In neither case did the Court investigate the assumptions of and reasoning behind Congress's decision to impose one set of standards on the provision of public benefits to the residents of the American states and another to the residents of the U.S. territories.

Historically, the U.S. Supreme Court has affirmed Congress' authority over the territories and their residents. This authority could be exercised directly, following specific legislation (as with territories being treated as states for the purposes of extradition dating since 1793, as litigated in *Kopel v. Bingham* 1909), or, more usually, indirectly, though the authority vested in the territorial governments established through acts of Congress (per the prohibition against double jeopardy under the Act of July 2, 1902, as litigated in *Kepner* 1904 and *Grafton* 1907). On other occasions the Court could infer congressional intent, as it did in *Rassmussen*. Were Congress to pass new legislation for the territories, however, as it did after the rehearing of *Lincoln v. United States* and *Warner Barnes* (1906), then the Court heeded the new federal law, per *Heinszen* (1907).

Government Sanction. The other two branches of U.S. government and the international community echoed Congress's approval of the Puerto Rico Constitution. All agreed that Puerto Rico had been delegated "considerable autonomy" in "local matters, [where] the sphere of action and the methods of government bear a resemblance to that of any State of the Union" (S. Rep. No. 1720, 82d Cong., 2d Sess., 6 [1952], quoted in *Sanchez Valle* 2016, 1882, Breyer, J., dissenting). The adjective "considerable" and the phrase "bear a resemblance" are significant: members of the 81st and 82nd Congress did not think that the presence of a republican constitution in Puerto Rico would "change Puerto Rico's political, social, and economic relationship to the United States" (Senate 1950b, 27); U.S. sovereignty and Congress's plenary power remained.

U.S public officials emphasized Puerto Rico's self-government; they did not claim Puerto Rico's independent sovereignty. Upon signing P.L. 600 and P.L. 447, President Truman declared that the new constitution "vest[s] in the people of Puerto Rico" complete "authority and responsibility for local self-government" (*Sanchez Valle* 2016, 1882, Breyer, J., dissenting). The Constitution of Puerto Rico was "a proud document that embodies the best of our democratic heritage" (Truman 1952). President Kennedy subsequently circulated a memorandum stating that Puerto Rico's relationship with the United States and its "Commonwealth structure" "provide for self-government in respect of internal affairs and administration, subject only to the applicable provisions of the Federal Constitution, the Puerto Rican Federal Relations Act [*i.e.*, P.L. 600], and the acts of Congress authorizing and approving the constitution" [*i.e.*, P.L. 447] (*Sanchez Valle* 2016, 1882, Breyer, J., dissenting). Neither president denied the United States' plenary power under the territory clause.

This was also what the international community believed. Chapter XI of the United Nations Charter obligated the United States and other countries with non-self-governing territories (e.g., Australia, Belgium, Denmark, France, Great Britain, the Netherlands, and Portugal) to establish self-government in their territories. Until then, they were to regularly inform the U.N. Secretary General of the conditions in the territories and (Heefner 2005, 551). U.S. officials said as much upon signing the U.N. Charter; "the United States would 'develop self-government' in its Territories" and "promised change" (Art. 73[b], 59 Stat. 1048, June 26, 1945, T. S. No. 993 [U.N. Charter], in *Sanchez Valle* 2016, 1880, Breyer, J., dissenting; also see González Berdecía 2016, 139 n.223).[26]

After the creation of the Commonwealth of Puerto Rico, a majority vote in the U.N. General Assembly on November 27, 1953, favored discontinuing the requirement that the United States issue annual reports on Puerto Rico as a "Non-Self-Governing Territory" (per the provisions of Article 73[*e*] of the U.N. Charter). U.S. Ambassador to the U.N. Henry Cabot Lodge, Jr. remarked on the significance of Puerto Rico's "new Commonwealth status": "This is the kind of progress to self-government contemplated by the United Nations Charter. This is the democratic pattern of the free world—of the goals set and hopes realized" (Lodge 1953). Yet, and revealingly, Ambassador Lodge's most powerful language did not come from his own words or those of President Truman, but the resolution of the Puerto Rican delegates at the Constitutional Convention: "Thus we attain the goal of complete self-government, the last vestiges of colonialism having disappeared in the principle of Compact, and we enter into an era of new developments in democratic civilization" (Lodge 1953).

Further indicative of the equivocal nature of Puerto Rico's political status, fewer U.N. member states supported the resolution (26) than—in combination—opposed (16) and abstained (18). Delegates from Third World states, especially from Latin America and the Soviet Bloc, understood that Puerto Rico's "new Commonwealth status" obtained at the sufferance of Congress and federal government. Only then would Puerto Rico enjoy a "democracy within a democracy" (U.S. Senate 1950b, 23). U.S. Rep. Frances Bolton, a member of the U.S. delegation to the U.N., was therefore overstating matters when she claimed, "there exists a bilateral compact of association between the people of Puerto Rico and the United States which has been accepted by both and which in accordance with judicial decisions may not be amended without common consent" (Bolton 1953).

The fact that Congress retained its authority under the territory clause and that Puerto Rico remained an unincorporated U.S. territory did not mean that there was not significant change—per P.L. 600 and P.L. 447, and President Truman's and Ambassador Lodge's statements. U.S. Presidents, their top advisers, State Department officials, and members of Congress were aware of the postwar wave of anticolonialism and decolonialization that pressured Great Britain, France, Spain, Belgium, the Netherlands, and other imperial powers to either reform their colonial laws or decolonize. American politicians and government officials sought to avoid the charge by Soviet Bloc and Third World politicians that the United States was denying its own territorial citizens—as well as African Americans, Latinos, and American Indians—the very same rights and liberties the United States was intent on promoting and demanding around the world (Heefner 2005, 549–55; Dudziak 2000; Layton 2000).[27] A constitution for Puerto Rico would "free both Puerto Ricans and the people of the rest of the States of the malicious accusation of colonialism so constantly wielded against them by Communist groups in Latin America," Puerto Rican governor Muñoz-Marín told U.S. senators (U.S. Senate 1950a, 8). And were the U.S. House of Representatives to reject the Puerto Rican Constitution, Rep. Frank T. Bow (R Ohio) warned his colleagues, it would "feed the propaganda mills of Soviet Russia" (CQ Almanac 1952).[28]

In sum, "Congress's plenary power over Puerto Rico" coexisted with Puerto Rico's newly established "American governmental structure, consisting of three independent branches of government—legislative, executive, and judicial," an associate justice of the Puerto Rico Supreme Court commented (U.S. Senate 1950b, 21). With its new constitution, Puerto Rico "ha[d] all the essential powers for effective local self-government, including the power of taxation...[and] like any State the power to enact, to enforce, and to interpret its own laws" (U.S. Senate 1950b, 22). Rather than merely giving "lip service to self-government as a principle," Congress now "translated theory into practice" (U.S. Senate 1950b, 22).

A few years later the Johnson administration confirmed Puerto Rico's changed relationship vis-à-vis the U.S. government. In 1967 State Department officials informed the U.N. General Assembly that Puerto Rico had achieved "the full measure of self-government" and that it would henceforth have "freedom from control or interference by the Congress in respect to internal government and administration" (*Sanchez Valle* 2016, 1882). The General Assembly accepted the statement as indicative of Puerto Rico's "new political status" (*Sanchez Valle* 2016, 1882-1883, Breyer, J., dissenting; Blocher and Gulati 2018, 254-256).

This is what Justice Breyer argued in his dissent: the creation of the Commonwealth of Puerto Rico as an "organized...body politic by the people of Puerto Rico under their own constitution" produced "significant changes in Puerto Rico's governmental structure" (*Sanchez Valle* 2016, 1883; Breyer, J., dissenting; Lewis 1953).[29] These differences in Puerto Rico's governmental structure were "subject to congressional regulation," to be sure, but the changes nonetheless "distinguish[ed] Puerto Rico's laws from those of other Territories" (*Sanchez Valle* 2016, 1883; Breyer, J., dissenting).

Specifically, Puerto Rico was "an independently sovereign source of its criminal laws" for the purposes of the double jeopardy clause, according to Justice Department officials (*United States v. López Andino* 1987). In *López Andino* the Court accepted the U.S. government's position that "Puerto Rico is to be treated as a state for purposes of the double jeopardy clause" [citation omitted] (*Sanchez Valle* 2016, 1883, Breyer, J., dissenting). For "over a period of more than 50 years," in fact, lower courts had recognized that "Puerto Rico's laws are 'state statutes' within the terms of the Three-Judge Court Act,"[30] and they had endorsed the position "that Puerto Rico's people (and not Congress) are the 'source' of Puerto Rico's local criminal laws" (*Sanchez Valle* 2016, 1883, Breyer, J., dissenting).

Not only had Congress authorized Puerto Rico to govern itself and not only had Congress, the Executive, and the judiciary for decades allowed it to do precisely that, but Congress had not done anything to amend or overturn its legislation of 1950 and 1952 and consequently undermine or negate Puerto Rico's self-government. It had not countermanded or revoked P.L. 600; it had not repealed or amended the Puerto Rico constitution; it had not placed the Puerto Rico Department of Justice in receivership; and it had not rewritten Puerto Rico's criminal laws. "[N]ever—I repeat, *never*," Justice Breyer stated, had Congress "vetoed or modified a local criminal law enacted in Puerto Rico" (*Sanchez Valle* 2016, 1883; Breyer, J., dissenting—italics in original). Congress had the authority to make such interventions—"there [being] no change of sovereignty" (U.S. Senate 1950b, 22)—but it had not chosen to do so.

The Court's rejection of Puerto Rico's sovereignty under the "separate sovereigns" doctrine in the *Sanchez Valle* ruling conflicted, then, with Congress's and the U.S. government's long-lasting existing policies. For the Court to assert that "the degree to which an entity exercises self-governance—whether autonomously managing its own affairs or continually submitting to outside direction—plays no role in the analysis" (*Sanchez Valle* 2016, 1870) thus ignores the laws of the 82nd and 83rd Congresses and neglects the precedents in *Kepner, Grafton, Kopel v. Bingham,* and *Board v. Ynchausti* decisions, where, as we have seen, the Court followed Congress's explicit territorial policy on double jeopardy, extradition, and the taking of property in the Philippines or Puerto Rico. Chief Justice White was unequivocal on this point of Congress's plenary power: when "a particular activity...is *as the result of power conferred by Congress*...it is obvious that the exaction of such a duty, as such prerequisite condition," cannot be unconstitutional (*Board v. Ynchausti* 1920, 405—emphasis added).

Justice Kagan ruled it was. Rather than deferring to decades of congressional and governmental policy and rather than following Congress's lead on the fundamentally political questions of how to apply the Constitution to the territories (Burnett and Marshall 2001; Rivera Ramos 2001, 11-22; Sparrow 2006, 80-85, passim; Vignarajah 2010), Justice Kagan held that the guarantee against double jeopardy depended on the "ultimate source" of sovereignty (following *United States v. Wheeler*). But—and this is the odd twist in the Court opinion—Justice Kagan claimed Congress to be the "ultimate source" of Puerto Rico's sovereignty, even though in none of the *Insular Cases* that litigated the guarantee against double jeopardy had the Court tried to establish the "furthest-back" or "ultimate" source of the territorial government's authority (*Sanchez Valle* 2016, 1875).[31] In the *Insular Cases* the Court had simply ruled on the direct or proximate source of governmental authority— whether federal law, national treaty, or presidential war powers.

Justice Kagan's reliance on the *Grafton* decision (*Sanchez Valle* 2016, 1873, 1873 n.5, 1874) brings the poverty of her ruling into further relief. What had mattered in *Grafton* and other *Insular Cases* was not the "ultimate source" of the guarantee against double jeopardy, as Justice Harlan determined, but Congress's enacted territorial policy: the Court was bound by the Act of July 1, 1902 (*Grafton* 1907, 345, 352)[32]—the same basis by which the Court had ruled to protect against double jeopardy in *Kepner* (*Grafton* 1907, 345) and *Mendezona* (1904).[33]

This was how the Court had previously made its decision in *United States v. Lara* (2004), a case concerning the sovereign power of Indian tribes to prosecute non-tribe Indians. Congress was authorized under the Constitution "to permit tribes, as an exercise of their inherent tribal authority, to prosecute nonmember Indians" (*Lara* 2004, 210). And Congress had done exactly that; thus, it could exercise its power "to modify the degree of autonomy enjoyed by a dependent sovereign that is not a State" in the instances of Hawai'i, the Northern Marianas, Puerto Rico, and the Philippines (*Lara* 2004, 203). "[T]he Spirit Lake Tribe's prosecution of Lara did not amount to an exercise of federal power, and the Tribe acted in its capacity of a separate sovereign. Consequently, the Double Jeopardy Clause does not prohibit the Federal Government from proceeding with the present prosecution for a discrete *federal* offense. *Heath*, 474 U. S., at 88" (*Lara* 2004, 210—italics in original). This was the situation upon the establishment of the Constitution of Puerto Rico and its three-branch republican government.

"Puerto Rico's people (and not Congress) are the 'source' of Puerto Rico's local criminal laws" (*Sanchez Valle* 2016, 1883, Breyer, J., dissenting).

At the same time, Puerto Rico was and remains subject to the territory clause, to Congress, and to the U.S. government. And even as Puerto Rico remains subject to congressional regulation, as with the passage of PROMESA and the creation of the Financial Oversight Management Board, Puerto Rico is able to pass and enforce its own criminal laws. And up until the *Sanchez Valle* decision, Congress and the U.S. government had given Puerto Rico the authority to exercise such powers, consistent with the states' carve-out for double jeopardy. Indeed, nothing prevented the Roberts Court from letting the government of Puerto Rico prosecute its own duly passed criminal laws, from following the processes and institutions established under the Puerto Rico Constitution and longstanding federal practice, and from simultaneously retaining the U.S. government's sovereignty over Puerto Rico.

Two recent lower court decisions bring the Supreme Court's puzzling finding in *Sanchez Valle* into further relief. The judges in *United States v. Vaello-Madero* (2020) and *Schaller v. U.S. Social Security Administration* (2020) held against the executive branch and revisited the application of federal law under the Fifth Amendment's equal protection clause of the Constitution. Notably, both courts explained why the U.S. government could not deprive the U.S. citizens of Puerto Rico and Guam of their SSI benefits, contrary to the Supreme Court's decisions in *Califano v. Torres* (1978) and *Harris v. Rosario* (1980).

In *United States v. Vaello-Madero* the First Circuit Court determined there were neither good economic reasons nor good social reasons—i.e., a "rational basis"—for Congress to discriminate against U.S. citizens of Puerto Rico. It explained that the *Torres* and *Rosario* decisions were made "without benefit of briefing or argument" (*Vaello-Madero* 2020, 9; *Harris v. Rosario* 1980, 654, Marshall, J., dissenting). The First Circuit Court further argued that Rehnquist Court's decision in *Rosario* relied on what Justice Thurgood Marshall described as the "questionable" merits of the *Insular Cases* (*Vaello-Madero* 2020, 9). The Social Security Administration was consequently *not* entitled to collect $28,000 in overpayments after the plaintiff moved back to Puerto Rico after living in New York for 28 years (*Vaello-Madero* 2020, 2–3; *Harvard Law Review* 2021; also see Cepeda Derieux and Weare 2020, 304–5).

Months later, the First District Court of Guam ruled there was no rational basis for excluding SSI benefits from a disabled woman, Katrina Schaller, when she moved from Pennsylvania to Guam. The Social Security Administration's "rational basis" was that SSI benefits are funded by federal income taxes and that U.S. territorial residents do not pay federal income taxes (*Schaller* 2020, 15). Including Guam would cost too much, the SSA contended, and extending SSI benefits to residents of Guam would disrupt the island's economy. But the First District Court of Guam disagreed. It made no sense for the U.S. citizens of Guam not to be allowed to receive SSI benefits, while those residing in the Northern Marianas would be allowed to get them (per the terms of the annexation of the Commonwealth of the Northern Mariana Islands in 1975). The district court found that the extension of SSI benefits to Guam residents would increase the SSI budget by a mere 0.03 percent (*Schaller* 2020, 13) and that there was no evidence that the payment of additional SSI benefits would adversely affect the Guam economy.

Both district courts carefully argued why there was no "rational basis" for the U.S. government's SSI program to discriminate against the U.S. citizens residing in Puerto Rico or Guam. By upholding the equal protection of the law, both decisions effectively overturned the *Torres* and *Rosario* decisions.[34] They also posed a stark contrast to the *Sanchez Valle* decision, where the Court did not explain why the logic of the "ultimate source" of Puerto Rico's prosecutorial authority (per *Wheeler*) prevailed over a decision based on the direct source (per *Lara*) or why it rejected the last seventy years of federal policy that had accepted Puerto Rico's self-government.

It was well within Congress's powers to delegate authority to Puerto Rico. Congress's grants of authority to Puerto Rico in 1950 and 1952 were relatively recent instances of what Justice Frankfurter in 1914 had identified as Congress's "inventive statesmanship" (*Sanchez Valle* 2016, 1876). In 1846, Congress had used statutory law to cede the Virginia portion of the ten-mile-square federal district, notwithstanding the enclave clause (Art. I, Sec. 8, Cl. 17). In 1863, Congress hived off West Virginia from the (then Confederate) state of Virginia, contrary to the terms of the admissions clause (Art. IV, Sec. 3, Cl. 1). From 1871 to 1874, Congress established a territorial government in federal district (under District of Columbia Organic Act, 16 Stat. 419 [1871]), despite the fact that the enclave clause (Art. I) and the territory clause (Art. IV) refer to distinct congressional powers. And Congress admitted Texas as a state and annexed Hawaii as a territory by joint resolution in each instance, even though the Constitution is silent on the admission or the annexation of independent republics.

Yet the Court did have a magic wand, one that was able to make extant caselaw, decades of governmental practice, and the history of postwar U.S. foreign relations disappear.

The Court's ruling in *Sanchez Valle* thereby ignored the driving principle of the *Insular Cases*: that congressional law determined how the Constitution was to apply to the people and government of the territories (also see *Sanchez Valle* 2016, 1879–80, Breyer, J., dissenting). Justice Kagan argued, instead, that the Court was obligated to find the original source of Puerto Rico's sovereignty for the prosecution of its criminal laws. She did not have a "magic wand" to make Congress's ultimate sovereignty disappear (*Sanchez Valle* 2016, 1876).

Yet the Court did have a magic wand, one that was able to make extant caselaw, decades of governmental practice, and the history of postwar U.S. foreign relations disappear. It made the *Insular Cases* and the incorporation doctrine themselves disappear.

III. The Precedent Vanishes

The Court's omission of the *Insular Cases* and the incorporation doctrine in its opinion in *Sanchez Valle* is puzzling, especially because in argument the assistant U.S. solicitor general and Justice Breyer both repeatedly referred to the *Insular Cases* and, specifically, to *Downes, Dorr,* and *Balzac* (Transcript 2016). Both litigants' briefs and several of the amici curiae briefs extensively cited the *Insular Cases*, whether collectively or individually, moreover.[35]

The fact that neither Justice Kagan, nor Justice Ginsburg, nor Justice Thomas, nor Justice Breyer referred to the *Insular Cases* in their opinions in *Sanchez Valle*[36] fits a pattern dating since *Boumediene v. Bush* (2008), when Justice Kennedy cited the *Insular Cases* at length (*Boumediene* 2008, 726, 756–61, 764, 768).[37] The Supreme Court has subsequently avoided bringing attention to the *Insular Cases*.[38] The Court has declined to hear cases on the constitutional and political rights of U.S. territorial residents on other occasions (*Tuaua v. United States* 2017) or has mentioned the *Insular Cases* only in passing (*Financial Oversight and Management Board for Puerto Rico v. Aurelius Investment, LLC et al.* 2020). In other territorial cases, as in *Sanchez Valle*, the Court simply stopped citing the *Insular Cases* (*Puerto Rico v. Franklin California Tax-Free Trusts et al.* 2016).[39]

The fact that Justice Kagan did not refer to the *Insular Cases* suggests that the *Insular Cases* have achieved a new status. They have joined a small number of cases[40] jurists have either stopped citing or that contemporary jurists no longer cite because the case opinions refer to outdated norms and unacceptable values (Schwarz 2007, 1475, 1492–4; also see Cepeda Derieux and Weare 2020, 296–7). The justices' opinions in these cases "speak a language that the [contemporary] court does not understand" or finds intolerable (Schwarz 2007, 1477). Jurists look at these cases "not with agreement and conformity," "but with hostility." Because of this antipathy, these cases "carr[y] no weight at all" among jurists, even as they remain good law (Schwarz 2007, 1477).

This was the fate of *Dred Scott v. Sandford* (1856) in the decades between the Civil War Amendments and the 1964 Civil Rights Act (also see Currie 1984, 131–86, 183). Justices avoided citing Chief Justice Taney's opinion, in which he made unacceptable statements on African Americans being "unfit to associate with the white race either in social or political relations" and "ha[ving] no rights which the white man was bound to respect" (*Dred Scott*, 407). *Dred Scott* was for decades cited in justices' opinions for the Court or in their dissenting opinions, as in *United States v. Wong Kim Ark* (1898, 662, 716, Fuller, C.J., dissenting); *De Lima v. Bidwell* (1901, 196, 209); and *Downes v. Bidwell* (1901, 246, 250, 257, 271–6; 291, 320, White, J., concurring; 360, Fuller, C.J., dissenting). Justices also cited *Dred Scott* in *Williams v. North Carolina* (1945, 274, Black, J., dissenting) and *Cohen v. Hurley* (1961, 142 n.23, Black, J., dissenting). For the most part, however, *Dred Scott* was ignored. Indicatively, Justice Brown's ruling in *Plessy v. Ferguson* (1896) did not refer to *Dred Scott*.[41]

It was also the fate of *Plessy v. Ferguson* between 1938 and *Brown v. Board of Education* (1954), at which point *Plessy* also became bad law. Whereas justices had cited *Plessy* with approval through the mid-1930s, after 1938 they cited *Plessy* in their counterarguments (*Sweatt v. Painter* 1950, 636; *Lombard v. Louisiana* 1963, 280; *Bell v. Maryland* 1964, 287), in their dissenting opinions (*Cohen v. Hurley* 1961, 142; Black, J., dissenting; *Wright v. Rockefeller* 1964, 62, Douglass, J., dissenting), and in their concurring opinions (*Bell v. Maryland* 1964, 287, Goldberg, J., concurring). Neither did the Court opinions nor the dissenting opinions in *Moore v. Dempsey* (1923) and *Brown v. Mississippi* (1936)—lynching cases in which the Court protected African Americans' right to criminal due process—refer to either *Dred Scott* or *Plessy*.

In *Reynolds v. United States* (1878), too, Chief Justice Waite quoted derogatory statements about polygamy and its victims in his ruling on the constitutionality of anti-polygamy laws (*Reynolds* 1878, 166–8). After the decision the Court has only cited *Reynolds* occasionally, whether to argue in favor of the "wall of separation" between the government and religion or to point out the anomalies of a case (consistent with the *Reynolds* challenge to anti-polygamy legislation). After 1995, the Court stopped citing *Reynolds* altogether.[42]

This is what has befallen the *Insular Cases*.[43] Jurists have sought to deliberately "distance...American constitutional law from the *Insular Cases*" (Issacharoff et al. 2019, 35; also see Erman 2021, 1239–40). The *Insular Cases* "cannot be disentangled from anachronistic and extra-constitutional considerations that are fundamentally at odds with present-day understandings" (Wolfson 2014, 24–5).[44] And the Court "need not and should not look to the *Insular Cases* for guidance" in its decision in *Sanchez Valle*, the Puerto Rico Bar Association wrote in its amicus curiae brief (Netter 2015, 5). To "rely in any way on the *Insular Cases*...would wrongly send a message to Congress, the Executive, and lower courts that the flawed reasoning of those cases remains valid" (Netter 2015, 24). In fact, constitutional scholars of all "methodological perspective[s]" have rejected the *Insular Cases* (Lawson and Sloane 2009, 1146).

Consistent with the *Insular Cases'* newly achieved status, several of the amicus curiae briefs in *Sanchez Valle* omitted any mention of the *Insular Cases* as precedent. Notably, the U.S. Solicitor General's influential amicus brief on behalf of the respondents did not refer to the *Insular Cases*, whether collectively or individually (Verrilli 2015). And neither did two other amicus briefs (Hrelic 2015; Srebnick 2015).

Such omissions do not make the *Insular Cases* any less the precedents of the Court's ruling in *Sanchez Valle*, of course. Neither do they make *Sanchez Valle* any less their progeny.

IV. Conclusion

In his ruling in *Balzac*, Chief Justice Taft remarked upon his search for expressions of Congress's intent, whether in federal law or U.S. treaty (*Balzac* 1922, 309). However, he could "find no features in the Organic Act of Porto Rico of 1917 from which to infer the purpose of Congress to incorporate Porto Rico into the United States with the consequences which would follow" (*Balzac* 1922, 313). On the contrary, because the incorporation into the Union of "distant ocean communities of a different origin and language from those of our continental people" was an "important" step to statehood, the Chief Justice was confident that when Congress takes that step it would do so "deliberately and with a clear declaration of purpose, and not [leave it] a matter of mere inference or construction" (*Balzac* 1922, 313).

Chief Justice Taft's regard for U.S. government policy characterized the Court's argument in most of the *Insular Cases*. With its powers under the territory clause, Congress could treat the United States' territories differently, depending on whether it viewed them as destined for statehood or as not being suited for incorporation. And the Court went along.

Unlike the Court's decision in *Balzac* and unlike its rulings in the other *Insular Cases*, however, Justice Kagan ignored existing and well-established federal law. Instead, the Court arrogated to itself the authority to decide how the Constitution applied (*viz.*, with respect to Puerto Ricans being prosecuted under both U.S. and Puerto Rico law). She ignored what Congress had legislated and what President Truman had identified as Puerto Rico's "authority and responsibility for local self-government." She neglected the precedents set in several of the *Insular Cases* with respect to the double jeopardy clause, cases in which the Court based its decisions on Congress's expressed own explicit grant to Puerto Rico of local self-government and, hence, "separate sovereign" status for the purpose of double jeopardy.

Even so, the *Sanchez Valle* decision echoes the Court's century-old ruling in *Balzac*: it likewise affirms the legacy of the prior *Insular Cases* and it similarly instantiates the incorporation doctrine by virtue of the Court's claim to its distinct authority for deciding which constitutional provisions apply to Puerto Rico and the other territories of the United States. As with *Balzac*, the *Sanchez Valle* ruling affirmed the U.S. government's "political apartheid" of treating geographically separate U.S. citizens unequally. No longer was Puerto Rico to be a "democracy within a democracy" (U.S. Senate 1950b, 23).

An assessment of *why* the Court ruled as it did in *Sanchez Valle* is beyond the scope of this article. One possibility, though, is what the U.S. government had at stake. The U.S. Solicitor General's amicus brief wrote of the United States "substantive interest" in the litigation, observing that the decision "may affect the federal government's defense of federal legislation and policies related to Puerto Rico across a broad range of substantive areas, including congressional representation, federal benefits, federal income taxes, bankruptcy, and defense" (Verrilli 2015, 1). In view of the ongoing efforts for Puerto Rico statehood, the increased migration of Puerto Ricans to the mainland United States, Puerto Rico's stagnant economy, its bankruptcy of the mid-2010s, and the fact that the ruling could potentially affect U.S. security interests in Guam and other territories (Sparrow 2015, 52–6; Sparrow and Lamm 2017, 308–9), the Obama administration had its reasons for leaving no doubt about Puerto Rico's sovereignty.

A more immediate explanation may have been the pending Puerto Rico Oversight, Management, and Economic Stability Act (PROMESA), which was to create a federally appointed oversight board with extraordinary powers over the finances of the Puerto Rico government. In the summer of 2016, the bill passed Congress, thereby essentially putting Puerto Rico under receivership. The justices would have been aware of this larger political current, especially with their decision on Puerto Rico's authority (more precisely, its lack of authority) to restructure its $70 billion in debt (*Franklin California Tax-Free Trust*) to be issued four days after *Sanchez Valle*. They and the Obama administration may both have gleaned that the 114th Congress little cared if they were to contravene long-lasting federal policy vis-à-vis Puerto Rico.

Whatever the reason and however unpalatable the *Insular Cases* may be to legal, media, and academic professionals, however contrary the *Insular Cases* may be to democratic principles, and however ignored they now may be, the *Insular Cases*, the incorporation doctrine, and the political apartheid of Puerto Rico live on.

ACKNOWLEDGEMENTS

Professor Sparrow appreciates the comments of and his conversations with William Blake, Christine Bird, Jonathan Blocher, Pamela Corley, Sam Erman, Jorge Farinacci, Mito Gulati, Gary Jacobsohn, Christina Duffy Ponsa-Kraus, Efrén Rivera Ramos, Allen Sumrall, several anonymous referees, and the guest editors of *CENTRO Journal*'s special number on the centenary of the *Balzac* case, José Javier Colón Morera and Charles R. Venator-Santiago.

NOTES

[1] The "Black Lives Matter" movement began with the death of Trayvon Martin in 2012, surged with Michael Brown's death in 2014, and resurged in the summer of 2020, following the deaths of Breonna Taylor and George Floyd. This list could also include the ongoing feminist movement, efforts for the rights of the disabled, and the movement for equality for members of the LGBTQ+ communities.

[2] The (territorial) incorporation doctrine should be distinguished from the "incorporation doctrine" of the "nationalization of the Bill of Rights," which extends the Due Process clause of the Fourteenth Amendment to the Constitution's first ten amendments.

[3] "Political apartheid" is here defined as a government's segregation of ethnic and racial minorities for political ends.

[4] Much of the analysis below could refer to the U.S. citizens of the other Caribbean and Pacific territories; American Samoans remain U.S. nationals.

[5] The *Insular Cases* have been identified as the first six cases of 1901 (Torruella 2001), as 23 cases (Rivera Ramos 2001, 2015), 27 cases (Burnett 2001), and 34 cases (Sparrow 2006).

[6] González Berdecía gives *Puerto Rico v. Franklin California Tax-Free Trust* (2016) nearly equal weight to *Puerto Rico v. Sanchez Valle* (2016). I concentrate on *Puerto Rico v. Sanchez Valle* as the earlier, more encompassing, and more radical decision.

[7] The opinion once mentions the "Territory Clause" (*Sanchez Valle* 2016, 1868).

[8] Chief Justice Taney confined the application of the territory clause to the U.S. territory as of 1787, holding that the United States could not "enlarge its territorial limits in any way, except by the admission of new states" (*Dred Scott* 1856, 446).

[9] The territory clause establishes that Congress has the "power to dispose of and make all needful rules and regulations respecting the territory or other property belonging to the United States; and nothing in this Constitution shall be so construed

as to prejudice any claims of the United States, or of any particular state."

[10] The case was decided 7-2; Justice McKenna dissented, joined by Justice White.

[11] Although none of the *Insular Cases* involved disputes over government-sanctioned favoritism among U.S. ports, the decisions in the cases on tariff and trade between the territories and the mainland states constituted implicit ruling on the preference clause (Art. I, §9, cl. 6).

[12] The Puerto Rico district court did not become an Article III court until 1966, and persons born in Puerto Rico did not become birthright, or *jus soli*, U.S. citizens until after January 13, 1941.

[13] Justice Holmes concurred in the decision but did not write a separate opinion.

[14] Contemporaries regarded Joseph McKenna as a political centrist, as not having a coherent judicial philosophy, and as being probably the least distinguished justice on the Supreme Court.

[15] The Puerto Rico Supreme Court thereby overturned the decision of the Puerto Rico Court of Appeals (Pet. App. 1a-69a. 2015), which had ruled in favor of Puerto Rico's separate sovereignty with respect to double jeopardy.

[16] Justice Scalia participated in the oral argument on *Sanchez Valle*, but he died in February 2016. I refer to the "Court opinion" and "Justice Kagan's opinion" interchangeably.

[17] The federal arms trafficking law under which the respondents were indicted has different language, distinct provisions, and greater scope than the Puerto Rico law, but the practical effects of the two laws were judged similar and their relative reach was not in dispute.

[18] Justice Stewart wrote for a unanimous Court; Justice Brennan took no part in the decision.

[19] President McKinley had previously extended the protection against double jeopardy to the Philippines with the Military Order of April 23, 1900.

[20] Both Spanish law and the Taft Commission (1900-1916) also prohibited double jeopardy in the Philippines.

[21] Although a civil court could not normally retry a court martial because the two typically had separate jurisdictions and occupied distinct spheres of justice, the territorial government was the creation of Congress (in contradistinction to the American states' independent sources of sovereignty), thus the martial court *did* have jurisdiction over Homer E. Grafton (*Grafton*, 353-354), an Army private who was charged with killing two Filipinos.

[22] In two other *Insular Cases*, *Trono v. United States* (1905) and *Gavieres v. United States* (1911), the Court rejected the plaintiffs' appeals on the grounds of being put twice in jeopardy. In *Trono*, Justice Peckham ruled that because the three plaintiffs had themselves appealed the original assault conviction—only for the Philippine Supreme Court to then convict them of homicide—the case should proceed "as if no trial had previously taken place" (*Trono* 1905, 533). In *Gavieres*, Justice Day argued that the two charges were distinct; the plaintiff's insult of a public official, contrary to Philippine code, "was not within the terms" of the plaintiff's charge of drunken and disorderly conduct, contrary to Manila city ordinance (*Gavieres* 1911, 345).

[23] "Treaty concerning the Cession of the Russian Possessions in North America by his Majesty the Emperor of all the Russias to the United States of America: June 20, 1867."

[24] The language of the treaty with Russia was consistent with that in the treaties for the Louisiana Purchase and the Oregon Territory, from Britain, but the latter areas were annexed in the early and mid-nineteenth century and were contiguous to the existing territories and states.

[25] Other post-1922 decisions also prominently cite the *Insular Cases*, such as *Reid v. Covert* (1956) and *United States v. Verdugo-Urquidez* (1990). Neither case involved the interpretation of congressional legislation.

[26] The Philippines achieved independence on July 4, 1946.

[27] Neither Mary Dudziak (2000) nor Azza Layton (2000) link anti-colonialism and decolonization to the U.S. government's relations with Puerto Rico or the other U.S. territories.

[28] Indicative of the political climate, the U.S government changed other territorial polices as well. Under the Guam Organic Act of 1950, Congress granted Guam a civilian government to replace the U.S. Navy's administration, and in 1952 Congress made "all persons born in the island of Guam on or after April 11, 1899" U.S. citizens (Public Law 82-414). In 1951 Congress transferred control of American Samoa from the Navy to the U.S. Department of the Interior, and in 1953 it established a new, four-tier Territorial Judicial System for the Samoan islands. In 1954 Congress passed the Revised Organic Act of the Virgin Islands, which established a local government consisting of an elected governor, a 15-member unicameral legislature, an appointed judiciary, and a Bill of Rights; the Act effectively serves as the U.S.V.I.'s constitution.

[29] Justice Breyer's dissenting opinion followed the arguments of the counsel for the petitioners, the Puerto Rico government (Landau 2015a, 2015b).

[30] See *United States v. López Andino* (1987) and *Puerto Rico v. Castro Garcia* (1988).

[31] The Court's reliance on *Wheeler* for the argument of Congress being the "ultimate

source" of Puerto Rico's prosecutorial authority neglects an important difference
between *Wheeler* and *Sanchez Valle*: Congress had not already delegated authority to the Navajo prior to the Court's decision in *Wheeler*. Were the cases actually
comparable, the Rehnquist Court (in this scenario) would have proceeded to ignore
Congress's previous delegation of authority and then ruled that the Navajo were not
sovereign for the purpose of double jeopardy.

[32] Justice Kagan omits the fact that *Grafton* is regarded as one of the *Insular Cases*
(Burnett and Marshall 2001, 390; Kerr 1982, 106–7; Lawson and Seidman 2005, 195
n.21; Rivera Ramos 2001, 118; Torruella 1985, 77–8; Sparrow 2006, 191–2).

[33] Unlike Puerto Rico, which already had a republican constitution, the Philippines
did not acquire a republican constitution until 1935, following a territory-wide
plebiscite, at which point sovereignty resided "in the people and all government
authority emanate[d] from them" (1935 Philippine Constitution, Art. II, §1).

[34] *United States v. Vaello-Madero* was granted cert by the Court of Appeals on March
1, 2021.

[35] The litigants' briefs each mentioned the *Insular Cases* eight times (collectively or
individually).

[36] Justice Sotomayor did not mention the *Insular Cases* in argument. She did not
insist that Justice Breyer include them in the dissenting opinion she joined. And
she did not include them in her dissenting opinion, joined by Justice Ginsburg, in
Puerto Rico v. Franklin California Tax-Free Trust, et al. (2016). Her questions in argument in *Sanchez Valle* showed her to be unfamiliar with the legislative history and
caselaw bearing on the rights and privileges of the people and government of Puerto
Rico (Transcript 2016). See Justice Sotomayor's views on Puerto Rico's status and
the "compact theory" in her concurring opinion in *Fin. Oversight & Mgmt. Bd. for
P.R. v. Aurelius Inv., LLC* (2020, slip opinion; see Ponsa-Kraus 2020).

[37] Justice Scalia also cited the *Insular Cases* in *Boumediene* (2008, 838–9, Scalia, J.,
dissenting).

[38] Nor did any of the justices writing in *Sanchez Valle* refer to Puerto Rico as a "non-
incorporated" (or "unincorporated") territory or as an American colony (González
Berdecía 2016, 112; Serrano 2018, 430).

[39] The same holds for the district court decisions in *Vaello-Madero* and *Schaller*.

[40] The five *Civil Rights Cases* are another set of landmark decisions that have been
treated as a single case. The decision in the *Slaughterhouse Cases* also consolidated
three separate cases.

[41] *Plessy* upheld the constitutionality of a Louisiana law establishing "equal but separate accommodations for the white and colored races" on railway carriages. Justice Harlan's dissenting opinion in *Plessy* did compare *Plessy* to *Dred Scott* (*Plessy* 1896, 559).

[42] Justices also cited *Reynolds* in controversies that concerned the use of prior-recorded testimony (*Dutton v. Evans* 1970, 97n.5) and that involved territorial law (*Palmore v. United States* 1973, 403n.10, 403n.11). I am grateful to Professor Gary Jacobsohn for recommending I include *Reynolds* among this set of cases.

[43] Schwarz's own list of deliberately "forgotten" cases consists of *International News Service v. Associated Press* (1918), *Shelley v. Kraemer* (1948), and *Schindler v. Schiavo* (2005) (Schwarz 2007, 1481, 1509).

[44] In *Financial Oversight Bd. v. Aurelius Investment*, Justice Breyer wrote that the Court did "not consider the request by some of the parties that we overrule the much-criticized 'Insular Cases' and their progeny" (*Aurelius* 2020, 21). The *Insular Cases* "did not reach this issue, and whatever their continued validity we will not extend them [here]" (*Aurelius* 2020, 21).

REFERENCES

Álvarez González, José Julián. 1990. The Empire Strikes Out: Congressional Ruminations on the Citizen Status of Puerto Ricans. *Harvard Journal of Legislation* 27(2), 309–60.

Armstrong v. United States. 1901. 182 U.S. 243.

Balzac v. Porto Rico. 1922. 258 U.S. 298.

Bell v. Maryland. 1964. 378 U.S. 266.

Board of Public Utility Commissioners v. Ynchausti & Co. 1920. 251 U.S. 401.

Boumediene v. Bush. 2008. 553 U.S. 723.

Brown v. Board of Education. 1954. 347 U.S. 483.

Brown v. Mississippi. 1936. 296, U.S. 278.

Burnett, Christina Duffy. 2005. *Untied* States: American Expansion and Territorial Deannexation. *University of Chicago Law Review* 72(5), 797–879.

_____. 2009. A Convenient Constitution? Extraterritoriality after *Boumediene*. *Columbia Law Review* 109, 973–1046.

Burnett, Christina Duffy and Burke Marshall. 2001. Between the Foreign and the Domestic: The Doctrine of Territorial Incorporation, Invented and Reinvented. In *Foreign in a Domestic Sense: Puerto Rico, American Expansion, and the Constitution*, eds. Christina Duffy Burnett and Burke Marshall. 1–36. Durham: Duke University Press

Cabranes, José A. 1979. *Citizenship and the American Empire: Notes on the Legislative History of the United States Citizenship of Puerto Ricans.* New Haven: Yale University Press.

Califano v. Torres. 1978. 435 U.S. 1.

Cepeda Derieux, Adriel I. and Neale C. Weare. 2020. After *Aurelius*: What Future for the *Insular Cases*? *Yale Law Journal Forum* 130(Nov. 2), 284–307. Accessed 28 June 2021. <https://www.yalelawjournal.org/forum/after-aurelius-what-future-for-the-insular-cases>.

Cohen v. Hurley. 1961. 333 U.S. 117.

Commonwealth of Puerto Rico v. Sanchez Valle et al. 2016. 136 U.S. 1863.

CQ Almanac. 1952. Puerto Rican Constitution. Accessed 5 July 2021. <library.cqpress.com.ezproxy.lib.utexas.edu/cqalmanac/document. php?id=cqal52-1381241>.

Cuison-Villazor, Rose. 2021. Testimony of Professor Rose Cuison-Villazor, Rutgers Law School, Before the Committee on Natural Resources Committee, Hearing on H. Res. 297 May 4. Accessed 18 June 18. <https://docs.house. gov/meetings/II/II00/20210512/112617/HHRG-117-II00-Wstate-Cuison-VillazorP-20210512.pdf>.

Currie, David. 1984. Constitution in the Supreme Court: Civil War and Reconstruction, 1865-1873. *University of Chicago Law Review* 51, 131–86.

De Lima v. Bidwell. 1901. 182 U.S. 1.

De Lima, Goetze v. United States and *Crossman v. United States.* 1901. 182 U.S. 221.

Dooley v. United States 1901. 182 U.S. 222 [*Dooley I*].

Dooley v. United States. 1901. 183 U.S. 151 [*Dooley II*].

Dorr v. United States. 1904. 195 U.S. 138.

Dowdell v. United States. 1911. 221 U.S. 325.

Downes v. Bidwell 1901. 182 U.S. 244.

Dred Scott v. Sandford. 1856. 60 U.S. 393.

Dudziak, Mary. 2000. *Cold War Civil Rights: Race and the Image of American Democracy.* Princeton: Princeton University Press.

Dutton v. Evans. 1970. 400 U.S. 74.

Erman, Sam. 2019. *Almost Citizens: Puerto Rico, the U.S. Constitution, and Empire.* New York: Cambridge University Press.

_____. 2021. Truer U.S. History: Race, Borders, and Status Manipulation. *Yale Law Journal* 130, 1188-249.

Financial Oversight and Management Board for Puerto Rico v. Aurelius Investment, LLC et al. 2020. 140 S. Ct. 1649.

Gavieres v. United States. 1911. 220 U.S. 338.

González Berdecía, Andrés. 2016. Puerto Rico Before the Supreme Court of the United States: Constitutional Colonialism in Action. *Columbia Journal of Race and Law* 7, 80–149.

Grafton v. United States. 1907. 206 U.S. 333.

Harris v. Rosario. 1980. 446 U.S. 651.

Harvard Law Review. 2021. Territorial Law: *United States v. Vaello-Madero.* *Harvard Law Review* 134, 1260–7.

Hawaii v. Mankichi. 1903. 190 U.S. 197.

Heath v. Alabama. 1985. 474 U.S. 82.

Heefner, Gretchen. 2005. 'A Symbol of the New Frontier': Hawaiian Statehood, Anti-Colonialism, and Winning the Cold War. *Pacific History Review* 74(4), 545–74.

Hrelic, Dana M. 2015. Brief of Amicus Curiae Virgin Islands Bar Association (VIBA) in Support of Respondents. Commonwealth of Puerto Rico, Petitioner, v. Luis M. Sánchez Valle and Jaime Gómez Vázquez, Respondents, On Writ of Certiorari to the Supreme Court of Puerto Rico, 22 December.

International News Service v. Associated Press. 1918. 248 U.S. 215.

Issacharoff, Samuel, Alexandra Bursak, Russell Rennie and Alec Webley. 2019. What Is Puerto Rico? *Indiana Law Journal* 94(1), 1–45.

Kent, Andrew. 2014. Citizenship and Protection. *Fordham Law Review* 82, 2115–35.

Kepner v. United States. 1904. 195 U.S. 100.

Kerr, James Edward. 1982. *The Insular Cases: The Role of the Judiciary in American Expansion.* Port Washington, NY: Kennikat Press.

Kopel v. Bingham. 1909. 211 U.S. 468.

Landau, Christopher 2015a. Petition for Writ Certiorari to the Supreme Court of Puerto Rico, The Commonwealth of Puerto Rico, Petitioner, v. Luis M. Sánchez Valle and Jaime Gómez Vázquez, Respondents, 136 S. Ct. 28 (2015) (No. 15-108), 17 July.

―――. 2015b. Brief for Petitioner, On Writ of Certiorari to the Supreme Court of Puerto Rico, The Commonwealth of Puerto Rico, Petitioner, v. Luis M. Sánchez Valle and Jaime Gómez Vázquez, Respondents, 136 S. Ct. 28 (2015) (No. 15-108), 16 November.

Lawson, Gary and Guy Seidman. 2004. *The Constitution of Empire: Territorial Expansion and American Legal History.* New Haven: Yale University Press.

Lawson, Gary and Robert D. Sloane. 2009. The Constitutionality of Decolonization by Associated Statehood: Puerto Rico's Legal Status Reconsidered. *Boston College Law Review* 50, 1123–93.

Layton, Azza Salama. 2000. *International Politics and Civil Rights Policies in the United States, 1941-1960.* New York: Cambridge University Press.

Lewis, Gordon. 1953. Puerto Rico: A New Constitution in American Government. *The Journal of Politics* 15(1), 42–66.

Lincoln v. United States; Warner, Barnes & Co. v. United States. 1905. 197 U.S. 419.

Lincoln v. United States; Warner, Barnes & Co. v. United States. 1906. 202 U.S. 484.

Lombard v. Louisiana. 1963. 373 U.S. 267.

Loughborough v. Blake. 1820. 18 U.S. 317.

Lowell, Abbott Lawrence. 1899. The Status of Our New Possessions—A Third View. *Harvard Law Review* 13(3), 155–76.

Mendezona v. United States. 1904 195 U.S. 158.

Moore v. Dempsey. 1923. 1261 U.S. 86.

Netter, Brian. 2015. Brief of Colegio de Abogados y Abogadas de Puerto Rico and the Puerto Rican Bar Association, Inc., as *Amici Curiae* in Support of Respondents, Commonwealth of Puerto Rico, Petitioner, v. Luis M. Sanchez Valle and Jaime Gomez Vazquez, Respondents, On Writ of Certiorari to the Supreme Court of Puerto Rico, December [n.d.].

Neuman, Gerald L. 2015. Introduction. In *Reconsidering the Insular Cases: The Past and Future of American Empire,* eds. Gerald L. Neuman and Tomiko Brown-Nagin. xiii-xvi. Cambridge: Human Rights Program Series, Harvard Law School.

Ocampo v. United States. 1914. 234 U.S. 91.

Ochoa v. Hernandez. 1913. 230 U.S. 139.

Palmore v. United States. 1973. 411 U.S. 389.

Plessy v. Ferguson. 1896. 163 U.S. 537.

Ponsa-Kraus, Christina. 2020. Forum: Political Wine in a Judicial Bottle: Justice Sotomayor's Surprising Concurrence in *Aurelius. Yale Law Journal* 130 (Nov. 2), 101–31. Accessed 28 June 2021. <https://www.yalelawjournal.org/forum/political-wine-in-a-judicial-bottle-justice-sotomayors-surprising-concurrence-in-aurelius>.

Porto Rico v. Rosaly. 1913. 227 U.S. 270.

Puerto Rico v. Castro Garcia. 1988. 120 D.P.R. 740.

Puerto Rico v. Shell Co. 1937. 302 U.S. 253.

Puerto Rico v. Franklin California Tax Free Trust et al. 2016.

Rassmussen v. United States. 1905. 197 U.S. 516.

Reid v. Covert. 1956. 354 U.S. 1.

Reynolds v. United States. 1878. 98 U.S. 145.

Rivera Ramos, Efrén. 2001. *The Legal Construction of Identity: The Judicial and Social Legacy of American Colonialism in Puerto Rico*. Washington, DC: American Psychological Association.

_____. 2015. The Insular Cases: What is There to Reconsider? In *Reconsidering the Insular Cases: The Past and Future of the American Empire*, eds. Gerald L. Neuman and Tomiko Brown-Nagin. 29–38. Cambridge: Harvard University Press.

Rowe, L. S. 1901. The Supreme Court and the Insular Cases. *The Annals of the American Academy of Political and Social Science* 18 (Sep. 1901), 38–62.

Schaller v. U.S. Social Security Administration. 2020. Civil Case No. 18-00044 (Dis. Ct. of Guam).

Schindler v. Schiavo. 2005. 403 F.3d 1223.

Schwarz, Timothy. 2007. Comment: Cases Time Forgot: Why Judges Can Sometimes Ignore Controlling Precedent. *Emory Law Journal* 56, 1475–1510.

Serrano, Susan K. 2018. Elevating the Perspectives of U.S. Territorial Peoples: Why the Insular Cases Should Be Taught in Law School. *The Journal of Gender, Race, and Justice* 21, 395–457.

Shelley v. Kraemer. 1948. 344 U.S. 1.

Smith, Rogers M. 2015. The Insular Cases, Differentiated Citizenship, and Territorial Statuses in the Twenty-first Century. In *Reconsidering the Insular Cases*, eds. Gerald L. Neuman and Tomiko Brown-Nagin. 103–28. Cambridge.: Human Rights Program Series, Harvard Law School.

Sparrow, Bartholomew H. 2006. *The* Insular Cases *and the Emergence of American Empire*. Lawrence: University Press of Kansas.

_____. 2015. The Centennial of *Ocampo v. United States*: Lessons from the *Insular Cases*. In *Reconsidering the Insular Cases: The Past and Future of American Empire*, eds. Gerald L. Neuman and Tomiko Brown-Nagin. 39–59. Cambridge: Human Rights Program Series, Harvard Law School.

Sparrow, Bartholomew and Jennifer Lamm. 2017. Puerto Ricans and U.S.
    Citizenship in 1917: Imperatives of Security. *CENTRO: Journal of the
    Center for Puerto Rican Studies*. Special Issue: One-Hundred Years of the
    Jones Act and Puerto Rican U.S. Citizenship. 29(1), 284–313.

Srebnick, Howard. 2015. Brief for *Amici Curiae* Florida Association of Criminal
    Defense Lawyers—Miami Chapter in Support of Respondents,
    Commonwealth of Puerto Rico, Petitioner, v. Luis M. Sánchez Valle
    and Jaime Gómez Vázquez, Respondents, On Writ of Certiorari to the
    Supreme Court of Puerto Rico, 22 December.

Sweatt v. Painter. 1950. 339 U.S. 629.

Terrasa, Gabriel A. 1997. The United States, Puerto Rico, and the Incorporation
    Doctrine: Reaching a Century of Constitutional Authoritarianism. *John
    Marshall Law Review*. 31(1), 55–93.

Thomas, Brook. 2001. A Constitution Led by the Flag: The *Insular Cases* and the
    Metaphor of Incorporation. In *Foreign in a Domestic Sense: Puerto Rico,
    American Expansion, and the Constitution*, eds. Christina Duffy Burnett
    and Burke Marshall. 82–103. Durham: Duke University Press.

Torruella, Juan R. 1985. *The Supreme Court and Puerto Rico: The Doctrine of
    Separate and Unequal*. Río Piedras: La Editorial, Universidad de Puerto
    Rico.

_____. 2007. The Insular Cases: The Establishment of a Regime of Political
    Apartheid. *University of Pennsylvania Journal of International Law* 29(2),
    283–347.

_____. 2013. Ruling America's Colonies: The Insular Cases. *Yale Law & Policy
    Review* 32(1), 57–95.

Truman, Harry S. 1952. Special Message to the Congress Transmitting the
    Constitution of the Commonwealth of Puerto Rico. 22 April. Accessed
    5 July 2021. <https://www.presidency.ucsb.edu/documents/special-
    message-the-congress-transmitting-the-constitution-the-commonwealth-
    puerto-rico>.

Tuaua v. United States. 2017. 951 F. Supp. 2d. 1.

Trono v. United States. 1905. 199 U.S. 521.

U.S. Senate. 1950a. *Puerto Rico Constitution: Hearing before the Committee on
    Interior and Insular Affairs, United States Senate, Eighty-First Congress,
    Second Session*. Washington, U.S. G.P.O. 13 March.

_____. 1950b. *Puerto Rico Constitution: Hearing before a Subcommittee of the Committee on Interior and Insular Affairs, United States Senate, Eighty-First Congress, Second Session.* Washington, U.S. G.P.O., 17 May.

United States v. Heinszen & Co. 1907. 206 U.S. 370.

United States v. Lara. 2004. 541 U.S. 193.

United States v. López Andino. 1987. 831 F. 2d 1164, 1168 [CA1 1987].

United States v. Vaello-Madero. 2020. No. 19-1390 (1st Cir.).

United States v. Verdugo-Urquidez. 1990. 494 U.S. 259.

United States v. Wheeler. 1978. 435 U. S. 313.

United States v. Wong Kim Ark. 1898. 169 U.S. 649.

Vignarajah, Krishanti. 2010. The Political Roots of Judicial Legitimacy: Explaining the Enduring Validity of the *Insular Cases*. *University of Chicago Law Review* 77, 781–845.

Weems v. United States. 1910. 142 U.S. 379.

Williams v. North Carolina. 1945. 325 U.S. 226.

Wolfson, Paul R. Q. 2014. Brief of Amici Curiae Scholars of Constitutional Law and Legal History in Support of Neither Party, Leneuoti Fiafia Tuaua, et al. v. United States of America, United States Court of Appeals for the District of Columbia Circuit. No. 13-5272.

Wright v. Rockefeller. 1964. 376 U.S. 52.

Puerto Rico without Puerto Ricans/"Puerto Ricans without Puerto Rico[1]": A Comment on *Balzac versus Porto Rico*, A Hundred Years Later

MADELINE ROMÁN

ABSTRACT

The case of *Balzac v. Porto Rico* is examined from the perspectives of the sociology of law and second-generation systems theory. Concerns about constitutionality, locality, and citizenship are examined in the context of a legal case and in the present tense. The problem posed by the discursive phrases "Puerto Rico without Puerto Ricans" and "Puerto Ricans without Puerto Rico" is discussed in the context of contemporary legal, political, and social scenery. [Keywords: modernity, systems, state of exception, sovereignty, citizenship, second generation systems theory]

Madeline Román (romanlopezmad@gmail.com) is a retired full professor from the Department of Sociology and Anthropology, University of Puerto Rico, Río Piedras Campus. She is the author of *Estados de violencia en Puerto Rico: abordajes desde la complejidad* (Publicaciones Puertorriqueñas, 2021); *Estallidos: polisemia y polimorfia del derecho y la violencia* (Publicaciones Puertorriqueñas, 2006); *Lo criminal y otros relatos de ingobernabilidad* (Publicaciones Puertorriqueñas, 1998); and *Estado y criminalidad en Puerto Rico: un abordaje criminológico alternativo* (Publicaciones Puertorriqueñas, 1993). Currently she coordinates the Mobile Observatory for the Study of Violence (observatoriomovil.com).

A series of qualifications

This essay reflects on how, as societies evolve, the complexities increase within and among function systems—legal, political, economic. These complexities show a process of coupling-decoupling within and among these systems of functions. The legal case of *Balzac v. Puerto Rico* shows one instance of the decoupling of legal, political, and societal processes.

Being a Puerto Rican, writing about *Balzac v. Porto Rico* is a theoretical and political challenge due to the alert raised by French theorist, Yves Michaud, in his book *Violencia y política* (1989). Michaud states that we must be careful not to fall into the enrollment of words at the service of convictions. This is important because, as stated by systems theorist Niklas Luhmann, the task of sociology is "to think through"; that is, to activate our capacity to study a domain in question, making analytical exception of the forms of power/knowledge that produce me as a subject. And this is not to aspire to neutral or objective knowledge but to recognize that there is more in the world than our convictions. In this essay, I refer to Michaud's contention to the urgency of developing the capacity to assume a reflection on the relevance or lack thereof of this legal case outside the prevailing political "mantras" (annexation versus independence).[2]

This is not a legal essay. Rather, it is an essay within the tradition of the sociology of law and sociology in general. As stated by Niklas Luhmann, "sociologists observe the law from the outside and lawyers observe the law from inside" (2004, 59). Consistent with second-generation systems theory,[3] a series of observations from a position of exteriority concerning the legal system will be discussed. That is, a series of observations from the social system as a whole (from the environment of the legal system) will be conducted, although I will also be making use of observations that, regarding this particular case, have been developed from within the legal system itself, from the capacity of the legal system to observe itself. This is also an examination of the reciprocal irritations (among the legal, political, and social systems as a whole) that have risen over time on the set of issues addressed by *Balzac v. Porto Rico*.

Observations from the standpoint of second-generation systems theory

From the standpoint of the second-generation systems theory, the evolvement of modernity includes the emergence of subsystems or specialized systems of functions (economic, political, legal, science system, among others) that operate autopoietically. That is, resting in their internal operations. In this sense, it is the systems themselves that identify what is their own (its legality). Therefore, the legal system operates as an autopoietic system, it reproduces itself according to its internal operations and, on account of this, it has operational closure. The other systems of functions constitute its environment.

The relationship between the system and its environment is complex in nature. In the environment, there is noise (information/communication), but the circulation of information in complex social systems does not take an input/output scheme.[4] For communication to flow from the environment to the system, it must first be recognized by the system in question as relevant communication. In the case of the legal systems, it must be recognized as legal communication. This is critical because, at times, while it is possible to identify a tight coupling among different systems (say, for example between the political and the legal system), it is also possible to identify loose couplings or no coupling at all. The observations made by legal scholars are conducted within the legal system and that's why they constantly refer to legal communication itself (court decisions, legislation, the Constitution) to validate a particular reading of the law. The law is validated by the law itself.

One hundred years in a person's life is a long time, but the question is whether or not one hundred years in legal or social life is considered a long time.

The call for papers to which this essay responds requests an analysis of the relevance, implications, or effects of the *Balzac v. Porto Rico* decision on the lives of Puerto Ricans—inside or outside of the island—on citizenship, on public policies, on civil and human rights struggles, etc. Niklas Luhmann, the main theorist of systems theory in sociology, argues that the only thing we know about the future is that it will not be like today. Furthermore, he suggests that the world is becoming more and more contingent.[5] The way this contingency is expressed within the legal system is in the understanding that a particular law is in force "until further notice" (Luhmann 2004, 469). How does it make sense of a legal case that was decided one hundred years ago? What sense does this analysis make in present times? These questions raise the issue of time as central within this analytical path and force us to address them.

All analysis of that which was debated in the past is intended to make sense of our present. However, the times of societies are not the times of individuals. One hundred years in a person's life is a long time, but the question is whether or not one hundred years in legal or social life is considered a long time. I asked this question to a young legal scholar, and she responded that 100 years in the legal field is "a world" and that in most juridical cultures, quoting cases so old is frowned upon.[6] As a result, the continuous review of legal cases functions as a re-entry, which is a process of returning to previously produced distinctions in order to produce new ones. Distinctions that could address the issues raised in this case should be much more current in nature.

There are a variety of analytical strategies that can be implemented when analyzing the relevance of an old legal case. Some focus on the year of its enactment to account for its context, the epochal forces in conflict, the rationalities that led to the determination of the case, etc. All of these strategies are important. I distance myself from a metaphysical reading of time both as a signifier of thought and as an immutably fixed point that gives foundation to what is moving. From this reading of time, *Balzac v. Porto Rico* (1922) is conceived as a foundational or overdetermining instance of Puerto Rico's politico-juridical framework. Perhaps it would be necessary to ponder the paradox that, although "only what happens happens," at the same time, everything could have been different, so it is necessary to explore both dimensions of this paradox.

According to Luhmann, as modernity evolves, stability erodes. Therefore, I will be discussing the paradox of the prevalence of this legal case within the context of "us back then" (as a collective and as a moment in time) are not the same as "us today"; neither are the forces, legal and nonlegal, in conflict.

Balzac v. Porto Rico: substantive issues

The following are a series of matters raised by the *Balzac* Supreme Court decision of 1922 in which I focus to stress the constitutive violence of the law.

The controversy in question

Jesús M. Balsac was the editor of a daily paper published in Arecibo, Puerto Rico, known as *El Baluarte*. He was charged with two counts of libel on publications made in April 1918. The case was debated in the District Court of Arecibo. Balsac demanded a trial by jury (not allowed in local courts for this offense) under the Sixth Amendment of the US Constitution. Nevertheless, his claim was overruled by the district court. Balsac appealed the decision to the Supreme Court of Puerto Rico, but the court affirmed the decision made by the district court (*Balzac v. Puerto* Rico 1922, 300, 302).

Substantive matters raised by the Supreme Court

On the question of US constitutional jurisdiction

The Supreme Court stated that the penal code in Puerto Rico divides crimes into felonies and misdemeanors. Only felony cases have the right to a jury trial. Given that libel falls under the misdemeanor classification, the Supreme Court upheld the determination of the district court. As to the question of whether the Sixth Amendment of the Constitution contemplates this case and/or Puerto Rico for all purposes, the Supreme Court stated "that they do not apply to territory belonging to the United States which has not been incorporated to the Union" (*Balzac v. Puerto Rico* 1922, 303–5).

The court supported its decision on the ruling in the case of *Dorr v. United States*, which in turn aligned with Article IV of the US Constitution, which states:

> ...that the power to govern territory, implied in the right to acquire it, and given to Congress in the Constitution ... does not require that body to enact for ceded territory, not made part of the United States by congressional action, a system of laws which shall include the right of trial by jury, and that the Constitution does not, without legislation and on its force, carry such right to the territory so situated. (1904, 305)

By stating this contention, the court departs from a previous understanding of the US judiciary, in the context of US expansion throughout the continental mainland, which holds the premise that "Constitution follows the flag." That is, the legal and political understanding of the time was that the expansion of the United States should be carried out through the project of incorporating territories providing full exercise of Constitutional rights, citizenship, and eventual integration as a state of the Union. In other words, once a territory is obtained by any means, the process of extending the Constitution in its totality, ending in the incorporation of the territory as a state of the Union would be inexorably initiated.

In this sense, the US sovereignty over Puerto Rico, and the other territories acquired in 1898, shows how a state of exception was implanted through a process by which the sovereign nation departs from the law with the permission of the law itself; that is, the law indicates what is inside or outside the law. As stated by Giorgio Agamben, both the paradox and the violence of sovereignty consist "in the fact that the sovereign is, at the same time, outside and inside of the juridical order" (1998, 15);   that is, the sovereign is the point of indistinction between violence and law. According to the *Balzac* decision, "the real issue in the insular cases was not whether the Constitution extended to the Philippines or Puerto Rico when we went there, but which of its provisions were applicable..." (1922, 312). Therefore, the imposed law is justified by the law itself, that is by the legal arguments raised and sustained in courts: full applicability of the Constitution for the US continental mainland, partial and selective application for the territory.

It is worth noting that the state of exception does not cancel the presence of the discourse on the rule of law. That is, the suspension does not entail elimination. Instead, it is how law employs exception from the standpoint of law itself, the way exceptional forms are politically and judicially justified. The example brought by Giorgio Agamben is the simultaneity of the enactment of the USA Patriot Act issued by the U.S. Senate on October 26, 2001, with the continuity of the rule of law both within US mainland and within the island.[7]

At a different level of analysis, it is important to note that, as stated by federal judge Juan Torruella, this legal reading was unconstitutional as it comes from the 1856 Supreme Court decision in the *Dred Scott v. Stanford* (1857) case:

There is certainly no power given by the Constitution to the Federal Government to establish or maintain colonies bordering on the United States or at a distance, to be ruled and governed at its own pleasure; nor to enlarge its

territorial limits in any way, except by the admission of new States . ... [N]o power is given to acquire a territory to be held and governed permanently [in a colonial] character. (1857, 446—quoted in Torruella 2016, 84–5)

Also, and as discussed by federal judge Gustavo Gelpí, Pedro Albizu Campos, prominent leader of nationalist and independence movements on the island, had argued in *Velázquez v. People of Puerto Rico* that the Treaty of Paris was an illegal act since Puerto Rico already enjoyed sovereignty before the treaty's enactment:

Puerto Rican patriots hold the Nationalist point of view that the Treaty of Paris and the subsequent acts of the United States in Puerto Rico are null and void so far as Puerto Rico is concerned, as the nation enjoyed at the time said treaty was signed international status, and Spain could not negotiate any treaty binding on Puerto Rico, unless negotiated by plenipotentiaries of Puerto Rico and ratified by the Parliament of Puerto Rico.

After the promulgation of the Autonomic Charter (*Carta Autonómica*), the relations between Puerto Rico and Spain were regulated by treaty, from sovereign to sovereign. (Gelpí 2018)

It is worth noting that "no idea of the law" (Luhmann 1998, 128) exists above the law for systems that operate autopoietically, that is, by establishing their boundaries. Therefore, Constitution operates as a "supra legal law" in the sense of being the final answer to what is legal or not, or what is inside or outside the law (illegal). In this sense, the ambivalence and the different readings regarding the applicability or not of the Constitution in its full force to the territories end to be a neuralgic one.

On the nonincorporated status of the territory

The *Balzac* court stated that the Organic Act of Puerto Rico of 1917, known as the Jones Act, does not indicate "that it has the purpose to incorporate the island into the Union" (1922, 306). Furthermore, it stated that, from the court's point of view, there is no clause which declares such purpose; therefore, "it strongly tends to show that Congress did not have such intention and, if the case was the contrary, Congress would have stated it "by plain declaration" and not have left it to "mere inference " (1922, 306). This is a relevant contention from the court but is also a time-sensitive one. As it is stated by Luhmann, as Modernity evolves and so does the legal system, the reliance on the strict letter of the law in the determination of cases is increasingly substituted by the growing relevance of the function of legal interpretation. As a result, I contend that what is based primarily on the strict letter of the law at some point in time tends to be challenged by a variety of interpretations, the end result of which can be the enactment of a new law. I will come back to this discussion.

The paradox of citizenship and locality

As stated in the *Balzac* decision, it was assumed that the inhabitants of Puerto Rico had the right to expect protection from the new sovereign (1922, 308). The conferring of American citizenship to Puerto Ricans was viewed as a way to provide this protection. Yet the exercise of full citizenship was conditioned to settling in the continental United States "and becoming residents of any state there to enjoy every right of any other citizen of the United States, civil, social and political" (1922, 308). It is important to note that Puerto Ricans cannot enjoy full rights of citizenship in Puerto Rico since "it is locality that is determinative of the application of the Constitution ...not the status of the people who live in it" (1922, 309).

After all, the emphasis on locality, the sovereignty over the territory—with the effect of discursively and symbolically erasing its inhabitants—appear as the judicial and political framework of a stage in capitalist economic evolution.

The above contention from the court is consistent with the argument wielded by different scholars, namely, that what the US judiciary was interested in was the land and not the people. In this sense, the comment made by publicist Edwin Miranda in Ricardo Rosselló's chat in 2019—which resulted in his resignation from the position of governor—is characteristic: "I saw the future, it's so wonderful, there are no Puerto Ricans" is an expression of what was effectively stated in this legal case. It is also possible to assert that, at the time this case was tried, there appeared to be a tight coupling between the legal, political, and economic systems in the United States, with possession/property serving as the primary *dispositif*. After all, the emphasis on locality, the sovereignty over the territory—with the effect of discursively and symbolically erasing its inhabitants—appear as the judicial and political framework of a stage in capitalist economic evolution. In this stage, the imaginary of the land as the main object of valorization, the acquisition of a territory with the correspondent property rights conflated are central. Reflecting on the issue of locality, Efrén Rivera Ramos identified in *Downes v. Bidwell* (1901) a complementary clue:

The inhabitants of the islands are not joint partners with the States in their transaction. The islands are "territory belonging to the United States," not a part of the United States. The islands were the things acquired by the treaty; the United States was the party who acquired them, and to whom they belong. The owner and the item owned are not the same thing. (1996, 292)

Note that inhabitants are positioned in the same place as acquired things. The subjects in the transaction were Spain and the United States. In the subject/object divide proposed by positive science, objects are placed in a subordinate position with respect to subjects.

At a higher level of analysis, the emphasis on locality resulted in an abstraction of people, because considering its inhabitants would activate the possibility of opening a space for an imaginary of a (sovereign) corporality attached to the acquired territory. This would eventually compete (as it effectively was and has been) with the imaginary of US sovereignty, whose corporality is linked to the mainland people. As stated by Georgio Agamben, the principle of sovereignty lies in the nation and nation as a signifier derives from *nacere* (to be born) in the nation (1998, 128). Therefore, and in principle, sovereignty would have to be conferred to those who have been born in a specific locality, but by almost stating the "locality is mine," inhabitants become disposed or placed as bare life (not being part of the sovereign body), that is, life without juridical protection. For Agamben and Jacques Rancière (2004), bare life constitutes itself as political as the law itself interpellates the person as a subject of law, but if the conferred US citizenship for Puerto Ricans cannot be fully embraced on the physical space occupied by the island, then this juridical-political potentiality is truncated.

The "inconvenience" of overseas

In commenting on the incorporation of Alaska to the states of the Union, the court in the *Balzac* decision stated that:

Alaska was a very different case from that of Porto Rico. It was an enormous territory, very sparsely settled, and offering an opportunity for immigration and settlement by American citizens. (1922, 309)

The above quote clearly illustrates that incorporation was always viewed from the perspective of the "true citizens," which were (and still are) the white people from the US mainland. The juridico-political imaginary of the epoch fully legitimizes the inferiority of Black American citizenship on account of the equal but separate doctrine. In this sense, and once again, the legal rationale appears to be inextricably linked to the evolution of political and economic systems. The interest was the land as a resource to be populated and exploited by white American citizens.

Balzac v. Porto Rico in contemporary scenarios

A judicial update

There are, indisputably, two cases that confirm the prevalence of the dispositions contemplated in the *Balzac v. Porto Rico*: *Commonwealth of Puerto Rico v. Sanchez Vázquez* (2016) and the law known as PROMESA, which marked the beginnings of the Fiscal Control Board in Puerto Rico.[8] In the first case, although it is recognized as Congress' relinquishment over local matters, which is a measure of self-autonomy comparable to that possessed by the States at the time, this law makes Congress the original source of power for Puerto Rico's prosecutors. As stated by Juan Torruella:

...the United States argues that the approval of self-government for Puerto Rico in 1952 did not change Puerto Rico's fundamental constitutional status as

a U.S. territory subject to the paramount authority of Congress under the Territorial Clause. (2016, 81)

As with the congressional legislation named PROMESA, which created a
non-elected entity oversight board to restructure the island's debt, there is
a consensus that it made the territorial character of the island a politically
transparent phenomenon:

This Board will have the power to impose a deadline on the Government of
Puerto Rico for developing a fiscal plan and budget that meet Congress's crite-
ria—as well as the right to reject Puerto Rico's proposals and substitute its own
instead. (Torruella 2016, 81)

The legislation also gives the Board the prerogative to demand any information and documentation it believes may be relevant from the Government
of Puerto Rico... and requires the Puerto Rico legislature to submit all acts it
passes, along with estimates of their cost, to the Oversight Board for evaluation in short order... If the Board determines that an act is not consistent with
the approved fiscal plan, it may unilaterally dictate that the act be changed or
simply overrule the Government of Puerto Rico to block its enforcement or application. (Torruella 2016, 82)

It is worth noting that one of the provisions of the PROMESA legislation
(section 405) allows for the selling of thousands of acres of land for development purposes, allowing the Secretary of the Interior to convey it to the government of Puerto Rico to sell. In this sense, it is plausible to conclude that,
ownership of the land, central to a sovereign that rests on locality in *Balzac v.
Porto Rico*, finds its continuation and equivalence in legislation that constitutes
both a tight coupling with, and a juridical arm for, capitalism in its current
stage, that is, financial capitalism. From the valorization of land characteristic
of the imperial stage capitalism, still resting on an imaginary of capital that
extracts its profits from the land (the territory) to the preeminence of financial
capitalism, the economic system finds in the prevalence of *Balzac v. Porto Rico*
a similar judicial-political efficacy for both historical contexts. At present, the
evictions conducted by financial capitalism within the context of the mortgage

crisis are, almost, symbolically equivalent to the dispossession of Puerto Ricans at the time of the *Balzac* unanimous decision delivered by Judge Howard Taft.

Furthermore, at present, the preeminence of financial capitalism makes viable the settlement of an increasing number of American entrepreneurs—in the areas of tourism, real estate and digital companies—which changes what in this case appears as an "overseas inconvenience":

Despite the complex government bankruptcy and the critical state of the infrastructure in Puerto Rico, as the money for the recovery arrives—and the debt restructuring culminates—the future outlook is encouraging and those knowledgeable about the business sector assure. They assure that it is time to invest in the Island.

'For an American citizen, to the extent that he stops paying US taxes, he finds it attractive. They move, they eliminate the high costs, but they maintain the US guarantees and with lower taxes... and to that you add that they can continue to maintain their lifestyle,' added Rivera. (Ramos Segarra 2021)

'The luxury market a few years ago was almost non-existent on the Island. There was an opportunity and we took it. It is an attractive destination for its natural beauty, educated population, cultural richness and motivation,' Peña said, while noting that the average price of luxury properties that are being sold is around $4 million.

'They are looking for large properties. Before, the time on the market for these properties was a year and a half and now it is six months. The most requested areas are San Juan, Guaynabo, Río Grande, Dorado and Humacao. We recently sold a residence in Dorado at the Ritz Carlton for $18 million and another for $30 million with five offers,' added Peña. (Ramos Segarra 2021)

In fact, some towns in Puerto Rico, such as Rincón, the Island of Vieques, and Dorado have distinct demographics from the rest of the island. A quick glance reveals a higher concentration of settled Americans in these towns, as well as housing complexes and businesses that are clearly connected to that presence. If the above economic factors are met, this demographic landscape could be expanded throughout the island.

Juridico-political skirmishes

The *Insular Cases*[9] and the *Balzac* decision of 1922 have been described as cases with a significant number of ambiguities, interpretations, and uncertainties in terms of their projection of Puerto Rico's future. More recently, there have been lawyers and legal scholars from different political persuasions who have tried to turn this legal case around to reinstitute an act of interpretation capable of changing this state of affairs. The law attempts to legitimize itself with the law itself, aiming at producing a different law. These efforts are a type of juridico-political skirmishing or legal discursive terrorism aimed at gaining a greater sense of justice through the acquisition of more rights or equality from what is discursively identified at the federal level. In this line of efforts, I situated Judge Gelpí's arguments on a diversity of subjects: his proposed parallel between the territorial clause and the doctrine of separate but equal utilized to legitimize racial segregation in the US,[10] the unconstitutionality of the non-applicability of the Uniformed and Overseas Citizens Absentee Voting Act for citizens in Puerto Rico,[11] the doctrine of the double exposition,[12] the consent of the governed,[13] and the right of the social security supplement for Puerto Rico, among others. The case of *U.S. v. Vaello-Madero*,[14] about the right of the social security supplement, is perceived as the most important one by people in Puerto Rico. The doctrine of separate but equal was abolished based on the acknowledgment that it affirmed that Black Americans have rights as citizens that they were barred from exercising. Being in a citizenship category defines your rights. For example, Puerto Ricans living in Puerto Rico do not have the right to supplemental security income as American citizens.[15] As stated by Judge Gelpí in this case:

[Article IV], however, is not carte blanche for Congress to switch on and off at its convenience the fundamental constitutional rights to Due Process and Equal Protection enjoyed by a birthright United States citizen who relocates from a state to Puerto Rico. Congress, likewise, cannot denigrate and stigmatize said US citizen while he is in Puerto Rico with a label of inferior citizenship to that of his brethren nationwide. To hold otherwise would run afoul of the sacrosanct principle embodied in the Declaration of Independence that 'All Men are Created Equal.' (*United States v. Vaello-Madero* 2019, 208)

Most important, Judge Gelpí's assertion in *Consejo de Salud, Playa de Ponce v. Rullan* (2009), that Puerto Rico has evolved from an unincorporated territory to an incorporated one due to "a monumental constitutional evolution based on continued and repeated congressional annexation" (*Consejo De Salud Playa De Ponce v. Rullan* 2009), seems like a legal skirmish with the goal of producing a different juridical and political reality. Although other legal scholars feel obliged to indicate that Gelpí was mistaken in his decision since only the US Congress can make that kind of declaration as stated in *Balzac* (Rivera 2008), I tend to disagree. I believe that Gelpí's decision appears as a reinstituted act of interpretation aiming to test the capacity of the US courts and Congress to assume an act of self-correction (for the territory) in the name of justice and democracy within the parameters of the US Constitution and judicial system. Also, Gelpí's judicial strategy rests in conquering as much rights as possible, aiming at reaching a stage where the *de facto* integration of the island could weigh more than its *de jure* situation.[16]

I believe that Gelpí's decision appears as a reinstituted act of interpretation aiming to test the capacity of the US courts and Congress to assume an act of self-correction (for the territory) in the name of justice and democracy within the parameters of the US Constitution and judicial system.

As stated by Jacques Derrida, "justice as law" can only be reached by a "fresh judgement":

To be just, a judge's decision, for example, must not only follow a rule of law or a general law, but must also assume, approve, and confirm its value through a reinstituting act of interpretation, as if ultimately nothing previously existed of the law, as if the judge invented the law in each case. No exercise of justice as law can be just unless there is a "fresh judgment".... for a decision to be just and responsible, it must, in its proper moment if there is one, be both regulated and without regulation: it must conserve the law and also destroy it or suspend it enough to have to reinvent it in each case... (1992, 23)

At the same time, it is worth noting that tensions between federal and local courts due to the territorial status of the island continue to be a subject of legal disputes, as is currently the case pertaining to the seizure of jurisdiction by the federal court in Puerto Rico of the indictment of boxer Félix Verdejo for the murder of Keishla Rodríguez on April 27, 2021 (Acevedo 2021). Federal jurisdiction is justified on account of the charge of carjacking resulting in death,[17] which is a federal one, although the main object of inquiry, in this case, was a murder:

> **The investigation and presentation of charges against the boxer Félix Verdejo again reflected the cracks that the territorial status can cause in the Puerto Rican penal law.... The problem is that in Puerto Rico, since the decision of the Sánchez Valle case in 2016, the situation is different since that same court decided that "the ultimate source of Puerto Rico's prosecutorial power" rests with Congress. Thus, it can only be prosecuted by one of the two jurisdictions for the same conduct, if it is the same crime. This does not necessarily imply that criminal conduct cannot be prosecuted in federal court and in the courts of Puerto Rico, but it will be required to be for different crimes and that can be a very difficult dividing line to draw in some cases, so the clause against double exposure could be violated, thus preventing further prosecution. If this is the case, the prerogative of our Department of Justice to prosecute Félix Verdejo for some crimes allegedly committed could be violated—hypothetically. (Fontanet 2021)**

For some local lawyers and scholars, the seizure of jurisdiction by a federal court in Puerto Rico raises suspicions of an intention to introduce the death penalty into the island's legal and media landscape, a punishment not contemplated by the Puerto Rican Constitution.[18]

Evidently, judicial agency regarding subjects such as the territorial clause, the status of citizenship and the rights of Puerto Ricans of the Island are entirely crossed with proposed political solutions being independence, annexation, or any simple or complex alternative formulations. Political solutions like independence, annexation, or any other formulation are in opposition to the juridical actions regarding the territorial clause and the current citizenship of Puerto Ricans. Some people see the fight for more rights within the US legal system as moving away from the horizon of independence. Others view the rights conquered within the US legal system as a moral and legal duty from the United States to pay what it owes to Puerto Rico. Others state the fight for more rights within the US legal system as expanding the democratic imaginary in Puerto Rico deriving from the complete application of US Constitution.

Irritations from the environment

An update on locality

I have previously stated that the comment made by publicist Edwin Miranda in Rosselló's chat, "I saw the future, it's so wonderful, there are no Puerto Ricans," is a faithful expression of the argument of "locality" in Balsac's case. Yet this expression confronted great and massive indignation on the part of thousands of protesters in the "15 days of fury" (Romero et al. 2019) leading to the collapse of Rosselló's government in 2019. How do we make sense of this phenomenon? Perhaps and intriguingly, something that is not a topic of conversation in Puerto Ricans' daily lives (US sovereignty over locality and the erasure of its inhabitants) acquires symbolic and political significance in the context of widespread dissatisfaction in the island. Perhaps what operates here is a collective corporeality (Puerto Ricans) that imagined itself as sovereign in complete disconnection with the prevalent juridical and political reality. For all practical purposes, the *Balzac* precedent promotes the idea of Puerto Rico without Puerto Ricans. At the same time, several combined and condensed factors promote the phenomena of Puerto Ricans without Puerto Rico illustrating that emptying the island has been a constant in US colonial governance (Negrón-Muntaner 2018). As examples, we confer to the following: full citizenship only to be exercised in US mainland, natural and political sagas that tend to the empty of the island,[19] the legitimate aspiration to a better life, and even the *Balzac* case itself. As it was recently stated by journalist, Benjamín Torres Gotay (2021):

In short, life in Puerto Rico is very complicated. A dying economy for more than 15 years. Institutional collapse. Corruption, favoritism, waste, superficiality…. Neither tomorrow nor the day after, there is no way out of the huge

crisis… But given how complex and easy it is to see over there from here, it is a miracle that people remain in Puerto Rico.

Simultaneously, there is a growing collective corporeality known as "Puerto Ricans," whose existential, cultural, social, and political trajectory (inside or outside the island) runs parallel to and on the margins of this juridico-political matter. This binary, Puerto Rico without Puerto Ricans/"Puerto Ricans without Puerto Rico," gets denser as more Puerto Ricans are on the US mainland than on the island. In 2018, the Puerto Rican population in the US was estimated at 5.8 million.

According to Negrón-Muntaner (2018), these 5.8 million people are not inhabitants of the diaspora since, for her, the diaspora as a signifier is related to an affective/political imaginary of a segment of the Puerto Rican population in the United States mainland that maintains a historical, affective, and consistent commitment to the island's trajectory and vicissitudes. This qualification is important because, "Puerto Ricans without Puerto Rico" could be viewed as a polysemic discursive phrase subject to being signified in a variety of ways: as a population (inside or outside the island) with a strong and contesting cultural cohesiveness interested in the exercise of full right citizenship for the people in Puerto Rico, or as a population living in the US mainland entirely disconnected from the social and or political becoming of the island. The phrase could also signified a population living in the US that has abandoned the imaginary of sovereignty. In this sense, being without Puerto Rico is entirely irrelevant, and even points to a future possibility as the ecological question includes the imminent disappearance of a considerable number of islands (Negrón-Muntaner 2018), therefore the need to imagine a different kind of sovereign or non-sovereign existence.

The binary Puerto Rico without Puerto Ricans/"Puerto Ricans without Puerto Rico" could be assumed from an essentialist standpoint. It takes some inexorability of belonging, a correspondence between land and people—Puerto Rico and Puerto Ricans. I am approaching the binary from an anti-essentialist reading that allows for both the recognition of historical/legal factualities and present tendencies.

To a certain extent, Puerto Ricans' inclusion by way of exclusion in the US sovereign imaginary is similar to the current relationship between citizens and noncitizens (immigrants) on the US mainland. The paradoxical condition of Puerto Ricans is that they are neither on the island, nor on the mainland in their "proper place" (as if there is one!). We are faced with historical and contemporary fears that revolve around the figure of the white American and the consolidation of what Arjun Appadurai (2006) referred to as a predatory identity. That is, an identity with a haughty hegemony that is concerned about the "browning" of the United States and/or the population growth of various minorities:

Most of the people who took part in the assault [January 6 Capitol] came from places, his polling and demographic data showed, that were awash in fears that the rights of minorities and immigrants were crowding out the rights of white people in American politics and culture. (Feuer 2021)

Many whites today, both conservatives and progressives, fear the shift in demographics and the browning of America to varying degrees.... During the 21st century, racial minorities will eventually outnumber whites. Many whites fear this phenomenon. (Lyght 2021)

Possibilities for democratic questions

At present, and as Niklas Luhmann states it, the main irritations of the legal system derive from the political system, mainly from the struggles for more democracy. There is a consensus among Puerto Ricans regarding what is perceived as a democratic deficit, which is constitutive of the island on account of the colonial legacy. This democratic deficit assumes the face of an exceptional state under the US on account of the clause of territoriality, a half-applied Constitution, and a subordinated citizenship based on locality. This has been entirely naturalized by broad segments of the population over the course of a century. On many occasions, political discourses (from various political persuasions) that denounce this juridical and political subjection do not connect with the people's immediate needs or with their life aspirations.

There has also been a tendency in Puerto Rico to consider the territorial/colonial issue mainly as a juridical problem.

At the same time, there is an increasing recognition that the law is losing its relevance and its value on the capacity of people to cope with their everyday life and challenges (Luhmann 2004, 417; Román 2006). Perhaps there will be ones who conclude that I am referring to a generalized "colonial" alienation of significant population segments. Still, for me, it is more a matter of realizing that politics could be somewhere else. There has also been a tendency in Puerto Rico to consider the territorial/colonial issue mainly as a juridical problem. As a result of this tendency, the political and legal classes tend to monopolize the discussion on the island's juridico-political status, while the issue tends to be circumscribed and confined to partisan politics.

There are quite a number of Puerto Ricans in the island that are burdened with party politics. The tendency of electoral abstention tends to be increasing, plebiscites are viewed as a waste of money. There is a profound disaffection due to generalized corruption, but there is also a longing for more equality and justice, not finding support in the available juridical-political discourses. In a survey on Puerto Rican values conducted in 2019, it is stated that:

A majority have no interest in politics (52%) and would not vote for any political party. (EFE 2019)

44% of Puerto Ricans consulted in a study believe that most of the people who make up the island's state authorities have links to corruption. (EFE 2019)

Within this complex social and political scenery, it is evident that the economic problem is the most prominent one:

Since 2006, Puerto Rico has experienced a disastrous economic crisis from which it still does not see a possible escape. That year, the US Congress suspended an agreement that favored US companies to establish on the island, which led to an exodus of companies and led to the beginning of the economic debacle. Tens of thousands of Puerto Ricans have emigrated since then, unemployment and poverty rates have skyrocketed, cuts and debt have multiplied, and the government has run out of funds. (Lima 2019)

Puerto Rico's priority is to get out of the quagmire, put the economy to produce jobs, and have a clean government that works well for everyone and not
for a few. (Prats 2020)

The series of events and massive protests that culminated in the resignation of then-Governor Ricardo Rosselló in 2019 shows a condensation of
disaffections linked to these fundamental problems and needs, rather than a
position against the territorial/colonial condition. As it is stated by political
science professor [José] Javier Colón:

"Some of the problems that are being aired in these protests have more to do
with a series of austerity policies, a series of cuts in public spending that have
been bothering the population for many years," says Colón. (Lima 2019)

Paradoxically, although these problems are, at least, part of the effects of
a historically subjugated economy,[20] this connection is not always present
in the conscious registration of the everyday lives of Puerto Ricans. Still,
the debt problem places Puerto Rico in a subjection similar to that of other
countries—whether sovereign or not—in the sense that there is, as David
Harvey puts it, a "debtocracy," which implies "an accumulation of dispossession" for the people who live through it:

In the neoliberal frames of privatization, financialization, and management of
the crisis, jobs are being taken away, hopes are obliterated, and bodies are
instrumentalized and worn out. (Butler and Athanasiou 2013, 12)

It should be noted that what has been referred to as the "status" problem
(the colonial/territorial issue) has traditionally harmed any discussion of
democracy in Puerto Rico for a variety of reasons. Majoritarian political parties
have a propensity to relate current problems associated with a democratic deficit to the "status" issue, almost as "if the status problem did not exist, we would
not have these other problems either." This does not take into consideration
that problems associated with democratic deficits exist all over the world, and
other countries do not have the choice to use this discourse (the "status" problem) to explain their actions; instead, they must deal with it directly.

It is also worth noting that this fluid social and political scenery detailed thus far contrasts with Judge Gelpí's linear and consistent strategy towards the juridical, political integration of the island. This paradox can be seen as an illustration of a significant decoupling between the legal, the social, and the political, but, perhaps, it also illustrates that beneath this fluidity lies a generalized dissatisfaction with the current juridical-political status, apart from the course it will finally embrace.

Another level of analysis: the global context in which sovereignty is weighed

Up to a point, the *Balzac v. Porto Rico* decision appears to be a completely separate phenomenon from some of the contemporary debates about sovereignty. These debates revolve around the theoretical and political viability of the concept of sovereignty in the light of a globalized society's predominance, the relative decline of nation-states as major political actors, the intensification of all kinds of cultural reconversions, and their effect on the increasing hybridity of collective and personal "identitites." It also revolves around how the centrality of the right to collective self-determination has been replaced by the right to individual self-determination, and there is a tendency of people moving around the world in search of a "better life" rather than staying to create a "better country" (Román 2017, 285–95).

This juridical-political subjection has a tragic undercurrent. It has to do with the tendency to misinterpret a legal-political issue as a moral one. For those who assume this subjection as an existential conflict, life can become agonizing. Perhaps, this is one of the highest psychic prices paid by the subjected people themselves. This is the point of intersection between the social and the psychic systems. At the same time, there is a growing literature that also stresses that the epoch for embracing great heroic causes has been eroded (Canclini 1995). Therefore, broad segments of the population installed themselves in the legitimate aspiration of a good life and a relatively efficient administration of government departing themselves from all-embracing ideals.

Concluding remarks

As modernity evolves, the tendency for systems to decouple increases. The legal, political, economic, and cultural systems, among others, increase in complexity from both internal and external differentiation. It is plausible to say that the *Balzac* juridical dispositions are placed in open tension with a local government system that is very similar in its structure to that of any state of the union, a highly cohesive Puerto Rican culture that coexists with a large level of cultural reconversions, a highly complex local legal system comparable in its structure to that of the United States, and an economy whose subjugation to the territorial/colonial context is already unsustainable.[21]

This complex combination of different and conflicting states of affairs requires us to analyze what can be said and/or done about the territorial/colonial status of Puerto Rico from the standpoint of the political system, from the perspective of the economic system, from the perspective of the cultural system, and so forth. This could be a way to recognize that changes in one of these systems do not necessarily have a "domino" effect on the others. This recognition adds another level of complexity for a country's trajectory and personal ones.

Niklas Luhmann refers to the reproductive value of unsolved problems. He also stated that paradoxes surround us and that paradoxes tend to be solved not at the level they were raised, but at a different level. Perhaps in the search for other ways to discuss these issues, we can gradually resolve some of these paradoxes. At the time I am writing this essay, the Chairman of the House Natural Resources Committee in charge of discussing Puerto Rico's affairs, Raúl Grijalva, has requested a call for a public hearing on the *Insular Cases.* "The hearing seeks to examine the resolution that proposes to the federal government to discard that jurisprudence that created the status of unincorporated territory" (Delgado 2021), and there are also two plebiscite proposals submitted (Cotto 2021). The way these events in course will make a difference for the Puerto Rican people and the ways Puerto Rican people in the island will respond to these events remains to be seen.

This analysis is part of ongoing research, which centers around the relationship between communications deriving from the legal system and communications emanating from other systems of functions and the social system in Puerto Rico.

NOTES

[1] The discursive phrase is coined by Frances Negrón-Muntaner (2018) in her essay "The Emptying Island: Puerto Rican Exposure in Post-Maria Time"

[2] That is, without having to mechanically relate an observation with a specific political persuasion, being that independence of statehood, once the complexity of the juridico political content of this and other legal cases has been understood, surpasses party politics.

[3] This discursive phrase, second-generation theory, refers to a theoretical field initially developed within the natural sciences dedicated to the study of highly complex systems. Those systems are characterized by their capacity to reproduce themselves from their operations and their self-referentiality. The physical universe, the organization of living beings, and the social and psychic systems are considered domains that can be studied from the standpoint of this theoretical field.

[4] That is, in the understanding that determined outputs correspond to determined inputs.

[5] That is, that there are no inexorabilities, that everything could be different, that nothing is impossible, and nothing is necessary.

[6] I thank public defender Iris Rosario for her observations on this subject.

[7] The history of Puerto Rico is a history of exceptionality that begins with a military government. The President of the United States appointed all officials, including the local governor. The United States passes laws not applicable in Puerto Rico, while the "local" constitution of 1952 leaves intact US sovereignty of the island. The Fiscal Control Board has recently kept the power to overthrow all legislation inconsistent with their fiscal plan.

[8] Although the official name is the Fiscal Oversight Board, it is clear that its capacity to dictate what is consistent or not with their decisions unilaterally made its task closer to control and not to supervision. Therefore, in recognizing this, people in Puerto Rico choose to name it the Fiscal Control Board.

[9] A series of opinions by the US Supreme Court about the status of the territories acquired in the Spanish-American War.

[10] According to Judge Gelpí, Puerto Rico's legal situation is similar to that of Black American citizens under the doctrine of separate but equal, which was overturned in the 1954 Supreme Court case *Brown v. Education*, which established that the doctrine of separate but equal was not, in fact, equal at all.

[11] This Act establishes the right of all US citizens to exercise the right of absentee

vote for federal elections. Puerto Rico is excluded from that right since that act establishes that the right is conferred by the states.

[12] Judge Gelpí takes its applicability in Puerto Rico as an expression of the extension of US constitutional rights to Puerto Rico. This doctrine establishes that a person cannot be prosecuted twice (state and federal level) for the same charges.

[13] As stated by Judge Gelpí, at present, federal prosecutions of Puerto Ricans are conducted without the consent of the governed since people in Puerto Rico have not participated in the creation of the laws applied to them.

[14] This case addresses the case of José Luis Vaello-Madero who lived in New York from 1985 to 2013 and received SSI benefits due to a disability. However, after he moved to Loíza, Puerto Rico in 2013, he was removed from the program. He continued receiving his routine payments until 2016 when the Social Security Administration learned of his relocation. The agency then proceeded to demand that he return all payments issued in those three years, a total of $28,081 (Garófalo 2020).

[15] The First Circuit of Federal Appeals determined in April 2020 that it is unconstitutional—for violating the equal protection of the laws—to deny the residents of Puerto Rico access to SSI. Lawyers argued that this exclusion is "arbitrary and irrational" because it fails to fulfill the purpose of the law to treat citizens with disabilities and the indigent in a uniform manner.

[16] There has been a parallel evolvement in other areas of the law. For instance, although this legal system continues to stress that there is a single law for everybody, the system moves toward all sorts of differential legislations: to the creation of laws that pertain to the specific needs or claims of the population and people.

[17] The punishment for the federal offense of carjacking is severe. If no serious bodily injury or death occurred, a carjacker may be sentenced to 15 years in prison. If a serious bodily injury occurred as a result of the carjacking, a carjacker may be sentenced to 25 years in prison. If a death occurred as a result of the carjacking, a carjacker may be sentenced to life in prison or may even receive the death penalty (<https://www.justice.gov/archives/jm/criminal-resource-manual-1110-carjacking-statute>; and <https://www.johnedwardslaw.com/newsletters/criminal-law-newsletters/federal-laws-regarding-carjacking/#:~:text=The%20punishment%20for%20the%20federal,to%2015%20years%20in%20prison.&text=If%20a%20death%20occurred%20as,even%20receive%20the%20death%20penalty>).

[18] In 1950, Congress enacted legislation (P.L. 81-600) authorizing Puerto Rico to hold a constitutional convention and in 1952, the people of Puerto Rico ratified a

constitution establishing a republican form of government for the island. Some understand that these tensions refer to the relationship between the federal and state levels. However, since Puerto Rico is not a state of the union, the concept of federalism does not have the explanatory solvency needed to account for the exceptional nature of this situation.

[19] Chronic unemployment, the aftermath of Hurricane María, the economic crisis, the seismic problem, etc.

[20] At least partly because I am taking into consideration the recurring argument in Puerto Rico regarding both the problem of inefficiency local governmental and private sectors' neglect in the perpetuation of economic problems of the island.

[21] This last issue being the one most openly in conflict with the territorial/colonial status.

REFERENCE

Acevedo, Nicole. 2021. As Puerto Rico Mourns Keishla Rodríguez's Death, Boxer Félix Verdejo Is Indicted in Her Killing. *NBC News* 6 May. <https://www.nbcnews.com/news/latino/puerto-rico-mourns-keishla-rodriguez-s-death-boxer-f-lix-n1266598>.

Agamben, Giorgio. 1998. *Homo Sacer: Sovereign Power and Bare Life*. Palo Alto, CA: Stanford University Press.

Appadurai, Arjun. 2006. *Fear of Small Numbers*. Durham, NC: Duke University Press.

Balzac v. Porto Rico 1922. 258 US 298.

Butler, Judith and Athena Athanasiou. 2013. *Dispossession: The Performative in the Political*. Cambridge, UK: Polity Press.

Consejo De Salud Playa De Ponce v. Rullan. 2009. 586 F. Supp. 2d 22 (D.P.R.).

Cotto, Ingrid. 2021. Congreso realiza primera vista sobre estatus de Puerto Rico con dos propuestas para el futuro de la isla. *Orlando Sentinel* 14 April. <https://www.orlandosentinel.com/espanol/os-es-puerto-rico-congreso-estatus-propuesta-primera-vista-20210414-5lvicb2nyrdohaf4wvas6fppua-story.html>.

Delgado, José. 2021. Raúl Grijalba convoca a una vista pública sobre los casos insulares. *El Nuevo Día* 7 May. <https://www.elnuevodia.com/corresponsalias/washington-dc/notas/raul-grijalva-convoca-a-una-vista-publica-sobre-los-casos-insulares>.

Derrida, Jacques. 1992. Force of Law: The Mystical Foundation of Authority. In *Deconstruction and the Possibility of Justice*, eds. Drucilla Cornell, Michel Rosenfeld and David Carlson. 3–67. New York: Routledge

Dorr v. United States. 1904. 258 US 305.

Dred Scott v. Sanford. 1857. 60 U.S. 393.

EFE. 2019. Un 44% de los puertorriqueños ve corrupción en la mayoría de las autoridades estatales. *El Nuevo Día* 26 June. <https://www.elnuevodia.com/noticias/locales/notas/un-44-de-los-puertorriquenos-ve-corrupcion-en-la-mayoria-de-las-autoridades-estatales>.

Feuer, Alan. 2021. Fears of White People Losing Out Permeate Capital Rioters' Towns, Study Finds. *The New York Times* 6 April. <https://www.nytimes.com/2021/04/06/us/politics/capitol-riot-study.html>.

Fontanet, Julio. 2021. El estatus territorial y el arresto de Félix Verdejo. *El Nuevo Día* 6 May. <https://www.elnuevodia.com/opinion/punto-de-vista/el-estatus-territorial-y-el-arresto-de-felix-verdejo>.

Garófalo, Giovanna. 2020. Puerto Rico Still on Hold for Suplemental Security Income. *The Weekly Journal* 11 March. <https://www.theweeklyjournal.com/politics/puerto-rico-still-on-hold-for-supplemental-security-income/article_cfbd95ca-634a-11ea-a13b-777259d86382.html>.

Gelpí, Gustavo A. 2018. Pedro Albizu Campos, el abogado federal y el notorio caso de *Velázquez versus People of Puerto Rico. Academia de jurisprudencia de Puerto Rico* 29 November. <https://www.academiajurisprudenciapr.org/discurso-de-instalacion-honorable-gustavo-gelpi>.

Legal Information Institute. n.d. Separate But Equal. Cornell Law School. <https://www.law.cornell.edu/wex/separate_but_equal>.

Lima, Lioman. 2019. Crisis en Puerto Rico: por qué los graves problemas en la isla no terminan con la salida de Rosselló. *BBC News Mundo* 25 July. <https://www.bbc.com/mundo/noticias-america-latina-49105928>.

Luhmann, Niklas. 2004. *Law as a Social System.* New York: Oxford University Press.

Michaud, Yves. 1989. *Violencia y política.* Buenos Aires: Editorial Sudamericana.

Microjuris. 2018. Detras de la toga: entrevista al honorable Gustavo A. Gelpí. 24 July. *You Tube* video, 1:06:52. <https://www.youtube.com/watch?v=_qEVqCAa5ho&t=2411s>.

Negrón-Muntaner, Frances. 2018. The Emptying Island: Puerto Rican Expulsion in Post-Maria Time. *Hemisphere Institute.* <https://hemisphericinstitute.org/en/emisferica-14-1-expulsion/14-1-essays/the-emptying-island-puerto-rican-expulsion-in-post-maria-time.html>.

Prats, Roberto. 2020. La encuesta final. *El Nuevo Día* 1 November. <https://www.

elnuevodia.com/opinion/punto-de-vista/la-encuesta-final>.

Ramos Segarra, Christian. 2021. Atractivo Puerto Rico para la inversion. *El Vocero*
16 March. <https://www.elvocero.com/economia/atractivo-puerto-rico-
para-la-inversi-n/article_bfca1514-85f7-11eb-ba5f-1faa4e77ad36.html>.

_____. Puerto Rico en el ojo del inversionista. *El Vocero* 12 April. <https://www.
elvocero.com/economia/puerto-rico-en-el-ojo-del-inversionista/article_
ec90d158-9b52-11eb-9433-1f76f0573ff4.html>.

Ranciere, Jacques. 2004. Who is the Subject of the Rights of Man. *The South
Atlantic Quarterly* 103(3/4), 297–310.

Rivera Ramos, Efrén. 1996. The Legal Construction of American Colonialism: The Insular
Cases (1901-1922). *Revista Jurídica Universidad de Puerto Rico* 65, 225–326.

_____. 2008. ¿Territorio incorporado? *Derecho al derecho* 19 November. <http://
derechoalderecho.org/2008/11/19/territorio-incorporado>.

Román, Madeline. 2006. *Estallidos: polisemia y polimorfia del derecho y la violencia.*
San Juan: Publicaciones Puertorriqueñas.

_____. 2017. Sovereignty Still? In *Sovereign Acts: Contesting Colonialism Across
Indigenous Nations and Latinx America,* ed. Frances Negrón-Muntaner,
285–95. Tucson: The University of Arizona Press.

Romero, Simon, Frances Robles, Patricia Mazzei and José A. Del Real. 2019. 15 Days
of Fury: How Puerto Rico's Government Collapse. *The New York Times*
27 July. <https://www.nytimes.com/2019/07/27/us/puerto-rico-protests-
timeline.html>.

Torres Gotay, Benjamín. 2021. El milagro puertorriqueño. *El Nuevo Día* 27 April.
<https://www.elnuevodia.com/opinion/las-cosas-por-su-nombre/el-mila-
gro-puertorriqueno>.

Torruellas, Juan. 2016. Outstanding Constitutional and International Law Issues
Raised by the United States-Puerto Rico Relationship. *Minnesota Law
Review: Headnotes* 41. <https://scholarship.law.umn.edu/headnotes/41>.

United States vs. Vaello-Madero. 2019. 356 F. Supp. 3d 208 (D.P.R.).

William Lyght. 2021. Letter: White Fears Shift in US Demographics and the
'Browning' of America. *Savannah Morning News* 6 May. <https://www.
savannahnow.com/story/opinion/2021/05/06/white-americans-support-
voter-suppression-and-gerrymandering-hold-power-demographics-fear-
shift/4921695001>.

Latino Orlando: Suburban Transformation and Racial Conflict

By Simone Delerme
Florida: University Press of Florida, 2020
ISBN: 978-0-81306-625-7
210 pages; $80.00 [hardcover]

Reviewer: Alessandra Rosa (amrosa1@usf.edu), University of South Florida

Latino Orlando provides the reader with a detailed description of Latino/a/x migration and the demographic changes that led to the transformation of the landscapes and soundscapes in a suburb community within Orlando, Florida. It complicates the U.S. racial categorizations of the black-white binary by narrating the stories of Puerto Ricans and other Latino/a/x residents as they resettled into the Greater Orlando area (i.e., Orange, Osceola, Lake, and Seminole counties) as well as the impact on the receiving population. The book carefully portrays how complex and heterogenous the Latino/a/x community is in the "New South" and how central it has become to its economic, cultural, political, and social life.

It is a short and enticing book with only 149 pages of text and 12 pages of endnotes. It's organized into a brief prologue, an introduction, five substantive chapters, and a conclusion. Each chapter builds on the previous one as Delerme's two-year anthropological fieldwork led her to unexpected directions exploring issues regarding the development of the suburb Buenaventura Lakes (BVL) and how social class and racial identities were constructed and represented in the area. As she conducted her ethnography, she also gathered data about Latino/a/x migrant integration, the process of Latinization and racialization, as well as language ideologies.

In the opening prologue, Delerme offers us a glimpse into her life growing up as part of the Puerto Rican diaspora, enabling us to become familiarized with her-story and how she began researching Puerto Ricans in the South, particularly the BVL suburb also known as "Little Puerto Rico." The introduction, "New Destinations," situates the book in the context of new gateway destinations in the U.S. South for Latino/a/x migration. Using census data, Delerme traces an overview of the history of Latino/a/x migration to the U.S., focusing on the Puerto Rican migration to Florida, particularly the BLV suburb where Puerto Ricans settled. Here, readers are introduced to her methodology, why she uses the terms Latino and Hispanic interchangeably throughout the book, and her book's limitations.

Chapter 1, "Buenaventura Lakes," introduces us to the development of the Buenaventura Lakes suburb in Osceola County, Florida. It chronicles how a Mexican real estate company, Landstar Homes, marketed BLV as country-club living with affordable prices and high-end amenities. Its advertisement of living a "Landstar Lifestyle" promised upward social mobility by becoming homeowners and effectively attracted Puerto Ricans from both the Northeast and Puerto Rico, forming an ethnic enclave.

In chapter 2, Delerme presents the Latinization of the Greater Orlando area by documenting the long-term impact of Latino/a/x migrations. Particularly, she focuses on how Puerto Rican migration led to cultural, political, economic, and social transformations to the landscape and soundscape in the area. Similarly, we are able to read about the local response of non-Latino whites to these changes, which made them feel like outsiders, and the development of language ideologies and white racial consciousness (e.g., being American means speaking English).

The next chapter, "The Fractured American Dream," covers the decline of a BLV suburb from a middle-class neighborhood. Through online sources, Delerme examines the perceived change in reputation of BLV from country-club living to "ghetto or slum" as Latino/a/x residents increased. Some of the factors Delerme identified that led to the current state, and for BLV not to be considered a good investment anymore, were because of crime, concerns about safety, unemployment, ageing homes that were not maintained, absence of a Home Owner Association (HOA) to enforce restrictions, loss of amenities like the country club and golf course, the foreclosure crisis, and for some people the concentration of Latinos/as/xs and the widespread use of Spanish language.

In chapter 4, Delerme examines the social class diversity of Latino/a/x migrants in the Greater Orlando area by attending events tailored to the Latino/a/x elite. In these events, she is able to meet upwardly mobile Latino/a/x professionals and entrepreneurs and observe how they create spaces for networking within the Latino/a/x community and with non-Latino whites.

Here, Delerme explores how belonging to Latino/a/x networking organizations provides its members with power and privileges. Through the stories of six participants, we are able to understand how cultural capital functions. That is, how it's constructed, reproduced, and policed by the participants and their class ideologies. Likewise, Delerme offers forms of everyday activism as a backlash to contest the exclusivity of these networking organizations.

The last substantive chapter, "The *Encargado* System," considers a system of underground real estate economy in which Latino/a/x homeowners rent out rooms to friends, families, and/or strangers as a way to pay the mortgage. This chapter introduces us to four participants who, as Delerme, are part of the *encargado* system either by being the homeowners or renting out rooms. She discusses some advantages and disadvantages to living communally such as establishing a familiar bond yet sacrificing personal privacy. By participating in this practice, Delerme was able to engage in informal conversations with Latino/a/x migrants about their identities and interethnic relations as well as observe their everyday activities as they barely made a living.

In the conclusion, Delerme reminds us of the complexities surrounding Latino/a/x ethnoracial identities (whether self-identified or ascribed) and existing U.S. census categorizations. She discusses the future directions of her work on Latinos/as/xs in the South by moving to the northern Mississippi/Tennessee border. With the "browning" of America, the book ends by recommending us to reconsider our notions of race, ethnicity, and what it means to be an American.

In *Latino Orlando*, Delerme weaves data from her extensive ethnography (e.g., participant observations), informal and semi-structured interviews, census data, newspaper archives, and online materials (e.g., Internet blogs and forums) to provide a much-needed analysis of Latinos/as/xs in a suburban context. She recalls that she set out to research upwardly mobile, middle-class homeowners; however, Puerto Ricans and other Latinos in the BLV community were perceived as working-class or low-income people. It wasn't until she attended different meetings and events of business networking organizations—such as the Puerto Rican Chamber of Commerce, Hispanic Chamber of Commerce, Amigos Profesionales, and Hispanic Young Professionals and Entrepreneurs (HYPE) in the Greater Orlando area—where she found upwardly mobile Latinos/as/xs. This served as a stark contrast to the daily struggles she observed through the *encargado* system she participated in where working homeowners rented out rooms in their homes in order to be able to pay the mortgages and generate economic capital. By her storytelling, Delerme is able to depict how social class position and language usage mediated relationships of Latinos/as/xs migrants among themselves and others in the Greater Orlando area.

Latino Orlando is an engaging book written in accessible language appropriate for general audiences. Being Puerto Rican and having lived in Deltona, Florida, during the years 1989-1991, I found myself reliving some of my personal memories throughout the book. In sum, it is a must read for any person interested in understanding and researching the complexities of Latino/a/x migration to the U.S.

It is important to note that at the time of writing Delerme mentions that Hurricane Maria had just impacted Puerto Rico, which we now know led to a mass exodus of Puerto Ricans precisely to Central Florida. This makes me question how different, if at all, her experience would have been conducting fieldwork with post-disaster migrants.

"El feminismo no es nuevo": Las crónicas de Clotilde Betances Jaeger

Edited and with an introduction by María Teresa Vera-Rojas
Houston, Texas: Arte Público Press, 2020
ISBN: 978-1-55885-908-1
200 pages; $21.95 [paper]

Reviewer: Cristina Pérez Jiménez (cperezjimenez01@manhattan.edu),
Manhattan College

"El feminismo no es nuevo": *Las crónicas de Clotilde Betances Jaeger*, edited by María Teresa Vera-Rojas, compiles the literary and journalistic writing of Puerto Rican author Clotilde Betances Jaeger. These writings primarily from the 1920s and 1930s had until now been scattered in archival Spanish-language periodicals. The edited collection is published by Arte Público Press's Recovering the Hispanic Literary Heritage of the United States project, at the University of Houston, which continues its important legacy of recovering, preserving, and making widely available pre-1960s US Latino print culture. *"El feminismo no es nuevo"* is a valuable contribution to the documentation of the culture of early twentieth-century New York's Hispanic *colonias*, especially the cultural work and views of women and middle-class figures, which arguably have been even further overlooked in favor of more militant and male working-class voices.

Clotilde Betances Jaeger (1890-197?) was born in San Sebastián, Puerto Rico, to a relatively privileged family. She was the grandniece of nineteenth-century independence leader Ramón Emeterio Betances, and initially moved to the United States to pursue an undergraduate degree at Cornell University, an opportunity available to few Puerto Ricans, let alone women. In 1923, she moved to New York City, becoming part of the city's tightly knit Hispanic middle-class cultural circles. She lived the rest of her life in the mainland United States, where she earned a graduate degree, married, had a career as a teacher and wrote for myriad publications within and outside the country. Most of the *crónicas* collected in *"El feminismo no es nuevo"* were originally published in three Spanish-language New York publications: the weekly *Gráfico*, the cultural magazine *Artes y Letras*, and the daily *La*

Prensa. Vera-Rojas also compiles dispersed writings published in Puerto Rican periodicals, and—most interestingly—in Spain's anarchist press, which helps readers situate Betances Jaeger's writing in broader transnational feminist and literary networks across periodical culture.

In her excellent introduction, Vera-Rojas highlights that Betances Jaeger's entry into journalism was tied to the appearance of the so-called women's pages in the Hispanic press. Many of Betances Jaeger's journalistic contributions appeared in these sections devoted to topics of family, food, furnishings, and fashion, which were of purported interest to women. If these sections primarily targeted women as passive consumers, appealing directly to them within a framework of stereotyped domesticity, writers like Betances Jaeger appropriated this public space to challenge patriarchal norms and traditional gendered roles. *"El feminismo no es nuevo"* also includes an appendix with a handful of responses to Betances Jaeger's crónicas. These examples of the contemporary reception of Betances Jaeger's work more fully contextualize the crónicas within debates about women's roles and responsibilities, as waged in the women's pages of the era's print culture. Betances Jaeger's direct exhortations to an explicitly female readership showcase her intent to cultivate a feminist community through her journalistic writing.

The crónica that gives the edited collection its title, "El feminismo no es nuevo," articulates Betances Jaeger's view of feminism as a personal and collective yearning that transcends any given campaign on women's issues, such as the suffrage movement, and which embodies instead women's innate and shared desire for intellectual, economic, political, and bodily autonomy. Through this expansive, almost universalizing view of feminism—more a matter of consciousness than a political movement—Betances Jaeger implicitly resituated feminism within the natural purview of the U.S. Hispanic woman. Unlinking feminism from the exclusive domain of Anglo-American modern womanhood, Betances Jaeger thus negotiated Hispanic women's culturally differentiated place in the cosmopolitan metropolis. "New" is a key word. As Vera-Rojas —the critic to have most thoroughly and extensively analyzed Betances Jaeger's work—argues here and elsewhere, Betances Jaeger's feminist views need to be understood in the context of the anxieties elicited by the emancipated New Woman, so frequently represented, discussed, and caricatured in the periodical press of the period (see Vera-Rojas 2018, 2016, 2014, 2010). If many leading Hispanic men saw the New Woman as a distinctly "American" (i.e., U.S.-derived) threat and sought to uphold traditional Latin American feminine ideals by relying on an anti-assimilationist rhetoric, Betances Jaeger's feminist writings contest that impulse by refusing facile and flawed binaries between Puerto Rican or "Latin" traditions and U.S. modernity. Feminism was not new, and neither was it foreign.

Organized around six interlocking thematic chapters and the appendix, the collected writings give evidence of the wide range of issues and cultural references that comprised Betances Jaeger's feminism and cultural milieu. Part I assembles Betances Jaeger's most explicitly feminist crónicas, addressing issues of sexuality, marriage, and motherhood, and in which her sense of ethnic difference from Anglo-American feminists recurs and stands out. Part II includes her profiles of notable Latin American and Spanish women, allowing us to map networks of transatlantic Hispanic feminism. Part III focuses on her political stances, evidencing her pro-independence sentiments and international outlook. Part IV groups crónicas around the theme of education, showcasing her embrace of the humanistic liberal tradition and classical Western culture. Part V presents an assortment of reviews of cultural events. Part VI features her uneven literary output, primarily short narratives and poems heavily influenced by *modernismo* and *criollismo*.

Betances Jaeger's literary style, like that of many of her contemporaries, has not aged particularly well. The language is florid, the allusions pompous, the syntax clunky. Yet readers willing to look past the outmoded prose are rewarded with the opportunity to situate themselves in the cultural world inhabited by Betances Jaeger, recovering references to authors no longer read, and polemics now forgotten. *"El feminismo no es nuevo"* offers a valuable panoramic snapshot of the events, figures, and performances that were on the radar of middle-class, professional Spanish-speaking New Yorkers during the 1920s and '30s.

From the vantage point of today, Betances Jaeger's crónicas are of further interest not only for what they document, but also for what they omit or overlook. The author brazenly challenges authority and mindless conformity, but never quite questions the idea of the home as an exclusively female realm, even as she calls for women to enter other domains. She decries the past evils of slavery and celebrates abolitionists like her grandfather, Ramón Emeterio Betances, but remains silent on Jim Crow, lynching, and the vicious prejudice experienced by her fellow Black and/or Spanish-speaking New Yorkers. She denounces fascism but says surprisingly little about the Spanish Civil War or the antifascist activism ablaze in New York City at the time. She supports Puerto Rican independence and favorably mentions Pedro Albizu Campos, but fails to really address the contemporary political struggles on the island, which were marked by an emboldened yet increasingly persecuted Nationalist movement. There are no explicit references to Franklin D. Roosevelt, the New Deal, or even the Great Depression that was ravaging the lives of so many compatriots on the island and the streets of New York. These omissions are particularly striking because they dominated headlines in mainstream and ethnic presses alike.

In light of her collected writings, can we consider Betances Jaeger a predecessor of what we today call women of color feminism? It is evident from her crónicas that her feminist views and stances were inflected by her self-understanding as a colonial subject and as a racialized *mujer latina*. At the same time, a clearly privileged perspective dominates, one which embraces aesthetics, cultural and intellectual refinement, and the appreciation of fine arts as means of attaining respectability and counteracting racialized hierarchies. She courageously advocates for women's professional development and public recognition but seems to neglect the struggles, needs, and demands of the legions of Hispanic women laborers. Tellingly, the crónica "El feminism no es nuevo" seems to address exclusively middle and upper-class Hispanic women who live in "jaulas doradas," and although freed from economic imperatives, yearn for financial independence and intellectual self-realization. Several crónicas, moreover, echo José Ortega y Gasset's contemptuous views of the masses. How do we reconcile her often rather elitist views of culture with her proximity to anarchism and to the socialist feminism of Violeta Miqueli and Federica Montseny, which Vera-Rojas so fascinatingly unearths? How do we make sense of her daring critiques of religious dogma and moral puritanism in light of the abundance of Judeo-Christian references, her involvement in Protestant Hispanic circles, and avowed Christian faith? How do we untangle the convergences and divergences between Betances Jaeger and labor leaders like Bernardo Vega and Jesús Colón, all of whom were involved in *Gráfico*, and the "Hispanic" communities they represent?

That we are able to recover cultural references, probe silences, formulate questions, and explore generative tensions and contradictions in Betances Jaeger's life and writing is a testament to the significance of this edited collection. Some of her views and feminist stances may grate on contemporary sensibilities, but many others surprise and gratify us with their pertinence. The *crónica* "Hay que respetar a la mujer," for instance, condemns the pervasiveness of sexual assault and harassment in our everyday culture and encourages women to take a stand. Its closing plea—"El hombre te cree su cosa sujeta a sus caprichos. ¡¡Desmiéntelo!!"—would not be out of place in the #MeToo and #NiUnaMenosNiUnaMás movements. María Teresa Vera-Rojas' wonderful edition, *"El feminismo no es nuevo": Las crónicas de Clotilde Betances Jaeger*, reminds us that feminism is not new, not foreign, and never out of date.

References

Vera-Rojas, María Teresa. 2010. Polémicas feministas, puertorriqueñas y desconocidas: Clotilde Betances Jaeger y sus "Charlas femeninas" en el *Gráfico* de Nueva York (1928-1930). *CENTRO: Journal of the Center for Puerto Rican Studies* 22(2), 4–33.

_____. 2014. Lecturas desde el margen: en torno a las cartas de María Mas Pozo en el diario *La Prensa* de Nueva York. *CENTRO: Journal of the Center for Puerto Rican Studies* 26(2), 80–109.

_____. 2016. De estudiantes, artistas y feministas: Reapropiaciones de la mujer moderna en la revista *Artes y Letras* de Nueva York. *Lectora: Revista de dones i textualitat* (22), 199–222.

_____. 2018. *"Se conoce que usted es 'Moderna'": lecturas de la mujer moderna en la colonia hispana de Nueva York (1920-1940)*. Madrid and Frankfurt: Iberoamericana Vervuert.

Poets, Philosophers, Lovers: On the Writings of Giannina Braschi

Edited by Frederick Luis Aldama and Tess O'Dwyer
Pittsburgh: University of Pittsburgh Press, 2020
ISBN: 978-0-8229-4618-2
168 pages; $45.00 [cloth]

Reviewer: Carmen Haydée Rivera (ch.rivera@upr.edu), University of Puerto Rico, Río Piedras

Giannina Braschi is one of the most multifaceted and innovative diasporic Puerto Rican writers of the past decades. Her literary works, published in English, Spanish, and Spanglish, and translated into various languages have revolutionized Puerto Rican Literature, both on and off the island. Born in San Juan, Puerto Rico, Braschi's creative and intellectual world extends far beyond geographic, linguistic, historical, and cultural boundaries to embrace another dimension of the tangible and the imagined in her efforts to form part of a literary tradition that she constantly renews and reinvents.

Braschi's literary production begins with verse in Spanish, reflecting her humanistic erudition and vast knowledge of literature, art, philosophy, and world history that feeds into her poetic imagery. Her poetry collection, *El imperio de los sueños,* published in 1988 coalesces previous collections (*Asalto al tiempo, La comedia profana,* and *El imperio de los sueños*). In 1994, the work was translated into English by Tess O'Dwyer. The University of Puerto Rico Press released a new edition in 2000, with an introduction by UPR professor and philosopher Francisco José Ramos.

Braschi moved on to hybrid narrative experimentation, developed through the juxtaposition of genres (fiction, poetry, drama) and languages (Spanish and English) that defy and problematize narratological categorization in her work titled *Yo-Yo Boing!,* published by *Latin American Literary Review* in 1998. She later followed up with a publication full of multiple narrative voices and characters that traverse historical eras and literary movements in an attempt to unravel life's significance within a transnational lens and postmodern perspective in *United States of Banana* (2011). In the same year of this publication, Amazon Crossing for World Literature also issued a collected works version of Braschi's writing that included *Empire of Dreams, Yo-Yo Boing!* and *United States of Banana.* In 2021, a version of *United States of Banana* appeared as a graphic novel, illustrated by Joakim Lindengren and published by Ohio State University Press.

Apart from her publications, Braschi has taught creative writing at various universities, including Rutgers, CUNY, and Colgate. She has also participated in translation and writing seminars in France and Sweden, in addition to her engagement as writer-in-residence in the Baltic Centre for Writers and Translators. Her prestigious awards and recognitions have come from varied sources: the National Endowment for the Arts, New York Foundation for the Arts, Ford Foundation, PEN American Center's Open Book Award, Peter S. Reed Foundation/InterAmericas, Instituto de Cultura Puertorriqueña, among others.

What we witness in Braschi is an artist that moves beyond the traditional im/migrant story in search of the American Dream, though the American Dream looms large in her writing. Her work reveals characterizations that constantly question the imposition of ideologies that obstruct an individual's realization and prevents them from experiencing their inalienable rights. Reading Braschi requires a reconceptualization of literary creativity and a realization of the power of a writer who instigates constant scrutiny of preconceived notions of identity, culture, tradition, and language. Her works are not passive reading but, rather, interactive and unsettling. To follow her multiple fluctuations between narrative voices, settings, ideologies, and philosophies results in a fascinating yet complex task. Seeing her in person and hearing her conferences on the process of literary creation and its significance in her life is to contemplate an artist who accepts her fragility and, simultaneously, embraces the need to express her ideas and convictions as freely and authentically as possible. Her use of dual languages and integration of multicultural experiences showcase her heterogeneous creative mindset and a play on words that is at once instinctive, casual, revealing, and a clear display of the contemporaneity of the creative process of one of the most innovative writers of our time.

It comes as no surprise that critical-theoretical approaches to Braschi's work thus must follow. One of the most recent is the collection titled *Poets,*

Philosophers, Lovers: On the Writing of Giannina Braschi, edited by Frederick Luis Aldama and Tess O'Dwyer, published by the University of Pittsburgh Press (2020), under the Latinx and Latin American Profiles series. To date, this is one of the most comprehensive and critically engaging publications that covers the breadth and scope of Braschi's literary production. A very brief preface by writer and critic Ilan Stavans opens the collection with a reflective rendition of one of his favorite quotes by Braschi, an "ode to ambiguity," that Stavans renders through his own use of strategic bilingual interplay. Aldama's concise and critically informative Introduction follows, situating Braschi's work within a comparative literary framework vis-à-vis other American, Latin American, and European writers with whom he sees Braschi conversing, while highlighting innovative approaches to the main thematic concerns in her major works. In addition to including brief summaries of the essays contained in the collection, Aldama also provides suggested further readings to contextualize Braschi's literary production.

The volume is then subdivided into three parts, with four to five critical articles included in each part. "Vanguard Forms and Latinx Sensibilities" leads the discussion in Part I, with authors such as Madelena Gonzalez, John "Rio" Riofrio, Anne Ashbaugh, Francisco Moreno-Fernández, and Maritza Stanchich commenting on varied topics that focus on Braschi's narratives, identities, and worldviews. The authors in this section critically assess Braschi's works and propose innovative interpretations of her writing that highlight topics such as poetry as resistance to cultural commodification, bilingual and translingual practices, breaking aesthetic schemas, dialogues with ancient prophets in the articulation of autonomy and freedom, translanguaging deployments, hemispheric American Latinx experiences, and new literary traditions as "global poetics of dissent."

Part II, "Persuasive Art of Dramatic Voices," displays critical discussions by Cristina Garrigós, Laura Loustau, Elizabeth Lowry, and Daniela Daniele on the polyphony of voices, rhetoric, identification, and symbolic representation that Braschi uses to move her audiences with cognitive reasoning, but also with emotion, that often produce a conflation between author and narrative voice, creating a type of "poet/artist, poet/reader dyad" within a cross-genre aesthetic that defies literary classifications and conventions. The post-traumatic, 9/11 global scene; subalternities, invisibilities, and the silencing of Puerto Rico, and Latinos, in general; the avant-guard art making tradition; and the brutalities of US imperialism are also topics explored and confronted in these essays.

Part III, "Intermedial Poetics and Radical Thinking," rounds up the last section of this volume and brings together the critical analyses of Dorian Lugo Beltrán, Ronald Mendoza-de Jesús, Francisco José Ramos, and an interview by Rolando Pérez. Topics deployed in this section include how Braschi's use of hybridized genres allows for other artistic representations of her works, such as graphic novel adaptations and slam poetry performances, among others, that create inter- and intra-textual references that move beyond the notions of in-betweenness. Other focuses include Braschi's common ground and worldviews with European philosophers (such as Jacques Derrida); politics and political satire; the sovereign self; the society of the spectacle; capitalism and its neoliberalist tenets, and how, according to Francisco José Ramos, Braschi takes literature to "the limits of its possibilities." This section ends with Rolando Pérez's poignant and incisive, yet ultimately emotional interview that allows Braschi to soar through her kaleidoscopic literary development and career while showcasing her aesthetics and deep convictions.

Giannina Braschi's multimodal texts stretch the boundaries of nationalist discourses, of genres and disciplinary studies in ways that continue to astonish reading audiences and invigorate contemporary literature. Her works offer unprecedented opportunities for intercultural and transdisciplinary studies that critically examine intersectionalities, multidimensional literary schemes, and shifting linguistic codes as well as the rich array of literary output that revolving-door migration produces. This collection of essays, edited by Frederick Luis Aldama and Tess O'Dwyer, perfectly aligns with Braschi's literary proposals and aesthetics by providing a variety of critical voices and commentary on her work that help contextualize and further comprehend the important legacy of Braschi's incomparable genius and craft.

Revolution Around the Corner: Voices from the Puerto Rican Socialist Party in the United States

Edited by José E. Velázquez, Carmen V. Rivera and Andrés Torres
Philadelphia, Temple University Press, 2021
ISBN: 978-1-4399-2055-8
408 pages; $32.95 [paper]

Reviewer: Efraín Barradas (barradas@latam.ufl.edu), University of Florida, Gainesville

Necesitábamos este libro. Teníamos ya algunos trabajos de interés que estudian el impacto de los Young Lords o el Young Lords Party. Poco se habían estudiado otros movimientos progresistas de los puertorriqueños en los Estados Unidos, específicamente el Partido Socialista Puertorriqueño (PSP) que durante algunas décadas fue un movimiento de importancia cuyo estudio nos sirve para entender el desarrollo político e ideológico de parte de nuestras comunidades. Este libro avanza grandemente ese estudio y por ello hay que darle la bienvenida y agradecer el trabajo de sus compiladores quienes ya nos habían dado otros que sirven para complementar y completar este.

El libro está dividido en tres partes. La primera, presenta un gran marco histórico con tres importantes capítulos. Es de especial interés el primero, "A brief history of the Puerto Rican Socialist Party in the United States" de Andrés Torres. Este es un trabajo minucioso y, a pesar que anuncia en su título que es "brief", en verdad es extenso; tiene unas ochenta páginas y, con unas cuantas posibles adiciones, podría convertirse en una monografía independiente. En esta primera parte también se incluye un trabajo sobre el PSP en Chicago. Estos dos y un tercero, "Milestones: Reflections on a life journey of activism in the PSP in New York" de José E. Velázquez, texto que cabría también en la segunda parte del libro, sirven de marco general a todo el libro.

La segunda parte titulada "Testimonies", para mí la más reveladora e interesante de todo el libro, está compuesta por nueve capítulos; cada uno recoge las memorias de sus respectivos autores sobre el impacto del PSP en sus vidas. Uno de estos capítulos, "Hostos Community College: Battle of the Seventies" de Ramón J. Jiménez, ya fallecido, no cabe en esta sección ya que no se enfoca en la acción del PSP mismo, como lo hacen los otros textos de esta sección, sino que el partido aparece aquí como una más de las organizaciones que participaron en la lucha por salvar este campus de la Universidad de la Ciudad de Nueva York. El texto de Jiménez, que ya había sido publicado en *CENTRO Journal*, es un excelente trabajo que narra de manera efectiva esa lucha por el acceso a la educación universitaria para los latinos en la Ciudad de Nueva York, especialmente para los boricuas y dominicanos. Recalco: el texto es excelente pero no cabe dentro de los parámetros del libro porque no se enfoca en el PSP. Otros textos incluidos en otras secciones recalcan, más que el de Jiménez, el papel que el partido jugó en esta lucha en particular.

La tercera parte, "Coalitions and alliances", recoge tres capítulos donde se presenta cómo el partido fue más allá de lo nacional y estableció lazos con otras comunidades y con individuos de otros grupos étnicos. Algunos están escritos desde el punto de vista de no puertorriqueños afiliados al partido y todos desde una perspectiva histórica de la relación del PSP con otros movimientos progresistas. Dos de los capítulos incluidos en esta sección, escritos respectivamente por Rosa Borenstein y Ted Glick, también se pueden leer como testimonios personales. El tercero, de Alyssa Ribeiro, estudia la rela-ción de los movimientos boricuas en Philadelphia con los afroamericanos en esa misma ciudad.

El conjunto de los trabajos que se recogen en el libro va constantemente de lo personal a lo colectivo; así logra darnos un amplio cuadro del PSP en los Estados Unidos, especialmente en New York, y de las repercusiones políticas de este movimiento político, tanto en la Isla como en el continente. Como decía al principio, necesitábamos un libro como este y, obviamente, el que Torres, Velázquez y Rivera nos han dado cumple con su propósito, a pesar de las críticas que se le pueden hacer.

Para mí, la parte más interesante de todo el libro es la segunda, la que recoge los testimonios mayormente de militantes de PSP. Estos le dan a la actividad política del momento una cara humana, muy precisa y definida. Esto hace al libro muy atractivo ya que a través de estos trabajos vemos la actividad política de manera concreta y personal, con sus logros, contradicciones y fallas. Por ello mismo, en estos testimonios se hallan acertadas y convincentes críticas al PSP y autocríticas de los autores mismos. Más que en ninguna otra parte del libro, aquí se ve al PSP de manera fehaciente y personal. Por ello concentraré mi atención en estos testimonios pero, para hacerlo y para hacerlo de manera honesta, tengo que aclarar mi relación con el PSP. Primero y sobre todo, nunca he sido militante de este partido, pero he cooperado con la organización de distintas formas. He contribuido monetariamente a diversas de sus campañas y, sobre todo, he publicado con relativa frecuencia en su periódico. Durante los breves periodos cuando viví en Nueva York, llegué a hacer trabajo voluntario para este periódico; hice traducciones para *Claridad Bilingüe*. Y, cuando era estudiante graduado en New Jersey y visitaba a amigos en Nueva York, hasta salía con ellos a vender el periódico en las calles del Loisaida. Más importante aún, fui y soy amigo, en algunos casos íntimo, de varios de los que eran entonces líderes del PSP. Por ello, hay incidentes que se cuentan en el libro donde por respeto a los participantes no se da su nombre; pero al margen de las páginas de mi ejemplar fui escribiendo sus nombres porque los conocí y estuve al tanto de los hechos en el momento mismo que se daba el acontecimiento referido. Tuve acceso a esa información sin ser militante del partido. Muy probablemente es por ello mismo que esa segunda parte donde se recogen los testimonios de estos miembros del PSP sea la que más me atrae.

No se crea que estos testimonios son dignos de una telenovela o de una película de detectives. Estos testimonios no hacen revelaciones políticas secretas ni trascendentales; sólo recuerdan la vida de sus autores en el PSP. Por ello, son textos de gran mesura pero, algunos más que otros, le dan una cara concreta a los episodios políticos que se narran. Algunos, aunque enmarcan lo narrado en la vida del autor, se centran más que nada en el hecho político. Ese es el caso del testimonio de Zoilo Torres, "What the Puerto Rican Socialist Party nurtured in me". A pesar de ello, este texto es uno de los que más clara y directamente hace un balance razonable y preciso de la función del partido en el crecimiento intelectual y político de sus miembros. Por otro lado, el testimonio de Digna Sánchez, "Mi camino", cabe perfectamente bien dentro de la corriente de la autobiografía, corriente muy fuerte en las letras latinoestadounidenses. Hay pasajes conmovedores en este testimonio que me gustaría que la autora ampliara, quizás hasta darnos un libro, una autobiografía completa y más detallada. "My nation is the struggle" de Maritza Arrastía, también muy revelador a nivel personal, es de gran interés por demostrar como el partido en Nueva York y en otros lugares estuvo relacionado con jóvenes cubanos de visión progresista. Otros, como el de Olga Iris Sanabria Dávila, "From El Barrio to the United Nations", combina muy efectivamente lo personal con lo político y rescata a un personaje olvidado, el profesor J.A. González-González, "el Profe". Sanabria se destacó en el PSP por su trabajo a nivel internacional y quizás el dato sirva para entender su posición poco crítica o excesivamente diplomática del proceso político en Nicaragua, país al que estuvo conectada con su trabajo internacional. Para mí, el testimonio de Alfredo López, "Journalism, organizing, and revolution", es el que mejor presenta el elemento de crítica y autocrítica. Este es un trabajo revelador y honesto. Dos de estos testimonios, uno colectivo, "The personal is political: children of the Puerto Rican Socialists Party speak" de Teresa Basilio Gaztambide y Carmen V. Rivera, y otro personal, "A pamper rojo Boricua baby of the Puerto Rican Socialist Party" de Lenina Nadal, presentan el impacto de la vida en el partido para los que entonces eran niños y ahora son parte de una nueva generación de adultos. "¡Puerto Rico libre y socialista! A Philarican in the struggle" de José Manuel Navarro es de interés, entre otras razones, porque presenta cómo el impacto del PSP no se limitó a la ciudad de Nueva York. Al principio de este comentario apuntaba a cómo el testimonio de Ramón J. Jiménez, "Hostos Community College: Battle of the Seventies", no debía ser parte del libro porque no se centra en su tema, pero, fuera de este contexto, como testimonio de otro activista boricua del momento, es un excelente texto y nos ayuda a entender el momento y rescata también figuras olvidadas.

La riqueza de información y, sobre todo, las visiones personales de los hechos que se narran es lo que, para mí, hace de estos testimonios textos de importancia que servirán en el futuro como documentos primarios y como claves para entender mejor este movimiento progresista y el momento cuando se dio. A la vez, mientras leía estos testimonios no podía dejar de pensar en muchas otras personas, militantes o simpatizantes, que pudieron haber cooperado con sus recuerdos. Pienso, entre muchos otros, en María Josefa Canino, en Luis Aponte Parés, en Sandra María Esteves, en Víctor López Tosado, en Armindo Núñez Miranda, quien dirigió una pequeña librería organizada por el partido en la calle 14, "Libro Libre", y en Alida Millán, actual directora del periódico *Claridad* quien por años vivió y militó en Massachusetts. Además, hemos perdido los posibles testimonios de importantes líderes del PSP que ya no está con nosotros. Pienso en lo mucho que nos podría iluminar con su testimonio Ramón Arbona, quien dirigió el PSP en los Estados Unidos y fundó *Claridad Bilingüe*. La lista de otros posibles o imaginados testimonios sería tan larga que sólo con ellos daría para publicar otro libro mucho más amplio que le daría una cara aún más humana al PSP y a otros movimientos progresistas en este importante momento histórico.

También habría que presentar –lo que desafortunadamente no se hace – la contribución que hicieron varios músicos y poetas a través de "El Grupo".

Este, fue un conjunto de artistas que extraoficialmente servían como el brazo cultural del PSP en la década de 1970. "El Grupo" actuaba en mítines políticos y otras actividades del PSP. Rafael Rodríguez Abeillez, simpatizante pero no militante del partido, fue su coordinador y con él cooperaban, entre otros, Pedro Pietri, Sandra María Esteves y Jesús Papoleto Meléndez. A "El Grupo" se le debieron dedicar aunque fuera algunas líneas. Urayoán Noel, en su estudio sobre la poesía neorrican, In visible movement... (2014), le ha prestado un poco de atención a este conjunto de músicos y poetas. Pero todavía hace falta estudiarlo con más detenimiento para entender mejor el desarrollo de la poesía neorrican y, en general, el trabajo cultural del PSP.

De los testimonios, y de los otros trabajos de carácter más histórico y político que se recogen en el libro, se obtiene la clara idea de que el acto celebrado el 27 de octubre de 1974 en Madison Square Garden, el "National Day of Solidarity with Puerto Rico" – ¡Orgullosamente declaro que allí estuve! – fue la cima del impacto político del PSP en los Estados Unidos. También se puede llegar a la conclusión, gracias a la lectura de estos textos, que el periódico *Claridad*, que ha sobrevivido al partido, fue su herramienta más útil y poderosa. El constante choque entre los puertorriqueños de la Isla y los del continente ha sido un insoluble problema que marcó el periodo que se estudia en este libro y que todavía nos marca. La confrontación con visiones nacionalistas y hasta chauvinistas, como con las racistas, las machistas y las homofóbicas, también se evidencia en la lectura de este libro. Habría que añadir que militantes y simpatizantes gais del PSP comenzamos a organizar en ese momento un intento de combinar la lucha por la independencia y el socialismo en Puerto Rico con la liberación homosexual. Habría que destacar cómo en ese pequeño y efímero movimiento nos enfrentamos a la necesidad de comenzar a ver con ojos boricuas lo que se veía sólo como otro movimiento gringo más; algo que tampoco se ha estudiado debidamente.

Este es un libro necesario y rico en información que, con sus perspectivas políticas, históricas y personales, sirve para aclarar un momento en nuestra historia. Es por ello que reconozco el valor que tiene a nivel colectivo y también personal. Por ello, y por los trabajos que muy probablemente estas páginas provoquen como respuesta crítica a sus postulados y otros que se inspiren en ellas para continuar la exploración aquí iniciada, es que hay que agradecerles a Rivera, Torres y Velázquez por esta importante contribución al estudio de una organización y un momento en el desarrollo de la comunidad puertorriqueña en los Estados Unidos. ¡Gracias!

CARIBBEAN STUDIES

Revista bianual del Instituto de Estudios del Caribe
Universidad de Puerto Rico

ÍNDICE • CONTENTS • SOMMAIRE

Vol. 48 No. 1 (January-June 2020)

Artículos • Articles • Articles

Vlastimil Bernas, Comparative Analysis of the Status of French Guiana, Mayotte and New Caledonia

Luis Raúl Cámara Fuertes, Liberal or Conservative, Left or Right: The Identification with Ideological Labels by Puerto Rican Legislators

Héctor Tavárez, Mildred Cortés y Carmen Álamo, Disposición a pagar por proyectos dirigidos a erradicar la escasez de agua en Puerto Rico: Resultados del método de valoración contingente

Fidel Rodríguez Velásquez, Excavando el pasado del Caribe insular venezolano: Historia e historiografía de los primeros 100 años de arqueología en las islas de Cubagua y Margarita, 1915-2019

Humberto Carvajal Chitty y Olga Rey, Aportes a la bioestratigrafía del Aptiense–Albiense en la cuenca oriental de Venezuela con base en foraminíferos y nanoplánckton calcáreo

In Memoriam

Ellen Schnepel. In Memoriam of Lambros Comitas

Oscar Zanetti. En memoria de Alejandro García Álvarez

Ensayos bibliográficos • Review Essays • Comptes Rendus

Michelle A. González Maldonado, Jana Evans Braziel. 2017. *Riding With Death: Vodou Art and Urban Ecology*. N. Fadeke Castor. 2017. *Spiritual Citizenship: Transnational Pathways from Black Power to Ifá in Trinidad*. Karen E. Richman. 2018. *Migration and Vodou*.

Anthony P. Maingot, DISECTING THE PLURAL SOCIETY. Selwyn Ryan. 2019. *Ryan Recalls. Selwyn Ryan: His Memoirs*. Rita Pemberton, Debbie McCollin, Gelien Matthews and Michael Toussaint, eds. 2018. *Historical Dictionary of Trinidad and Tobago. New Edition*

Reseñas de libros • Book Reviews • Comptes Rendus

Edgardo Meléndez. 2017. *Sponsored Migration: The State and Puerto Rican Postwar Migration to the United States (Aldo A. Lauria-Santiago)*

Von Díaz. 2018. *Coconuts and Collards: Recipes and Stories from Puerto Rico to the Deep South (Cruz M. Ortiz Cuadra)*

Rubén Nazario Velasco. 2018. *La historia de los derrotados: Americanización y romanticismo en Puerto Rico, 1898-1917. (Pedro L. San Miguel)*

Aarón Gamaliel Ramos. 2016. *Las islas migajas: los países no independientes del Caribe contemporáneo (Ángel L. Viera-Tirado)*

Sharon Milagro Marshall. 2016. *Tell My Mother I Gone to Cuba. (Pedro L.V. Welch)*

Suscripción Anual

Instituciones $50.00 / Individuos $25.00

Cheque o giro postal pagadero a

Universidad de Puerto Rico

INSTITUTO DE ESTUDIOS DEL CARIBE
UNIVERSIDAD DE PUERTO RICO
9 AVE UNIVERSIDAD STE 901
SAN JUAN PR 00925-2529

Tel. 787-764-0000, ext. 87738
caribbean.studies@upr.edu

 **CSRC Press**

Two award-winning anthologies, now in ebook format ...

Knowledge for Justice
An Ethnic Studies Reader

David K. Yoo, Pamela Grieman, Charlene Villaseñor Black, Danielle Dupuy, and Arnold Ling-Chuang Pan, editors

● **2021 OUTSTANDING BOOK AWARD, ASSOCIATION FOR ETHNIC STUDIES**

Knowledge for Justice focuses on the intersectional intellectual, social, and political struggles of the communities represented by UCLA's four ethnic studies research centers: African American Studies, American Indian Studies, Asian American Studies, and Chicana/o Studies. The articles and essays in this anthology articulate the specificity of each group's struggle while interrogating the ways in which ethnic and racial labels and categories are inadequate.

The Chicano Studies Reader
An Anthology of Aztlán, 1970–2019

4th edition

Edited by Chon A. Noriega, Eric Avila, Karen Mary Davalos, Chela Sandoval, Rafael Pérez Torres, and Charlene Villaseñor Black

● **BRONZE MEDAL, WEST-PACIFIC—BEST REGIONAL NON-FICTION, 2022 INDEPENDENT PUBLISHER BOOK AWARDS**

● **GOLD MEDAL, MULTICULTURAL NONFICTION ADULT, 2021 INDEPENDENT PUBLISHER BOOK AWARDS**

The Chicano Studies Reader has been a standard text in ethnic studies classrooms since 2001. This latest edition offers thirty-nine essays that document the foundation of Chicano studies, testify to its broad disciplinary range, and explore its continuing development.

Distributed for CSRC Press by University of Washington Press
Available in electronic format from your favorite ebook vendor

 **UCLA CHICANO STUDIES RESEARCH CENTER PRESS**
www.chicano.ucla.edu

 **UNIVERSITY OF WASHINGTON PRESS**
Seattle uwapress.uw.edu

CENTRO
Journal of the Center
for Puerto Rican Studies

SUBSCRIBE ONLINE
http://www.centropr-store.com/journals

OR CONTACT
Center for Puerto Rican Studies
Hunter College—CUNY
695 Park Avenue, Room E-1429
New York, NY 10065
212.772.5686
FAX: 212.650.3673

SUBSCRIPTION RATES
Institutional: $90/year
Individual: $45/year

Centro Publications

2022 CATALOGUE

Puerto Rican Studies in the City University of New York: The First Fifty Years

Edited by María E. Pérez y González and Virginia Sánchez Korrol
ISBN: 9781945662492 | LCCN 2021948909
Pbk. 2021; 308 pages
$25.00

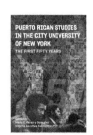

Authored by leading scholars in the field of Puerto Rican and Latinx Studies, this volume features a comprehensive fifty-year trajectory in the field of Puerto Rican Studies at the City University of New York in a series of critical essays on scholarship, the social sciences, bilingual education, media, and its counterparts beyond CUNY, in addition to retrospectives from founders of the field, current professors, and alumni.

Patria: Puerto Rican Revolutionary Exiles in Late Nineteenth Century New York

Edgardo Meléndez
ISBN 9781945662287 | LCCN 2018052581
Pbk. 2020; 308 pages
$25.00; $9.99 Kindle

Patria examines the activities and ideals of Puerto Rican revolutionary exiles in New York City at the end of the nineteenth century. The study is centered in the writings, news reports, and announcements by and about Puerto Ricans in the newspaper *Patria* of the Cuban Revolutionary Party. The book looks at the political, organizational and ideological ties between Cuban and Puerto Rican revolutionaries in exile, as well as the events surrounding the war of 1898. The analysis also offers a glimpse into the daily life and community of Puerto Rican exiles in late nineteenth century New York City.

Liberalism and Identity Politics: Puerto Rican Community Organizations and Collective Action in New York City

José E. Cruz
ISBN 9781945662089 | LCCN 2017006438
Pbk. 2019; 218 pages
$25.00; $9.99 Kindle

This book is a recollection and analysis of the role of ethnic identity in Puerto Rican community institutional development and collective action in New York City between 1960-1990. The book demonstrates that through institutional development and collective action, Puerto Ricans articulated and promoted a liberal form of identity politics in which ethnic identity and the idea of group rights provided a platform for the production of both individual and collective goods.

http://www.centropr-store.com

Centro Publications

2022 CATALOGUE

Not the Time to Stay: The Unpublished Plays of Víctor Fragoso

Víctor Fragoso; Selected, Edited, Translated and with an Introduction by Consuelo Martínez-Reyes
ISBN 9781945662249 | LCCN 2018034538
Pbk. 2018; 244 pages
$25.00; $9.99 Kindle

Not the Time to Stay brings to light for the first time the marvelous work of Puerto Rican playwright Víctor Fragoso. Eight plays, edited and translated by Consuelo Martínez-Reyes, portray the socio-cultural issues Fragoso sought to expose: the choice and difficulties of migration, the clash between American and Puerto Rican societies, the oppression suffered by Latinos in the USA, homelessness, and domestic violence, among others. Fragoso played a key role in the New York City theater scene in the 1970s, and in the overall interrogation of Puerto Rican and Latino identities in the USA.

Race, Front and Center: Perspectives on Race Among Puerto Ricans

Edited by Carlos Vargas-Ramos
ISBN 9781945662003 | LCCN 2016030601
Pbk. 2017; 403 pages
$30.00

Race, Front and Center is a collection of essays that captures in a single volume the breadth of research on the subject of race among Puerto Ricans, both in Puerto Rico and the continental United States, and in the migration between the two. Its twenty-two chapters divided into seven sections address the intellectual, aesthetic and historical trajectories that have served to inform the creation of a national identity among Puerto Ricans and how race as a social identity fits into the process of national identity-building.

Before the Wave: Puerto Ricans in Philadelphia, 1910–1945

Víctor Vázquez-Hernández
ISBN 9781945662027 | LCCN 2016047262
Pbk. 2017; 129 pages
$25.00

This book recounts the genesis of the Puerto Rican community in Philadelphia during the interwar years (1917-1945). It connects the origins of this community to the mass migration of the post-WWII years when Puerto Ricans consolidated their presence in Philadelphia (1945-1985). This study compares the experiences of Puerto Ricans with that of the Italians, the Polish, and African Americans in Philadelphia during the early twentieth century.

http://www.centropr-store.com

Centro Publications

2022 CATALOGUE

Rhythm & Power: Performing Salsa in Puerto Rican and Latino Communities

Edited by Derrick León Washington, Priscilla Renta and Sydney Hutchinson
ISBN 9781945662164 | LCCN 2017038687
Pbk. 2017; 88 pages
$20.00; $9.99 Kindle

The story of New York salsa is one of cultural fusion, artistry, and skilled marketing. A multi-disciplinary collective of scholars illuminate how immigrant and migrant communities in New York City—most notably from Puerto Rico—nurtured and developed salsa, growing it from a local movement playing out in the city's streets and clubs into a global phenomenon.

State of Puerto Ricans 2017

Edited by Edwin Meléndez and Carlos Vargas-Ramos
ISBN 9781945662126 | LCCN 2017021705
Pbk. 2017; 138 pages
$25.00

This book provides an updated overview of some of the most salient subjects and themes about the Puerto Rican population in the United States. It highlights the continued mobility and expansion of the Puerto Rican population throughout the country, including state-to-state migration, migration from Puerto Rico in light of the economic crisis in the island, as well as the role of service in the armed forces in anchoring new areas of settlement.

2016 Almanac of Puerto Ricans in the United States

Editors Jennifer Hinojosa and Carlos Vargas-Ramos
ISBN 9781945662072 | LCCN 2017002040
Pbk. 2016; 167 pages
$25.00

LLearn more about the recent changes in the Puerto Rican community on the mainland United States through national and state-specific demographic data. The almanac compiles information on social, economic, and civic conditions of the Puerto Rican population in nine key states, and includes maps, tables, and descriptions of the population nationwide.

http://www.centropr-store.com

Centro Publications

2022 CATALOGUE

The Bodega: A Cornerstone of Puerto Rican Barrios (The Justo Martí Collection)
Carlos Sanabria
ISBN 9781945662065
Pbk. 2016; 43 pages
$20.00

This photo book is a compilation of photographs of bodegas in 1960s New York City shot by Cuban photographer Justo Martí. The photos are part of Centro's Justo Martí collection, which documents the life and activities of the individuals, families and organizations that made up the Puerto Rican experience in New York.

Gilberto Gerena Valentín: My Life as a Community Activist, Labor Organizer, and Progressive Politician in NYC
Edited by Carlos Rodríguez Fraticelli; Translated by Andrew Hurley; With an Introduction by José E. Cruz
ISBN 9781878483744
Pbk. 2013; 316 pages
$25.00

Gilberto Gerena Valentín is a key figure in the development of the Puerto Rican community in the United States, especially from the forties through the seventies. He was a union organizer, community leader, political activist and general in the war for the civil-rights recognition of his community. In his memoirs, Gilberto Gerena Valentín takes us into the center of the fierce labor, political, civil-rights, social and cultural struggles waged by Puerto Ricans in New York from the 1940s through the 1970s.

Puerto Ricans at the Dawn of the New Millennium
Edited by Edwin Meléndez and Carlos Vargas-Ramos
ISBN 9781878483799
Pbk. 2014; 319 pages
$25.00

This edited volume features chapters by Centro researchers and outside scholars presenting new research on social, economic, political and health conditions of the Puerto Rican population in the United States and highlighting the improvements and the challenges in this rapidly changing and growing community.

Centro Publications

2022 CATALOGUE

Soy Gilberto Gerena Valentín: memorias de un puertorriqueño en Nueva York
Gilberto Gerena Valentín; Edición de Carlos Rodríguez Fraticelli
ISBN 9781878483645
Pbk. 2013; 302 pages
$25.00; $6.00 Kindle + ePub

Gilberto Gerena Valentín es uno de los personajes claves en el desarrollo de la comunidad puertorriqueña en Nueva York. En sus memorias, Gilberto Gerena Valentín nos lleva al centro de las continuas luchas sindicales, políticas, sociales y culturales que los puertorriqueños fraguaron en Nueva York durante el periodo de la Gran Migración hasta los años setenta.

The AmeRícan Poet: Essays on the Work of Tato Laviera
Edited by Stephanie Alvarez and William Luis
ISBN: 9781878483669
Pbk. 2014; 418 pages
$30.00

A collection of thirteen essays, an introduction, and a foreword, by fifteen established and emerging scholars. The essays discuss diverse aspects of Laviera's life and substantial body of work that includes five published collections of poetry, twelve written and staged plays, and many years of political, social, literary and healthcare activism. The book also includes four unpublished poems and the play "King of Cans."

The Stories I Read to the Children: The Life and Writing of Pura Belpré, the Legendary Storyteller, Children's Author, and New York Public Librarian
Pura Belpré; Edited and Biographical Introduction by Lisa Sánchez González
ISBN: 9781878483805
Pbk. 2013; 286 pages
$25.00; $7.99 Kindle

The Stories I Read to the Children documents, for the very first time, Pura Belpré's contributions to North American, Caribbean, and Latin American literary and library history. Thoroughly researched and clearly written, this study is scholarship that is accessible to general readers, students, and teachers. Lisa Sánchez González has collected, edited, and annotated over 40 of Belpré's stories and essays, most of which have never been published. Her introduction to the volume is the most extensive study to date of Belpré's life and writing.

http://www.centropr-store.com

Made in the USA
Las Vegas, NV
09 July 2022

51292987R00157